T0414012

The Bounds of Myth

Value Inquiry Book Series

Founding Editor

Robert Ginsberg

Editor-in-Chief

J.D. Mininger

VOLUME 364

Studies in the History of
Western Philosophy

Series Editor

Jon Stewart, *Slovak Academy of Sciences*

Assistant Editors

Alina Feld
Peter Mango

The titles published in this series are listed at *brill.com/vibs* and *brill.com/shwp*

The Bounds of Myth

The Logical Path from Action to Knowledge

Edited by

Gustavo Esparza and Nassim Bravo

BRILL

RODOPI

LEIDEN | BOSTON

Cover illustration: Image by Stefan Keller, pixabay.com.

Library of Congress Cataloging-in-Publication Data

Names: Esparza, Gustavo, editor. | Bravo, Nassim, editor.
Title: The bounds of myth : the logical path from action to knowledge /
    edited by Gustavo Esparza and Nassim Bravo.
Description: Leiden ; Boston : Brill, [2021] | Series: Value inquiry book
    series, 0929-8436 ; volume 364 | Includes bibliographical references
    and index. | Summary: "This book shed light on the internal shapes of the
    mythological discourse, showing the way in which myth borders religion,
    science, literature, theology, i.e., other forms of rationality. The
    contributing authors of the volume claim that myth is a valid form of
    thought and that the former evolves within other forms of discourse,
    even though its composition is independent and even precedes the
    latter"– Provided by publisher.
Identifiers: LCCN 2021001689 (print) | LCCN 2021001690 (ebook) |
    ISBN 9789004448667 (hardback) | ISBN 9789004448674 (ebook)
Subjects: LCSH: Myth.
Classification: LCC BL304 .B685 2021 (print) | LCC BL304 (ebook) |
    DDC 201/.3–dc23
LC record available at https://lccn.loc.gov/2021001689
LC ebook record available at https://lccn.loc.gov/2021001690

Typeface for the Latin, Greek, and Cyrillic scripts: "Brill". See and download: brill.com/brill-typeface.

ISSN 0929-8436
ISBN 978-90-04-44866-7 (hardback)
ISBN 978-90-04-44867-4 (e-book)

Copyright 2021 by Gustavo Esparza and Nassim Bravo. Published by Koninklijke Brill NV, Leiden,
The Netherlands.
Koninklijke Brill NV incorporates the imprints Brill, Brill Hes & De Graaf, Brill Nijhoff, Brill Rodopi,
Brill Sense, Hotei Publishing, mentis Verlag, Verlag Ferdinand Schöningh and Wilhelm Fink Verlag.
Koninklijke Brill NV reserves the right to protect this publication against unauthorized use. Requests for
re-use and/or translations must be addressed to Koninklijke Brill NV via brill.com or copyright.com.

This book is printed on acid-free paper and produced in a sustainable manner.

Long before the world is given to consciousness as a whole of empirical 'things' and as a complex of empirical 'properties,' it is given to consciousness as a whole of mythical forces and effects.

ERNST CASSIRER, "Zur Philosophie der Mythologie."

∴

Contents

PART 3
The Myth in Action

Acknowledgements

This volume owes a debt of gratitude to the Universidad Panamericana. We are thankful for all their help and support in furthering our line of research on myth studies, which has resulted in this work. In this regard, we would like to thank in particular Ramiro Velázquez, Nicolás Esparza and Mariana Herrera for their continuous encouragement and all the trust they have deposited on us.

We would also like to thank professors Jon Stewart, Claudio Calabrese, Ethel Junco and Fernanda Rojas for their kind suggestions and corrections. We are thankful with our authors for all their effort and their splendid contributions to this volume. We also thank Katalin Nun for her suggestions regarding the cover of the volume. To produce this work we have received generous financial support from the government of Mexico through the sn1 (Sistema Nacional de Investigadores). We are thankful for that.

This volume was produced at the Department of Humanities at the Universidad Panamericana, within the line of research "Mito, conocimiento y acción".

Notes on Contributors

Nassim Bravo

Researcher and professor in the Department of Humanities at the Universidad Panamericana. He is the head of the line of research on philosophy of religion at the same university. He is the founder and coeditor of the journal *Estudios Kierkegaardianos*. He has translated several works by Søren Kierkegaard into Spanish such as *Para un examen de conciencia* (2008), *Postscriptum no científico y definitivo a Migajas filosóficas* (2009) and *Prefacios* (2011). He is currently the head translator of the Spanish translation of Kierkegaard's journals and papers (2011-). He has published a number of articles and chapters in the field of Kierkegaard studies and Golden Age Denmark, including "Kierkegaard y el proyecto sobre el ladrón maestro (1834–1835): el rebelde marginado frente al orden establecido," (2019) "Heiberg's 'A Soul after Death': A Comedic Wake-Up Call for the Age" (2020) and "The Faust Project in Kierkegaard's Early Journals" (2020).

Claudio Calabrese

Professor at the Universidad Panamericana, Department of Humanities. He specializes in ancient philosophy (particularly Neoplatonism), patristics (especially the works and thought of Augustine) and phenomenology. He is the head of the research line "Myth, Knowledge and Action." He has published papers in journals such as *Graeco Latina Brunensia* and *Σχολή*. His latest book, coedited with Ethel Junco, *La recepción de Platón en el siglo XX: Una poiesis de sentido*, was published by Peter Lang in 2020.

Teresa Enríquez

Professor at the Universidad Panamericana. She works on philosophy of action in Aristotle, Thomas Aquinas and Harry Frankfurt. Her book *De la decisión a la acción* was published by Olms in 2011. She was the editor of the book *Racionalidad práctica y dimensión social de la acción humana*, published by Porrúa in 2012. She authored the chapters "Imperium, Instinct and Natural Law" (Cambridge Scholars Publishing, 2008) and "Mixed Actions in the Work of Harry Frankfurt" (Olms, 2016).

Gustavo Esparza

Researcher and professor of philosophy in the Department of Humanities at Universidad Panamericana. An expert on Cassirer's philosophy, he has published several scholarly articles on myth criticism and literary problems. His book *Mito, conocimiento y acción. Continuidad y cambio en los procesos cultura-les* was published by Peter Lang in 2019.

Ethel Junco

Professor at the Universidad Panamericana, Department of Humanities. Her field of study is the hermeneutics of classical culture. She is the author of publications on philosophy and literature in the ancient world; she also works on European and Latin American literature. She has coedited (with Claudio Calabrese) the book *La recepción de Platón en el siglo XX: Una poiesis de sentido*, published by Peter Lang (2020).

Enrique Martínez

Professor at the Universitat Abat Oliba CEU (UAO) at Barcelona, Spain. He is the Dean of the Faculty of Communication, Education and Humanities. He is also a member of the Pontifical Academy of Saint Thomas Aquinas and Director of the Thomistic Institute of Barcelona. He works on metaphysics, epistemology and philosophy of education. He has published articles in journals such as *Espíritu, Anuario Filosófico, Sapientia* and *Revista Española de Filosofía*. He has also written chapters published by Brepols, Springer and Classiques Garnier.

Cecilia Sabido

Researcher and professor at the Faculty of Social Sciences and Humanities at the Universidad Autónoma de San Luis Potosí (UASLP). Her research topics include poetics, aesthetics and human action; she also studies practical and political themes in Aristotelian philosophy and its reception during the Spanish fifteenth century, humanism, Novohispanic and Mexican philosophy. Some of her publications include *El pensamiento ético politico de Alfonso de Madrigal* (2016), and articles such as "Reflexiones sobre el principio de la acción y el placer como auxiliar en la formación de las virtudes en la ética aristotélica" (2019) and "El ideal humanista de mejoramiento humano y su influencia en Vasco de Quiroga" (2019). She is also coautor and editor of *La primera transformación de México, análisis de los argumentos filosóficos preindependentistas* (2020).

Jon Stewart

Researcher at the Institute of Philosophy at the Slovak Academy of Sciences. He is the founder and general editor of the series, *Kierkegaard Research: Sources, Reception and Resources, Texts from Golden Age Denmark*, and *Danish Golden Age Studies*. He is the co-editor of the *Kierkegaard Studies Yearbook* and *Kierkegaard Studies Monograph Series*. He has authored a number of works, including, *The Emergence of Subjectivity in the Ancient and Medieval World: An Interpretation of Western Civilization* (Oxford, 2020), *Hegel's Interpretation of the Religions of the World: the Logic of the Gods* (Oxford, 2018), *Søren Kierkegaard: Subjectivity, Irony and the Crisis of Modernity* (Oxford, 2015), *Idealism and Existentialism: Hegel and Nineteenth and Twentieth-Century European Philosophy* (Continuum, 2010), *A History of Hegelianism in Golden Age Denmark, Tomes I-II* (C.A. Reitzel, 2007), *Kierkegaard's Relations to Hegel Reconsidered* (Cambridge, 2003), and *The Unity of Hegel's Phenomenology of Spirit: A Systematic Interpretation* (Northwestern, 2000).

Prologue

Emily Grosholz

In order for philosophy to be effective and have a beneficial and profound impact on the world, we must bring science and mathematics together with traditional forms of knowledge, and indeed with tradition itself. During the twentieth century in the Anglophone philosophical community, the emphasis was on logic, and the power of deduction and to a certain extent induction to organize knowledge. This philosophical focus was, I think, driven by the rise and power of the physical sciences and their mathematical models, as well as a rather formalist and universalist political philosophy: we need universal principles from which we can reason downwards as a kind of demonstration. However, this approach leaves out human action in two ways. One way in which we come to understand the meaning of life, as Plato well understood, is to tell stories, as the importance of myths in all cultures shows: we tell and re-tell important stories that organize our understanding. A second way, also well understood by Aristotle, is to engage in debate, practical deliberation, about what we should do next, bringing together opponents united by good will. Many myths include dramatic accounts of such debates (that succeed or fail) as examples of the importance of talk, which is also a kind of action. I might add that right now human action is having an especially great impact on the environment; myth also often considers our relation to other living things, sometimes portrayed in magical or godlike ways, in ethical and metaphysical terms.

The philosopher Ernst Cassirer reminds us of the importance of myth in his four-volume *Philosophy of Symbolic Forms*, where it appears as the topic of the second volume. He saw the importance of the failure of practical deliberation in the two World Wars that he lived through, the second of which decimated the human population of the planet. Physics and chemistry helped us to create more and more effective weapons and fly planes to deliver them, but isn't the point of life to stay alive, and help others live?

Part 1: Exemplarity, Analogy and Expression in Myth

In this introductory essay, "The Bounds of Myth: The Logical Path from Action to Knowledge," Gustavo Esparza explains how the volume will show the indispensable role of myth as a symbolic form in human culture. In order to understand the history of culture and the transmission of culture, we must look to myth as part of the explanation; it is compatible with philosophy, history and science and provides insights that they could never arrive at on their own. Myth has its own rationality; among other things, it helps us see the importance of deliberation on the pathway from intention to achieved action. It also inspires us to systematic inquiry, asking, for example, the cosmological question about the cause of all causes: even if we cannot answer it, this is a question we cannot escape. So, this book aims at deepening our understanding of myth in relation to other ways of knowing.

One especially rich source is the interaction of myth and philosophy in ancient Greece. Both Plato and Aristotle see that poetry and drama play an important pedagogical role in philosophy, bringing feeling into relation with reason and the wide world, and linking language to experience. In Christian culture, St. Augustine reminds us that knowledge cannot pursue its ends without belief, as it looks for the causes of the world, because otherwise it falls into skepticism. The myths in the Bible are a useful basis for moving forward: belief may be the first step on the road to knowledge. And even in the modern era, myth as the archaic basis of culture helps us understand our relation to each other, to address the conundrum of human freedom, and to develop better, less destructive habits. Myth is a cultural form that we cannot do without, as we try to understand our own experience and move closer to truth.

In the essay "Considerations on the Visibility of Action in Aristotle," Cecilia Sabido and Teresa Enríquez offer a complex account of various classical texts. Aristotle notes that music can help young people learn and dramatic theatre (typically presenting mythical history) can help all of us become both citizens and people because it teaches us about character, virtue and action. Even though the actions presented are "mimetic," they are less confusing and better organized than the situations we find ourselves in as reality explodes around us. So they help us learn how to interpret and evaluate actions. A theory of action cannot do without ethics and poetics, because of the way they bring intelligence and perception together.

Theatre, epic and Platonic dialogues present exemplary characters who are both strong and dutiful, often in difficult circumstances which they must address: a good disposition and education helps them combine passion and action, and address others in constructive ways, though not always successfully since the outcome depends on the context. Their sufferings or successes, presented on the stage or in the text, remain with us in memory and orient us afterwards in real life. Our real action requires an education that includes mimetic and intelligible action, whether tragic or beautiful. The composition of the plot also helps us discern ethical and civic principles.

Enrique Martínez begins the essay "The Philosopher is Somehow a Lover of Metaphors" by reminding us that Aristotle claimed that a philosopher is in a sense a lover of myth, and then explores the writings of Christian writers, with special emphasis on St. Thomas Aquinas and St. John of the Cross. Wisdom searches for ultimate causes, and that kind of speculation can use metaphor as a resource. Metaphor allows us to think synthetically, to bring sensation and reason together without contradiction and with insight. When we say that old age is the sunset of life, we only assert a similarity, but it is not false. Old age offers its own especially beautiful light.

The use of metaphor is especially important, these thinkers argue, when we try to understand God. Given our finitude, when we seek ultimate causes metaphor is a good and pleasurable means to the end, helping us move from the limitations of body and sensation to the divine. As Aquinas notes, to call God a lion reminds us of the strength; to call him the Sun reminds us how he illuminates everything, the earth in one sense and the mind in another, analogous sense. We should remember that some of our best words for addressing God are psalms. "I will lift up my eyes unto the hills …"

Part 2: The Problems of Interpretation

The second section of the book explores issues and insights that arise in the interpretation of myth written in both religious and literary contexts. In the essay "The Meaning of Doctrine in *De Doctrina Christiana*," we learn from Claudio Calabrese that in this book St. Augustine combined the stories of the Bible with the intellectual tools, like rhetoric, that he learned from his classical education, in order to bring his countrymen into the Christian church. Both the power of argument, well organized and supported by evidence and good will, and the power of compelling tales that introduce Jesus and show him as a living presence, were required to achieve the ends of St. Augustine.

In the era of Late Antiquity, on the African side near the Mediterranean Sea on the banks of the Oued Hamise river, St. Augustine combined both continuity and rupture. Inspired by Cicero and Quintilian, he elaborated their rational eloquence through the expressive reading of scripture that added to the lived experience of others in the community. And he knew that the ambiguity of human language meant that reading is a difficult interpretive action, and so with hard work reading could transform a reader.

In the essay "The Myth of Self-Knowledge in Genesis 1–2: The Fascination of the Encounter," Gustavo Esparza explores the Biblical tale of Adam and Eve. Just as talking is a kind of action, so reading can be a kind of experience,

Esparza argues, that can inform and open one's life. The second section explores the wonder of Adam: Cassirer observes that consciousness of being is the first cause of wonder. But Adam was also lonely, after naming all the animals and realizing none of them are like him, so God, declaring that "it is not good that man should be alone," borrowed his rib and created another human being, not male but female. When he meets Eve for the first time, his exclamation "bone of my bone, flesh of my flesh" expresses his fascination with their complementary duality. She is also fascinated by him, and the emotion they feel is a recognition of two relations, of their bodies and the way they share consciousness.

The commentary of John Paul 2 about this biblical tale reminds us that the story, where the man and the woman realize both their likeness and their otherness, is about their awakening to each other and to self-understanding. This story counters the thought-experiment in Descartes' *Meditations*, which lacks the presence of another person, the drive of emotion and the play of imagination: all are needed for the correct understanding of the self, as part of a pedagogical process that helps us to learn who we are.

In his essay "The Notion of Subjectivity as Reflected in Early Notions of the Afterlife," Jon Stewart traces a compelling development of the understanding of human subjectivity across three thousand years in mythical accounts of the afterlife from the *Epic of Gilgamesh* to Dante's *Inferno*. He notes that in the Sumerian underworld, everyone is miserable, sitting in darkness. The situation is similar in the *Old Testament* Sheol, the Pit.

When Homer's Odysseus calls up dead souls from the underworld with the help of Circe, he sees that they are no longer physical beings: the human soul is immaterial and separable from the body. Still, they seem to eat and drink, and they are afraid of Odysseus' sword, and like the Mesopotamian and Hebrew dead, they are miserable, inactive, and languishing. Plato modifies this picture in the *Gorgias*: there in the underworld souls are judged for their behavior when they were living and subject to reward on the Isles of the Blessed or punishment in Tartarus. Zeus takes action to correct incorrect legal judgments: divine justice. However, Plato's Socrates' suggests that repentant sinner might be reincarnated, with the hope of redeeming themselves in the next life.

This increase in human individuality and inwardness increases in Virgil's underworld, when Aeneas crosses the river Styx and learns that Minos runs a court with a jury, to correct earthy judgments and decide who will go to Elysium and who to Tartarus, where Rhadamanthus punishes the sinners, and makes them confess their guilt. Moreover, all the souls carry out specific activities: in Elysium they listen to music and dance; and Aeneas' father tells him even souls there first had to pay for their minor sins. This sets the stage for Dante and his Christian account of the afterlife, where the developing recognition of human subjectivity is made clear and dramatic, showing its impact on the conceptions of morality and responsibility.

Part 3: The Myth in Action

The third section explores myth in action in important narratives written by authors who were quite reflective about the use and creation of myth. In the essay "Oedipus and Perceval: The Enigma as a Hermeneutical Principle," Ethel Junco reminds us that Claude Lévi-Strauss saw an inverse symmetry in the ancient Greek narrative of Oedipus and the medieval narrative of Perceval: confronted with an enigma, Oedipus responds with an answer and Perceval remains silent. Both of them have been raised outside their families, with a kind of disorientation, and both suffer for it. Oedipus unwittingly kills his father and marries his mother; Perceval unwittingly pursues the path of this lost father, which leads to the death of his abandoned mother, and fails to help the Fisher King. Both of them go on important quests and in the end find peace with God in the context of a forest.

Junco traces a network of images and explores how the darkness of the enigma leads to clarity. Oedipus' ability to correctly answer the riddle of the Sphinx leads to his triumph in Thebes, which also becomes his doom, and eventually he learns the truth, at which point he blinds himself. But in Colonus he finds purification when he recognizes the presence of Apollo and dies in a forest which will bless the land. Perceval's enigma is a procession that includes the Holy Grail in the company of maidens and the Fisher King, but he says nothing and thus fails to alleviate the suffering of the Fisher King. At the same time, he learns his mother has died. He too goes out in the forest to the sanctuary of his hermit uncle where he finds a kind of resolution and knowledge. Both men regain their identity and understanding by learning the truth.

Likewise, we learn about Kierkegaard's philosophical use of the legend of Robin Hood in Nassim Bravo's essay "Reinterpreting Medieval Lore through the Modern Prism: The Myth of Robin Hood in Kierkegaard's Early Journals." Why was Kierkegaard fascinated by what he referred to as the "Master-Thief"? Many scholars have noted his philosophical use of Biblical figures such as Abraham and Isaac or Job, Greek and Roman figures like Antigone, Nemesis or Prometheus, or Nordic figures like Thor or Loki, as well as modern personages like Hamlet. Halfway between poetry and philosophy, Kierkegaard was most interested in the development of the idea of the individual self and the evolution of character, rather than politics at a time when Denmark was in a crisis over its national and cultural identity.

In the journals he kept as a young man, Kierkegaard often turns to the model presented by Sir Walter Scott's novel *Ivanhoe*, a work inspired by medieval ballads about Robin Hood, which was published in 1819 and translated into Danish soon afterwards, in 1822. (This essay gives a fascinating picture of early 19th-century Copenhagen.) Although Scott as well as many of those interested in his book in Denmark understood Robin Hood politically, as a rebel against tyranny, Kierkegaard understood the good thief, who steals from the rich to give to the poor, as an expression of generosity of spirit. Estranged from his fellow thieves, his hostility to the established order is personal: Kierkegaard's Robin Hood uses other criminals to help him unwittingly, and to fight tyranny with humor, satire and ridicule. He might remind us of the great philosophical ironist, Socrates; like Socrates, the good master thief accepts his ultimate fate with serenity.

These days we need optimism, not least because now we see that we are responsible not only for ourselves, but for the other living things that share this planet with us. The rise of philosophy of biology in the past few decades, informed not only by philosophers in Europe but also in Latin American, Africa, India and China, often emphasizes the importance of traditional knowledge. Wangari Maathai makes good use of narrative in *Unbowed* where she first learns about the importance of trees from her mother. Vandana Shiva offers accounts of history at crucial junctions in *Making Peace with the Earth*, explaining the wisdom of traditional agriculture; and Philip Kitcher and Evelyn Fox Keller organize their book about climate change, *The Seasons Alter*, as a series of dialogues with vivid characters engaged in intense deliberation that moves from opposition to common ground. It is very important for philosophers to recognize the importance of mythical discourse, and so this collection of essays is a welcome addition to current discussion.

Introduction

Gustavo Esparza and Nassim Bravo

The general context behind this research is the classic anthropological question "What and who is man?" However, it attempts to respond through a broader philosophical spectrum than what is traditionally offered. Beyond answering the question based on a particular philosophical tradition or discipline, the purpose of this work is to expand the means of access that allow a more pluralistic investigation of human subjectivity, which underlies the question of the concept of the self. According to Lluís Duch,[1] the effort of human history (of culture) can be organized around a common progressive guiding axis: the inherent dialectic between subjectivity and objectivity This interrelation is culturally expressed around the expressions and social forms that arise from the μῦθος and the λόγος. In other words, all the effort in the history of the ἄνθρωπος begins with the origin, extends through his existence and continues with his future. Thus, the history and philosophy of culture tries to unify the *origin, progress* and *project* around a narrative identity that expresses the cohesion of human nature.

The need for self-understanding is so vital and constitutive to the human being that even all efforts to distance himself from his original origin constitute part of his identity. The human being "is" his history, not only in an ontological but also in a narrative sense. To look at what has been done reveals the project undertaken in the essential arc that invokes the re-calibration of the forms through which it is possible to orient the individual towards his anthropological essence. The human being is, therefore, a tension between its present time, its past and its future, but whose interrelation does not admit a split between the beginning, the middle and the end, but rather advocates a harmony that is revealed within the framework of a cultural hermeneutics.

We do not ignore other previous efforts made by Ernst Cassirer and Lluís Duch. In their respective works, the starting point for the measurement and distance of the progress of the history of the human being has been placed in the "archaic origin." In particular, Duch has created a research methodology that recognizes in the history of culture a dialectics of the tensions in which *myth* and *logos* are challenged, giving coherence and meaning to the *unity of*

---

1 Lluís Duch, *Mito, interpretación y cultura. Aproximación a la logomítica*, trans. by Francesca Babí y Domingo Cía, Barcelona: Herder 2002.

© GUSTAVO ESPARZA AND NASSIM BRAVO, 2021 | DOI:10.1163/9789004448674_002

opposites, through which the human essence is revealed: "the complementarity for which we advocate as optimal ... consists primarily of the firm conviction that what qualifies the human being as such is (should be) *polifacetism* ... because man is a unit of opposites (*coincidentia oppositorum*): therein lies his greatness."[2] Cassirer has delineated the phenomenological framework of nature and culture as the fundamental (essential) means for the development of the human person; within these tensions—the expression of these interrelationships—the formal symbolizations appear, among which the archaic form has recognized in *myth* and in *science* its most finished form. But only in the harmony of the tension of opposites, in the plural inclusion of their forms, is the form of the human "being" delineated: "Man is no longer considered as a simple substance which exists in itself and is to be known by itself. His unity is conceived as a functional unity. Such a unity does not presuppose a homogeneity of the various elements of which it consists. ... For this is a dialectic unity, a coexistence of contraries."[3]

Thus, if in this dialectical tension we acknowledge the need to approach "all" the forms of culture as a *necessary* contextual framework for the investigation of human nature, would this not imply an attack on such plurality to choose "only" the *myth* as an anthropological resource for investigation? How can one undertake a hermeneutic of culture that aims at an anthropology of all possible human forms of expression? As authors, we consider that a phenomenology of culture is not reduced to opposing its synthetic progression towards the absolute, but that it has to tighten the dualities in order to preserve the differences between mythical expressions and logical expressions, and then articulate them in a synthetic unit of meaning. Only in the framework of a universal essence is the transit from the phenomenal towards interpretation possible.

For this reason, the studies that are collected here, when placed within the myth, propose to appreciate the distance between the *already accepted* constitution of man and the *narrative* through which it is constituted as such. We consider that the interpretative conflict that has historically arisen to unify these extremes is revealed and better understood in the melting pot of culture and the variety of its forms. Although cultural unity is constituted in the process of symbolization and its own "points of view" (*Gesichtspunkte*), as Cassirer suggested, in each of these angles the dialectical unity of culture must

---

2 Duch, *Mito, interpretación y cultura*, p. 507.

3 Ernst Cassirer, *An Essay on Man: An Introduction to a Philosophy of Culture*, New York: Doubleday Anchor 1945, p. 280.

be reflected as a whole.[4] Therefore, the denial, exaltation or selectivity of one form over the others brings the danger of the disarticulation of the general form of the human world.

However, it is also true that each cultural form maintains its own legitimacy, which, in its dialectical progress, is offered as a valid form for the interpretation of the world that it devises; thus, myth or art cannot do without, for example, science or technology, but, in their harmonic progression, they appropriate resources offered by other cultural expressions with the aim of accentuating their particular identity and their own referent of interpretation. In this manner, myth is not understood as a denial of the general forms of culture, but rather a certain archaic gateway to the rest of its expressions.

If we observe in all the articles—beyond the nuances that differentiate one or another point of view—the interest in exposing how cultural harmony is possible in the boundaries that define the human world, then a door is opened to the possibility of recognizing in the mythical narratives a valid hermeneutical resource for the interpretation of the vital manifestations that the individual faces. Therefore, it is not the purpose of the present investigation to validate the idea that *mythical rationality* operates outside, or in spite of, *logical rationality*; on the contrary, we would like to argue that within mythical thought there is a peculiar logic that has as its object the investigation of the truth.

The distancing from the original myth, the act of literary mediation, the prehistorical and post-narrative consistency, which expands by poetic image, triggers the mythical μαθεῖν, in which memory is the fundamental comprehensive resource, both for its updating and its activation in culture. Thus, the myth, knowledge and action correlation should not be understood as a successive disposition of steps—a rational discourse—but as a simultaneity of meaning that is present by the reception-intuition of mythical narratives. The myth is a language of memory.

In this sense, the discernment of rationality, the point that requires our attention with more urgency, rests in the fact that the consideration of the myth itself implies raising the requirements of the logos beyond its vertebrate or architectural consistency (the deductive condition that we assign to *ratio*). If the myth is, in Greek semantics, an inexhaustible ποίησιζ in its possibilities, then the challenge will be to establish an interrelation with what we call, on the one hand, "theory," and, on the other hand, "praxis," according to the ethical claim of all human activity. According to this perspective, myth is not a

---

4 Ernst Cassirer, *Philosophy of Symbolic Forms. Volume III: Phenomenology of Knowledge*, trans. by Ralph Manheim, New Haven and London: Yale University Press 1955, p. 12.

path that is exhausted in the pre-logical quality of intuiting the entity, but as an existential path in which reason reaches its peak.

If for the enlightened mentality the myth is that pre-logical emergency, history is the knowledge that properly confronts it, as a progressive change towards the entelechy called the future. This idea of history arises in a controversy against the ideas of immutability and eternity, that is, against the proper identity of being. This implies that, ultimately, time is a transformation and not a step from being to non-being, as Plato considers it and as Aristotle defines it. The law of the conservation of matter ("Nothing is created, nothing is lost, everything is transformed") that is commonly attributed to the chemist Antoine Laurent Lavoisier, is one of the ways in which the concept of life of an infinite and eternal substance is translated. Undoubtedly, this notion of matter unfolds in a context that we could call presocratic and that, therefore, is so similar to Anaxagoras: "Nothing is created or disappears, but things already existing are combined and then again separated."

By accepting that, in the enlightened mentality, history is opposed to myth, we should also accept that "history" has a unique meaning, that is, only teleological or epistemological; therefore, it is appropriate to remember that in Latin the concept of "history" is presented by the phrase *res gestae*, the approximate translation of which is "things having been accomplished or performed." In Spanish we use the terms *"gesta," "gestación,"* and the verb *"gestar,"* accompanied by its intransitive form *"gestarse."* If we associate these concepts with each other, their semantic field leads us unequivocally to "birth" and, hence, to the evident meaning of being as being born and dying. From this perspective, "history / *res gestae*" is not a merely progressive development but the complete identity of a being (of Being) with itself. Inasmuch as it is a matter of "giving birth," of "understanding the gestation" of the entity as an actual being (distinct from an essential non-being), we might speak of a history of the gods in the sense of the Hesiodic *Theogony*.

Thus, myth is history: a story that is transformed into knowledge of what is gestating or being developed. It is no longer, then, "pure fictional history," but original history of what it is: the real condensed in the original / originating experience of language. Therefore, we can only predicate of the entity that it is "being in itself" because, in relation to being, it is meaningless (the religious experience takes us back to that absolute sense of being). Science can give us the partial meaning (the *in itself*) of the entity and consider it as a completeness.[5]

---

5   Edgardo Albizu, *Verdades del arte*, Buenos Aires: Baudino/UNSAM 2000, pp. 115–31.

We will take into account the following considerations in the approaches collected here: 1. As the original myth is unknown, we proceed from alterations, all generated by artistic mediation. The myth is a story and occurs primarily through literary transformation. By attributing the first hermeneutic to the compiler or author, we understand that this step of omission and selection leads to the discernment of constants that are essential for interpretation.

2. The narrative identity of myth, although it is put into historical perspective, is constituted by a reaction to history. The relation of approximately verifiable events is potentially a model of thought, but only insofar as they are assumed reflexively, whereas the myth is a complete and *a priori* model of thought. The myth is present in history as an event of language, prior to the human temporal occurrence or located in the arcane principle; this contrasts the assumptions of the story and conditions its interpretation. In history, action and story are deferred, the action is the source of the story, while in the myth the action is born with the story, it is the story.

3. The distance between the mythical mode and historical explanation, in contrast, marks the former's proximity to the religious explanation; the myth involves a relationship between the acute perception of human contingency and the desire for purpose and meaning, in short, for a certainty of divine justification.

4. The eminent language of this way of thinking is the image, that is, the sign of the poetic as a term of mediation and proposition. This condition gives the myth components that can be associated with the "fantastic" or "wonderful," as data, presences or indications not conceivable by rational simplification: to talk about the real thing it is necessary to take literal distance.

5. The constitution by images, that is, its imaginative character, offers freedom of movement and intercultural flexibility, variable as long as the fundamental premise of seeking reliable knowledge is fulfilled.

Bibliography

Albizu, Edgardo, *Verdades del arte*, Buenos Aires: Baudino/UNSAM 2000.

Cassirer, Ernst, *An Essay on Man: An Introduction to a Philosophy of Culture*, New York: Doubleday Anchor 1945.

Cassirer, Ernst, *Philosophy of Symbolic Forms. Volume Three: Phenomenology of Knowledge*, trans. by Ralph Manheim, New Haven and London: Yale University Press 1955.

Duch, Lluís, *Mito, interpretación y cultura. Aproximación a la logomítica*, trans. by Francesca Babí and Domingo Cía, Barcelona: Herder 2002.

PART 1

Exemplarity, Analogy and Expression in Myth

∴

The Bounds of Myth

The Logical Path from Action to Knowledge

Gustavo Esparza

Abstract

The purpose of this article is to delve into the role of myth in human culture as its archaic form. Despite the common conception that considers the mythical as a prelogical form that needs to be overcome, here it is argued that, regardless of the evolution of human thought, it continues to be based on its foundations that are expressed in mythological form. In this paper, three different historical conceptions are analyzed, together with their corresponding epistemic expressions achieved throughout their cultural evolution: their metaphorical base, the sign as a way of believing, and the ability to universalize. I would like to argue that myth allows us to understand the archaic as a logical path from action to knowledge. In the end, it will be argued that the myth has its own rules of knowledge and is a valid form of understanding.

1 The Space of Myth: Between Action and Logos

Lluís Duch claims that when we consider the history of culture, the philologist is the one who focuses the most on myth as a narrative way of expressing basic human experiences;[1] his objective is to understand how the "word" has developed as a means of oral expression and how this resource diverges from the written form. According to this author, the former was the most common means to communicate tradition in the early ages, and, therefore, ancient tribes have used it as a tool to maintain the most important aspects of daily life. In this way the human has been able to stabilize the signs of nature. In order to achieve this, it was necessary to bequeath the vocal word to the new generations so they could hear the formula that organizes the emotions caused by the presence of nature.

The second route, that of written expression, has allowed us to maintain human experiences beyond sound, even though this form was reserved for

---

1 Lluís Duch, *Mito, interpretación y cultura. Aproximación a la logomítica*, trans. by Francesca Babí and Domingo Cía, Barcelona: Herder 2003, pp. 65–131.

© GUSTAVO ESPARZA, 2021 | DOI:10.1163/9789004448674_003

some privileged groups that could access the secrets on how to stabilize the emotions and experiences promoted by nature, the usual space where deities communicated their designs. Duch states that the evolution of the history of culture developed overlapping oral and written words, resulting in a philological problem: considering that the experiences behind the vocal word are different from those that lead to the written expressions, is this mixture legitimate? There is no evidence that allows us to offer a plausible answer to this question; however, there is a favorable field for the study of these archaic forms and motifs of world configuration.

We can frame this question from another point of view. For Herbert Read,[2] the "image" should be considered the first way of conceiving the world. According to historical evidence, there is no reason to think that the first humans thought with words rather than with icons; the human being is naturally inclined to conceive the world through his abstractions and the first result is not the "word" (in any of its forms), but a "sign" in the pictorial sense. Fernando Zamora suggests a similar but more radical idea.[3] The image and the word are two worlds of expression that have been mixed throughout history, but each one has a space of adequate meaning. The consequence of the struggle to unite the results is the subordination of the image to the word, but, due to the force of the image, this entanglement has been repeatedly broken throughout the history of culture. However, although the image has proven to be fruitful in its own developmental space, an image of philosophy is increasingly necessary to relocate its place in the cultural environment.

The general background of these approaches is that there is a wide spectrum of representations to refer to the world, but in all of them we face a variety of problems that derive from the very nature of each way of knowing. Nonetheless, the objective remains the same: how is the affirmation of the truth possible? How can we argue that the path considered will reveal what lies behind the experience of the world? Ultimately, how are we sure that what I am thinking is really what is happening? This is once more the Cartesian question that investigates the possibilities of genuine knowledge.[4] The questions place us in the general problem and seek to investigate the form and contexts in which knowledge can be affirmed. As soon as we consider the issue

---

2 Herbert Read, *Icon and Idea: The Function of Art in the Development of Human Consciousness*, New York: Schocken Books 1965, pp. 17–35.

3 Fernando Zamora, *Filosofía de la imagen*, Mexico City: Universidad Nacional Autónoma de México 2013, pp. 105–232.

4 Mark C.R. Smith, "Cartesian Epistemology and the Authority of Norms," *History of Philosophy Quarterly*, vol. 27, no. 2, 2010, pp. 125–44.

from its historical form, various struggles between individual disciplines and positions emerge. But when we look at the debates from a purely philosophical prism, the question about the genesis and essence of what is knowledge repositions its central problem. Where, then, would be a good point to start? How is it possible to establish a common point of view to evaluate the space that myth occupies in culture?

The scholars of myth as a social phenomenon consider the ritual a starting point. The actions practiced continuously by an individual enable the spiritual entry into the community that justifies and shapes them. The action demonstrates the relationship between the activities practiced and a general proposition that coordinates these habits. The importance given to "action" is none other than the idea that, through it, it is possible to evaluate the mythical expressions of a particular community.

Another essential characteristic, although less conventional than the previous one, is the idea that myth does not lack rationality; on the contrary, it is a pre-logical way of thinking,[5] or a logomythic way,[6] developed by the so-called "*animal symbolicum*,"[7] whose essence is discursive reason. The central idea is that this expression is not alien to the human being; rather, it is its own nature that acts. Thus, even though the mythical is the first form of organized thinking in the history of mankind, it is not a systematic way of thinking.

In the words of Andoni Ibarra and Thomas Mormann, to determine something as an act of knowledge there must be a network of representative relationships through which it is possible to evaluate that the perceptual act of a data of the world is such that there is a cognitive representation of the world.[8] Although the authors present a broader thesis as they evaluate the scientific representations, we can take two basic ideas from their proposal: (1) Any theory of the world is supported by a complex network of intermediate representations that allows the postulate to be considered as a representation of an event. In this way, then, knowledge, or what scientific communities define as such, needs a functional relationship that links a practical fact with some theoretical structure or a "symbolic fact." (2) Derived from the interwoven nature

---

5   The three volumes of Cassirer's *The Philosophy of Symbolic Forms, Volume I: Language; Volume II: Mythical Thought; Volume III: Phenomenology of Knowledge*, trans. by Ralph Manheim, New Haven and London: Yale University Press 1955, are henceforth quoted as *PSF*, I–III; *PSF*, II, pp. 27–70.

6   Duch, *Mito, interpretación y cultura*, pp. 65–131.

7   Ernst Cassirer, *An Essay on Man. An Introduction to a Philosophy of Culture*, New York: Doubleday Anchor 1945, p. 44.

8   Andoni Ibarra and Thomas Mormann, "Scientific Theories as Intervening Representations," *Theoria*, no. 55, 2006, pp. 21–38.

of the representation, an interpretive model with which to interpret cognitive representations is necessary. The objective of this iterative process is to understand the theoretical relationship between the intellectual postulates of the world and the natural consequences of these representations.

This previous statement is important for our exposition because in maintaining that there is a logical form within the expressions of myth, we claim at the same time that for this archaic form there is a rationality proper to myth. Therefore, we postulate that mythical thinking is a complex network of signs that needs to be interpreted within the framework of a horizon of meaning; although myth is not a scientific form of knowledge, it is a representative theory of the world. In this way, we understand myth as a representation whose problematic core lies in these aspects: What is the nature of the network in which the myth is intertwined? What kind of representation of the world does this archaic form of knowledge offer?

Our purpose is to deepen the concept of myth, its nature and its way of relating to the rest of the epistemological resources with which we conventionally study the world. We conceive myth as a form of valid logical rationality, which is why we consider that mythical postulates cannot be assumed as a diminished "scientific logos." This form operates in its own realm. In this sense, it is understandable that the tension between mythical expressions and scientific concepts appear in efforts to validate mythical assertions and scientific results. We note that, so far, the most common aim has been to oppose them as two irreconcilable sides that try to subdue each other. Our goal is to study the epistemic validity that archaic expressions offer.[9]

We are convinced that (human) reason is not without myth and, as a consequence, operates with a peculiar logic; partly because of this, we are not interested in a specific period of time in the history of culture, but in the logical space in which these interactions occur. Since we accept the idea that the context is not only the "history of actions" but also the form of language, art, science and other cultural forms, we focus on the very nature of myth as a form that is expressed in the same social space in which it develops. In other words, we will argue that through myth it is possible to evaluate the cultural motives that enable "expression," of which the main mode of cultural presentation is an archaic or mythical thought. However, our starting point argues that not all

---

9 See, for example, Ursula Renz, "From Philosophy to Criticism of Myth: Cassirer's Concept of Myth," *Synthese*, vol. 179, no. 1, 2011, pp. 135–52; Gustavo Esparza, "Forma y legalidad del conocimiento mítico en Ernst Cassirer," in *Mito, conocimiento y acción. Continuidad y cambio en los procesos culturales*, ed. by Claudio César Calabrese, Gustavo Esparza and Ethel Junco, New York: Peter Lang 2019, pp. 41–74.

intuitive thinking is necessarily mythical; we believe that to reach a universal criterion that specifies a norm that lets us identify a true postulate from a false one, it is necessary to frame our reflection in the historical context of the ideas; in this way, time becomes a first criterion of evaluation of the form and postulates of the mythical.

This would explain why Cassirer claimed that only a critique of culture could assess the extent to which the diversity of mythical expressions could be legally integrated into a cultural form recognized as a general law.[10] However, we will not attempt to develop a philosophy of myth or culture. We will only study how various mythical expressions have manifested and been incorporated into their contexts to be considered as a valid logical postulate of their particular culture. Therefore, when considering the context of culture as a space of interactions where myth is fermented, we will investigate three cultural contexts in which mythical thinking has been expressed more clearly.

Through this path, we intend to delimit some of the most relevant historical stages of culture in order thereby to assess whether the form of the myth maintained over time can be considered a symbol that has mutated to adapt as a new and perceived format, or whether it is different from its origin.

2   Mystery and Myth in Greece: The Way of Language

Olga Freidenberg, in her *Image and Concept,* suggests the following thesis:

> the appearance of ancient poetic categories originates in the appearance of concepts, since the ancient concept is only a form of the image; and in this form of the image the concept has the function of "transferal" (... translation of concrete meanings) of the image into abstract meanings, "transferring" (... figural, metaphorical) meanings, which gives rise to metaphors and poetic figurality.[11]

We begin by distinguishing the main ideas of this quotation: (1) The image is a primitive form of the ancient concept. This implies—as suggested by Read and Zamora[12]—that perceiving is the first act of knowledge. (2) The function of the primitive concept is to translate perceived simple images into thought complex

---

10   *PSF*, I, pp. 78–81.

11   Olga Freidenberg, *Image and Concept: Mythopoetic Roots of Literature,* trans. by Kevin Moss, Amsterdam: Harwood Academic 1997, p. 20.

12   See Read, *Icon and Idea,* pp. 17–35; Zamora, *Filosofía de la imagen,* pp. 105–232.

images. (3) In order to achieve the previous point, a contextual (cultural) network is necessary in which the modes of linking between images and concepts are established. This implies a cultural world in which the final interpretations are constituted of conventional meaning in social and logical terms.[13] There is a fourth aspect that is evident throughout Freidenberg's study: (4) Language is the path through which it is possible (a) to connect the previous ideas (1–3) as well as (b) to establish a historical materialization of images and concepts in the social life of the community.

Nonetheless, a basic problem arises: what is perceived through the image? The question immediately puts us in a metaphysical environment that, while aspiring to answer the "what" of the question, takes us away from the immediate psychological experience that produces the image. Can we argue that the experienced image lacks a "metaphysics" and a "psychology" that operates in harmony just because we are not able to find an intermediate path of unification? According to Fernando Zamora, the history of thought has endeavored to distinguish between images and words (oral and written). It seems as if while the "word" adheres to the reason to offer an expression in a logical manner, the "image" is only able to remain as a primary (archaic) way of perceiving the world.[14] If the former is characterized by its discursive essence, the latter operates as the very presence of existence.

According to these ideas, then, the general problem of inquiry is no longer "what is perceived through the linguistic image," but "is an image that is not linguistic possible?" We argue that the genesis of the image does not begin with the metaphysical definition of "what is this," but in the space of the daily experience of "something I perceive in the world." Thus, within this framework it is necessary to ask what kind of "events" gives rise to what kind of "images." For the primitive human being there would not be an adequate response to what this (my) experience means, but the importance lies in the contextualization of where, when, and how I feel this experience. In this way, Freidenberg's thesis is closer to the interactions that produce images and eventual metaphors that give meaning to a particular experience than to the exploration of its metaphysical nature.

Eliminating the political and economic conditions of her study, Freidenberg argues that Greece is the place where images became concepts, not because of the material conditions surrounding the Greek language, but because of the cultural function with which they were endowed. The author is convinced

13   See Cassirer, *An Essay on Man*, pp. 278–85.
14   See Zamora, *Filosofía de la imagen*, pp. 27–102.

that what was done by the Greeks allowed for the understanding of the role that language plays in its expression of the phenomena of the world: "Why did Classical drama come out of cult? And if drama absolutely had to come out of cult and become tragedy, then why did tragedy appear only among the Greeks, if all the ancient cultures had cults? Why is it that not one folk theater had tragedies, but all presented only comedies?"[15]

Although Freidenberg offers an answer to these previous questions, some of her approaches are developed at the core of the language. What Greece had achieved revolutionized the expressive form because, instead of mimicking nature with oral or written signs, she organized a new system of intellectual representation that was able to manifest a new spiritual world. According to this, the great Greek tragedies are those that harmonically integrated the structure of the natural world and, at the same time, offered new means to build new cultural resources for expression. The new linguistic boundaries reached by the Greek poets brought to mankind other ways to express the *mysterium tremendum* experienced in everyday life; tragedies reveal the essential core of fear, anguish, despair and, in general, any human experience. When representing the natural events of the world, the Greek language becomes something new. Now the mysterious event hidden in the vicinity of archaic thought can be represented with phonetic and written signs. Therefore, instead of asking "what is this experience I feel," Greek thought redirects reflection to the new possibilities offered by the linguistic experience. With the representations of this path, an identity function is produced that unifies the facts, language and form of the event into a complete unit.

Freidenberg emphasizes that in this new spiritual context, myth operates as the primary foundation of language and, therefore, what is achieved by this culture is based on mythical thinking organizing new intellectual resources that we now consider to be essential in the daily development of our society. Since the poet understands the experience and at the same time is able to represent it, he or she is no longer forced to separate the two worlds, but through the poem he or she offers us a dialectic between the object, the image and the context: "Although mythological image and concept are two different means of knowing the world, at a certain historical stage they mutually conditioned one another."[16]

At this point we evoke the theory of the concept developed by Cassirer,[17] for whom the concept is always a universal form that operates as a law for

---

15   Freidenberg, *Image and Concept*, p. 21.
16   Freidenberg, *Image and Concept*, p. 27.
17   See *PSF*, III, pp. 281–327.

the constitution of meaning. Events, as singularities, are interrelated with the universal form only if they meet the criteria of the universal; therefore, the concept becomes a criterion that must be met in order to be included in the group. Here the problem arises of what are the criteria to evaluate that the relationship has been completed and, therefore, if the singular has been assumed as a peculiar mode of the concept. In this regard, Thomas Ryckman has stressed that "Cassirer argued that intuition is not a self-standing substrate or independent source of knowledge, but enters into knowledge only insofar as it is 'unified' by 'pure thought' under a 'series concept' as a system of relations and functional dependencies."[18] In other words, knowledge, and in particular the concept, relates to a network of functions that must satisfy a set of criteria given by the context, which, in turn, shape the regulations that regulate the practice of language.

Following these ideas we can argue that the Greek language through its tragedies does not present pure experiences, but a narrative path to experience these emotions about the world. This does not imply that the representation conditioned the form of expression by limiting the communication of experiences to their preset forms; on the contrary, in the Hellenic cultural context the language and the understanding of the meaning of the experiences arise as a unitary act, although both develop from a parallel form.

The latter implies a new problem: how to link both spaces (language and experience) and maintain that they form a dialectically harmonic unit? On the one hand, we have said that the act of thinking that the world begins with is intuition, and, according to Cassirer,[19] this primary act is a symbolic impregnation of the world because in every act of perception we find an archaic preconception of the vital environment that lets us understand an event as a unique experience. Therefore, for Cassirer, looking at the world is not only living in it, but perceiving a phenomenal fact that carries a primary sense, while guiding us towards a specific spiritual direction.

In this regard, Freidenberg reminds us that in the genesis of language there is an interaction between the image (perceptions) and the primitive concepts (explanations) about what is happening in the world: "The image, like the concept, is a logical cognitive category; but its essence lies in the fact that mythological image thought does not separate the knower from the known, the phenomenon (object) from its properties (symptoms), the represented from

---

18   Thomas Ryckman, "*Conditio sine qua non? Zuordnung* in the Early Epistemologies of
          Cassirer and Schlick," *Synthese,* vol. 81, 1991, pp. 61.

19   *PSF,* I, pp. 198–277; *PSF,* II, pp. 71–152; *PSF,* III, pp. 43–104.

the representing."[20] If, as Cassirer noted, the lack of distinction between subject and object had been the main weakness of the myth for many thinkers, it should now be considered its main source of meaning.[21] Inasmuch as the "image" does not distinguish between "representation" and "object," the subject not only names the thing, but lives the experience of the fact. Instead of using language as a way to separate experience and then symbolize it (as science does), in myth we experience the thing itself.

Finally, Freidenberg states that in the Greek context the image and its linguistic representation arose from the dialectical interactions between τὸ αἰσθητόυ (what is known by the sensory organs) and τὸ νοητόυ (what is known by speculation). According to her, there is no pure form of the two in the abstract since speculation is a perception of the world of sense, while the cognition of the sensory organs semantically represents thought. In this way, abstractions depend on sensations, while sensations are held in abstract universal ways to express a coherent meaning. Thus, although the images maintain the mystery in their own space of origin, they now rely on language to reveal what had been kept hidden in the perception of the image of the world.[22]

3   Language as a Space of Belief: Sign and Truth in St. Augustine

We begin this section with the admonition with which Augustine opens his *Confessions*:

> Grant me Lord, to know [*scire*] and understand [*intelligere*] which comes first—to call [*invocare*] upon you or to praise you, and whether knowing you precedes calling upon you. But who calls upon you when he does not know you? For an ignorant person [*invocat nesciens*] might call upon someone else instead of the right one. But surely you may be called upon in a prayer that you may be known. Yet how shall they call upon him in whom they have not believed? And how they shall believe [*credunt*] without a preacher [*predicante*]? They will praise the Lord who seek for him.[23]

---

20   Freidenberg, *Image and Concept*, p. 26.

21   See *PSF*, III, pp. 43–57.

22   Freidenberg, *Image and Concept*, pp. 26–27.

23   Augustine of Hippo, *Confessions*, trans. by Henry Chadwick, Oxford and New York: Oxford University Press 2008, book I, § 1.

Here the central question is how do we know we know? If we were sure of our own "knowledge" [*scire*] there would be no need to request "understanding" [*intelligere*]. But according to Augustine, it is important to investigate beyond our human nature to understand if what we know [*scire*] is true. However, we find ourselves in a circular problem that involves the following: (a) knowledge begins with the awareness of ignorance. (b) Ignorance is not an impediment to seek what we do not know, but in which we believe. (c) In order to inquire if it is possible to obtain something we do not have, it is necessary to compare what we know and that in which we believe so as to overcome the original state of ignorance. However, since this process does not guarantee a complete knowledge of the truth, we acknowledge that our ignorance remains. (d) Unlike the initial moment, in this stage of the process we see belief as a valid epistemic resource that allows us to resume our inquiry about the truth, even though we are aware of our own ignorance. In this manner, a new inquiry about the truth starts over, which, as it is incapable of guaranteeing such truth, shall repeat itself continuously.

In this sense, the *Confessions* refer us to the problem described as a paradox in *De Magistro* about how it is possible to achieve new knowledge if there is no way to learn something new, since only the true (internal) teacher can teach us.[24] The tension appears when Augustine begins to ask his son Adeodatus if it is possible to teach something with signs and words, and concludes that language in itself leads us to the truth; with signs and words there is no other end than the sounds of words. In this regard Jonathan Teubner argues that this path implies the impossibility of language acquisition because if only the "true teacher" is able to teach the "signs" of the "words," how can we "know" if something is true: "if nothing new can be taught by words, how does Augustine learn that it is Christ who is dwelling in the inner man?"[25]

The answer corresponds to the distinction between "belief" and "knowledge." If Augustine can learn something new, it is not by the power of words as such, but by the object that their signs point out; what the student acquires is not the sound, but its meaning in accepting and recognizing as true what is happening. Thus, Teubner notes that "while the majority of things cannot be known, Augustine still knows how useful it is to believe them. The conclusion is that the so-called 'historical knowledge' is, in fact, merely belief—it is not something he knows by direct appreciation."[26] In this sense, the essence of the

---

24   Augustine of Hippo, *Concerning the Teacher and On the Immortality of the Soul*, ed. by George G. Leckie, New York: Appleton-Century-Crofts 1938, pp. 11–12.

25   Jonathan Teubner, "Augustine's *De Magistro*: Scriptural Arguments and the Genre of Philosophy," *Studia Patristica*, vol. 54, 2012, p. 5.

26   Ibid., p. 8.

sign resides, on the one hand, in the act of believing and, on the other hand, in the act of defining what is known since the essence of knowledge is not to encompass universality, but only to point it out.

While it is true that there is no way to move towards the knowledge of the truth through the path displayed by skepticism, it must also be affirmed that there is no possibility of accepting that the true is given by the very essence of words. What we believe about language is not the sound or what is written physically, but the truth implies the act of believing and the act of the wisdom of solitude to distinguish between "calling" and "knowing." Thus, a way to move towards the truth will be revealed. In this interrelation we do not find the answer to how the process of language acquisition is possible, but the framework in which this occurs. The tension between "believing-knowing-understanding" makes it possible, to those who implore, to advance in the search for their path to the knowledge of the truth.

How do these reflections refer us to myth? At the beginning we established that the mythical form is a means for the knowledge of the truth, and, according to these results, we confirmed that this archaic form knows not by the words with which it narrates the events it describes, but by its signs. It is worth noting that in *De Magistro* Augustine explains—alluding to the biblical story of Shadrach, Meshach and Abednego[27]—that the nature of understanding is based on the usefulness of believing rather than positive demonstration with arguments.[28] The reason we can achieve knowledge of the truth is none other than the ability to "believe to understand, understand to believe" [*credo ut intelligam et intelligo ut credam*]. In the same way, then, myth is not what we can demonstrate, but a useful basis in which reason can stop to begin to indicate the essence of truth. The truth, therefore, does not belong or come from the physical display of the objects or the rationality of the subject, but from the interrelation of both and the genuine search for that universal form.

For Darrel Jackson, in the "sign," as it is understood by Augustine, there is a reference to a "natural" object, but not in a physical sense, but in relation to its "intention." Whereas the material sign can be perceived, its intention must be interpreted to be understood, and this process can only be achieved by the human being. Thus, the "sign" will always be an intentional relation completed by the perceiver, but, at the same time, the general meaning of what is sought

---

27   See Daniel 1:6–16.

28   See Augustine, *Concerning the Teacher*, chapter 11, § 37.

will be achieved only to the extent that what has been achieved reveals the essence of the investigation. In this way, we are faced with a paradox that develops a dialectical tension between (i) how it is possible to understand what the (ii) true intention is, and if such an objective (iii) was achieved "truly" by the interpreter. At this point it might be useful to remember a soliloquy that Augustine presents in his *Confessions*:

> How shall I call upon my God, my God and Lord? Surely when I call on him, I am calling on him to come into me. But what place is there in me where my God can enter into me? God made heaven and earth. Where may he come to me? Lord my God, is there any room in me which can contain you? Can heaven and earth, which you have made and in which you have made me, contain you? Without you, whatever exists would not exist. Then can what exists contain you? I also have being. So why do I request you to come to me when, unless you were within me, I would have not being at all? Accordingly, my God, I would have no being, I would not have any existence, unless you were in me. Or rather, I would not have no being if I were not in you of whom all things, through whom all are things, in whom all are things.[29]

This long paragraph is important for the thesis that we want to support because, according to the author, the purpose of the inquiry is not to establish that the language with which we "ask" is, properly speaking, the truth sought, even if it works as a path that leads the "human being" to the full understanding of what he or she seeks. Therefore, the "truth" will never be in "language" as such, but through it; neither is it "in the search," but by virtue of it. Applying this to our theme, we claim that myth cannot be considered as the essential objective of understanding, but the path through which the human being acquires the truth.

This path, as the history of thought has shown us, will not be free from contradictions and tensions in the methodological process. Nonetheless, at least a better transit route is developed by accepting that believing is not the end of knowledge, but its first step on the road. The same applies to the myth; this does not represent the opposition of the logos, but the beginning of the long path that we have to travel systematically until we reach the truth.

---

29   Augustine, *Confessions*, book I, § 2.

4   The Myth of Space: The Universality of Culture and the Basis
     of Truth

Throughout the "Introduction" to his *Phenomenology of Knowledge* Ernst
Cassirer establishes the genesis of knowledge in the field of perception.[30]
According to him, it is unquestionable that this is the primary stage where
the phenomenological act of knowledge begins. But this is also problematic.
Cassirer claims that in the history of thought many efforts have been made to
understand the process of knowledge as a path susceptible to objectification,
so it has been treated as a psychological expression, studied in its metaphysical
essence, presented as its physiological process and described as a metaphysical reality that can be achieved through the intellect, although none of these
approaches has been successful in its effort to explain in its complex reality
what "knowledge" is:

> This introduction was not intended to solve these problems, but rather
> to designate the difficulties and to point out the peculiar dialectic inher-
> ent in the mere question of immediacy, regardless of the direction from
> which it is raised. We have seen that neither epistemology nor metaphys-
> ics, neither speculation nor experience, whether taken as outward or as
> inner experience, can wholly master this dialectic. The contradiction can
> be moved further back, it can be shifted from one part of the spiritual
> cosmos to another, but it cannot in this way be resolved once and for
> all. Here philosophical thinking must not content itself with a premature
> solution; there is nothing it can do but resolutely take this very contradic-
> tion upon itself. The paradise of immediacy is closed to it.[31]

What knowledge faces is not only the understanding of itself, but the way in
which universality is related to singularity, so it is necessary to evaluate the
dialectic through which knowledge is constituted. According to Cassirer, "if
thought cannot directly apprehend the infinite, it should at least explore the
finite in all directions."[32] In this way, it is set as a criterion not to discard anything with the interest of moving towards the universal totality of truth. The
general path (the entire phenomenological process) must express the truth
and its interrelation through the totality of singularities that constitute it.

---

30   See *PSF*, III, pp. 1–42.

31   *PSF*, III, p. 40.

32   *PSF*, III, p. 41.

Even though the results of recent studies have followed this path, this result is not necessarily referring to the "universal truth," but to the "apparent truth." The final concern should not be the integration of "finitude" to achieve the "infinite" of perceptions, but, according to Cassirer,[33] we would have to unify the expressions of culture as a resource of inquiry to know the essence of human nature.

However, in Skydelsky's view, Cassirer's aspiration of a philosophy of culture has been limited, since it has been considered that such an infinite path is impossible.[34] In this regard, we can consider the statement that Heidegger makes on Neo-Kantianism about the fragmentation that led to the fragmentation of "Being" by current scientific research. Instead of looking towards the universality of cultural forms as a reflection of the truth, now the interest is in the specialization of scientific knowledge as the most reliable means to achieve certainty:

> The genesis [of Neo-Kantianism] lies in the predicament of philosophy concerning the question of what properly remains of it in the whole of knowledge. Since about 1850 it has been the case that both the human and the natural sciences have taken possession of the totality of what is knowable, so that the question arises: what still remains of Philosophy if the totality of beings has been divided up under the sciences? It remains just knowledge of science, not of beings.[35]

Cassirer was aware of this problem, since he considered that both the scientific field and the rational methods opened new means of investigating the truth, thereby expanding the resources for understanding the truth.[36] However, the core of the problem was not the lack of a model of universal understanding that would unify diverse points of view, but because of the eradication of a general law that integrates the complete scheme of knowledge into a functional unit, they had diluted the guarantees of a universal vision. For Cassirer, if there was no philosophical project that evaluated and integrated this cultural power, there would be a risk of losing sight of the entire cultural form. The

---

33   See Cassirer, *An Essay on Man*, pp. 87–96.

34   Edward Skidelsky, *Ernst Cassirer: The Last Philosopher of Culture*, Princeton: Princeton University Press 2011, pp. 25–35.

35   Martin Heidegger, "Davos Disputation between Ernst Cassirer and Martin Heidegger," in *Kant and the Problem of the Metaphysics*, trans. by Richard Taft, Bloomington and Indianapolis: Indiana University Press 1997, p. 193.

36   See *PSF*, I, pp. 85–114; *PSF*, II, pp. 1–26; *PSF*, III, pp. 1–43.

power of culture, then, is in balance as long as all forces recognize the proper space of each form and how all of them can coexist.[37]

How does myth contribute to the universal understanding of culture? The first step is to remember that the human being is an animal that acts, a ritual being that tries to achieve community or personal goals, but is always in search of ideals.[38] The danger is not the singularity or universality, but the radicalization of these forms in selfishness or communism. Forgetting the essence of the person and their interrelation with the form of culture could bring favorable results for the development of the human being. Cassirer systematically insisted on this when he stressed that knowledge in all its forms should lead to the cultural exercise of goodness. There is no reliable research program if (intellectual) understanding takes us away from (human) understanding of otherness.[39]

Among other contexts, this idea was sustained by Cassirer in the Davos debate. We will reproduce it here and then systematically analyze it:

> If we keep the whole of Kant's work in view, severe problems surface. One of these is the problem of freedom. For me, that was always really Kant's main problem. How is freedom possible? … the Categorical Imperative must exist in such a condition that the law set up is not valid by chance just for human beings, but for all rational entities in general. Here suddenly is this remarkable transition. The restrictedness to a determinate sphere suddenly falls away. The ethical as such leads beyond the world of appearances. Yet this is so decisively metaphysical that a breakthrough now follows. It is a matter of the transition to the *mundus intelligibilis*.[40]

Two concepts are important: the "apparent" and the "intelligible." With the first term, we return to the general intention of the *Phenomenology of Knowledge,* which proposes a general investigation of the process of the constitution of knowledge starting with (mythical) perception until its (scientific) conception. Although the aim of this third volume of the *Philosophy of Symbolic Forms* was to explain how scientific knowledge was constituted and

---

37   See Cassirer, *An Essay on Man*, pp. 87–96.

38   This is the core idea of Cassirer's *The Myth of the State*, New Haven: Yale University Press 1946.

39   See Ernst Cassirer, "The Concept of Philosophy as Philosophical Problem," in *Symbol, Myth and Culture. Essays and Lectures of Ernst Cassirer (1935–1945)*, ed. by Donald Philip Verene, New Haven and London: Yale University Press 1979, pp. 49–63.

40   Heidegger, "Davos Disputation between Ernst Cassirer and Martin Heidegger," p. 194.

its logical primacy over the rest of cultural expressions, this does not imply that the previous phases of the road should be subsumed once the stages have been overcome. For Cassirer, the essential difference of the scientific function is to present a resource through which the methodological under-standing of the truth is guaranteed. Even though science is not such only if it is "true," we cannot accept as valid a methodological process that does not strive to demonstrate its internal veracity. Since science has been forced to reach "infinity" in all its processes, therefore, each of the previous spheres (mythological and linguistic) operates as a firm step that maintains the same ultimate goal.

On the intelligibility, when Cassirer speaks of "transition" he is thinking that the action must be "ethical," but considering its (human) contexts. In this sense, then, the responsibility does not depend on the objectivity of the known, but on the cultural forms that are developed to produce daily habits. The core of this proposal is not to promote the development of an ethical theory of knowl-edge, but a hermeneutic of life, the objective of which is the interpretation of how singularities are related to a global law that governs each singular mem-ber. Cassirer does not aspire to control individualities, but instead proposes to place them within the framework of a general form that guarantees the inte-gration of singularities into the universality of the ideal form.

Therefore, the general objective is placed by Cassirer in the cultural func-tion, where the mythical form contributes with its archaic postulates to the understanding of the infinity of the experiences of the world. In this way, the myth operates as an archaic phase of the world of intelligibility, thus becom-ing the basis of later cultural forms. Culture, truth and myth, then, become branches of the same complete phenomenological path—a path that can only be interpreted as a hermeneutics of life

5   The Bounds of Myth: Final Thoughts

What we have claimed so far is that myth is a cultural form with its own legacy and that the general intention of this form of expression is the truth. We also argue that myth must be considered as a spatial form and not as a temporary understanding of phenomena that appear fleetingly. This does not imply that this cultural form operates above specific historical periods; rather, it is a form that develops on its own terms, regardless of temporal considerations. As we have seen, although there are other cultural forms on which the myth is based (language, art, science), its postulates are offered according to their internal form, without counteracting the interrelation with other cultural objects; the function of myth is, then, to provide the basis for understanding the general form of human experiences.

The objective of considering myth in its spatial development allowed us to explore different approaches to understand the way in which this form at different times (in the Greek world, the Patristic world, and the contemporary world) continuously seeks truth as its highest and most genuine goal. While its first objective is to universally connect basic human experiences, this does not imply that the unique ways in which the truth appears are unknown. We explained that neither the Greek metaphor nor the Augustinian statement nor Cassirer's analysis change the foundations of myth, but that all these cases consider myth as the natural way in which the perception of the world of intuition is present. What we have expressed here is not the supremacy of this form, but its archaic position within the general path that has to be traveled to know the universality of knowledge. On the horizon truth always presents itself as the true goal of myth.

However, at the same time we are aware that, like all human activity, this form can deviate from its path to follow morbid fantasy and reject reality. In this sense, we face a human condition that may believe that the immediacy of appearance is true knowledge; but the risk is not only for the myth, but also for all cultural forms. We face the general problem of how to access the Universal Being through particular experiences.

Therefore, although the myth offers a fruitful way through many of its mythical narratives, we face the dilemma of how to integrate the guidelines for universal validation to overcome unique experiences. If we want to see in the narrative structure only literary fantasies, we can lose the main objective of the discursive expression; there is only one spiritual force trying to find its own place in the world. It is only the rational nature of the human being and the continuous interpretation of the phenomena that can complete this task. Therefore, only going along the long cultural path of myth towards logos can guarantee the knowledge of the truth, and its first step is offered to us as mythical rationality.

Translated by Carlos Rafael Domínguez

Bibliography

Augustine of Hippo, *Confessions*, trans. by E. Pussey, London: J. Dent & Sons 1939.
Augustine of Hippo, *Concerning the Teacher and On the Immortality of the Soul*, ed. by George G. Leckie, New York: Appleton-Century-Crofts 1938.

Cassirer, Ernst, *An Essay on Man: An Introduction to a Philosophy of Culture*, New York: Doubleday Anchor 1945.

Cassirer, Ernst, *The Myth of the State*, New Haven: Yale University Press 1946.

Cassirer, Ernst, *The Philosophy of Symbolic Forms. Volume I. Language*, trans. by Ralph Manheim, New Haven and London: Yale University Press 1955.

Cassirer, Ernst, *The Philosophy of Symbolic Forms. Volume II. Mythical Thought*, trans. by Ralph Manheim, New Haven and London: Yale University Press 1955.

Cassirer, Ernst, *The Philosophy of Symbolic Forms. Volume III. Phenomenology of Knowledge*, trans. by Ralph Manheim, New Haven and London: Yale University Press 1955.

Cassirer, Ernst, *Language and Myth*, trans. by Susanne K. Langer, New York: Dover Publications 1946.

Cassirer, Ernst, *The Logic of Humanities*, trans. by Clarence Smith Howe, New Haven: Yale University Press 1961.

Cassirer, Ernst, "The Concept of Philosophy as Philosophical Problem," in *Symbol, Myth and Culture. Essays and Lectures of Ernst Cassirer (1935–1945)*, ed. by Donald Philip Verene, New Haven: Yale University Press 1979, pp. 49–63.

Duch, Lluís, *Mito, interpretación y cultura. Aproximación a la logomítica*, trans. by Francesca Babí and Domingo Cía, Barcelona: Herder 2002.

Esparza, Gustavo, "Forma y legalidad del conocimiento mítico en Ernst Cassirer," in *Mito, conocimiento y acción. Continuidad y cambio en los procesos culturale*s, ed. by Claudio César Calabrese, Gustavo Esparza and Ethel Junco, New York: Peter Lang 2019, pp. 41–74.

[Heidegger, Martin], "Davos Disputation between Ernst Cassirer and Martin Heidegger," in *Kant and the Problem of the Metaphysics*, trans. by Richard Taft, Bloomington and Indianapolis: Indiana University Press 1997.

Freidenberg, Olga, *Image and Concept: Mythopoetic Roots of Literature*, trans. by Kevin Moss, Amsterdam: Harwood Academic 1997.

Ibarra, Andoni and Mormann, Thomas, "Scientific Theories as Intervening Representations," *Theoria*, no. 55, 2006, pp. 21–38.

Frazer, James, *The Golden Bough: A Study in Magic Religion*, London: MacMillan 1900.

Levene, Nancy K., "Sources of History: Myth and Image," *Journal of the American Academy of Religion*, vol. 74, no. 1, 2006, pp. 79–101.

Makkreel, Rudolf A. and Luft, Sebastian, *Neokantianism in Contemporary Philosophy*, Indianapolis: Indiana University Press 2010.

Read, Herbert, *Icon and Idea: The Function of Art in the Development of Human Consciousness*, New York: Schocken Books 1965.

Renz, Ursula, "From Philosophy to Criticism of Myth: Cassirer's Concept of Myth," *Synthese*, vol. 179, no. 1, 2011, pp. 135–52.

Ryckman, Thomas, "*Conditio sine qua non? Zuordnung* in the Early Epistemologies of Cassirer and Schlick," *Synthese,* vol. 81, 1991, pp. 57–95.

Skidelsky, Edward, *Ernst Cassirer: The Last Philosopher of Culture*, Princeton: Princeton University Press 2011.

Smith, Mark C. R., "Cartesian Epistemology and the Authority of Norms," *History of Philosophy Quarterly*, vol. 27, no. 2, 2010, pp. 125–44.

Teubner, Jonathan, "Augustine's *De Magistro*: Scriptural Arguments and the Genre of Philosophy," *Studia Patristica*, vol. 54, 2012, pp. 1–10.

Zamora, Fernando, *Filosofía de la imagen. Lenguaje, imagen y representación*, Mexico City: Universidad Nacional Autónoma de México 2013.

Considerations on the Visibility of Action in Aristotle

Cecilia Sabido and Teresa Enríquez

Abstract

In this paper we analyze some passages of Aristotle's *Problems* related to the perception of movement and action, and then put them in relation to the theory of the dramatic composition of the *Poetics*. Exemplarity is an indispensable resource in moral formation for the ancient Greeks, in particular for Plato and Aristotle. However, there are only a few studies that consider the process of perception of movement and moral action. Ultimately, we explain why the imitation of actions present in the dramatic art is a valuable resource to understand the complexity of practical life precisely because of its ability to present human actions before the eye in its organic wholeness.

1 Introduction

One of the problems that Aristotle's *Politics* considers is the education of young people through music because of its relation with emotions and, through them, with human actions.[1] In the *Nicomachean Ethics,* the meaning of this formation is specified: virtue. And it specifically addresses young people, as older people have already acquired their habits from their own experience.[2] The acquisition of habits and moral formation are not only achieved by personal exercise, but also by a certain exemplarity.[3] This shows precisely the

---

[1]   *Politics,* VIII-3, 1337b 23ff, 1338a 13–25; VIII-5, 1339a 10ff. (For Aristotle's works, we are going to use the edition of Jonathan Barnes: *The Complete Works of Aristotle*, Princeton: Princeton University Press 1991.) Starting from Chapter 5, the rest of Book VIII is devoted to considering the musical formation of young people and its elements, such as appropriate rhythms, instruments, themes and so on, since this will teach them to choose what should be loved by any good citizen, and reject what should be hated and prepare them to make competent judgments. About this, see Nancy Sherman, "The Habituation of Character," in her *Aristotle's Ethics: Critical Essays,* Maryland: Bowman & Littlefield 1999, pp. 242–3.

[2]   *Nicomachean Ethics,* I-3, 1095a 3–5; II-1,1103b24-25; VI-8, 1142a 12–20; X-9, 1179b 30ff.

[3]   *Nicomachean Ethics,* IX-9, 1169b 30-1170a 1; *Politics,* VIII-5, 1340a 5ff; *Poetics,* 4, 1448b 5–20. This argument is also found in Emilio Lledó Iñigo, "Introducción a las éticas en Aristóteles," in *Ética nicomáquea, Ética eudemia,* Madrid: Gredos 1998, p. 33. On the exemplarity, especially *Prior Analytics,* II-23, 68b 9–14; *Posterior Analytics,* I-18, 81a 39-b42;

© CECILIA SABIDO AND TERESA ENRÍQUEZ, 2021 | DOI:10.1163/9789004448674_004

concern—both Platonic and Aristotelian—that young people are driven by music appropriate to the goals of their political formation.

For Aristotle, a powerful instrument of formation by exemplarity is theater. There the characters are not limited to saying only what they think, but "the imitator represents actions" [πράττοντας]. In effect, they carry out concrete actions in specific situations,[4] from whose contemplation the spectator acquires a series of learning experiences and their annexed pleasures, which he shares collectively.[5]

All of this suggests that there is the possibility of sensibly perceiving human actions or at least some elements thereof,[6] and that this perception contributes to the interpretation of the reality of the action that, outside of the mimetic context, is often cryptic. In everyday life, we perceive only the physical movement that a person performs and, unless he declares us the motivating end, we can only assume the reasons behind these movements. A high percentage of what we usually *call human actions* is the result of the interpretation we make of a series of movements and the *declarations*—or, if that fails, the assumptions—of what motivates them.[7] Otherwise, the interpretation of the action does not stop in this construction, but adds a judgment that considers the adequacy or inadequacy of the action for the supposed or declared purposes.[8]

    Nicomachean Ethics, VI-3, 1139b 27; and in *Rhetoric*, I-2, 1356b 5, 1357b 25–36, II 20, 1393a 26-1394a 18, and III-17, 1418a 1–22, just to mention some passages.

4   *Poetics*, 3, 1448a 27–29; 6, 1449b 24-1450a 7; 9, 1451a 36-b11.

5   *Politics*, VIII-7, 1341b 34-1342a 27; 5, 1340a 1–25.

6   *Politics*, VIII, 1340a 29–43: "The objects of no other sense, such as taste or touch, have any resemblance to moral qualities; in visible objects there is only a little, for there are figures which are of a moral character, but only to a slight extent, and all do not participate in the feeling about them. Again, figures and colours are not imitations, but signs, of character, indications which the body gives of states of feeling ... even in mere melodies there is an imitation of character, for the musical modes differ essentially from one another, and those who hear them are differently affected by each. ..."

7   *Nicomachean Ethics*, I-3, 1094b 20-1095a 10.

8   For example, I see a person leave the classroom with a phone in his hand. I may assume that my lecture is boring him, or that he disagrees with my ideas; but if I see him leave in a hurry, I can also think that it is an emergency. Later, he may tell me himself: "Excuse me, it was an emergency and I had to answer." I will also assess whether his conduct was correct or incorrect in the conditions in which we are. I might think "it was rude" or, on the contrary, I wish that the alleged emergency is nothing serious and that everything is fine. If he were not just any audience but a student in my classroom, it would seem incorrect to me that he had been paying attention to his cell phone instead of paying attention to the class, and given the formative expectations of my role as a teacher, I would even admonish him. Then he could tell me "it is an emergency, a family member is in the hospital and

Human actions are complex, and, despite having empirical evidence of them, there is a high degree of uncertainty in the elements we use to judge their entirety.[9] However, it seems that we learn to act by observing the actions of others and imitating them,[10] using judgments based on assumptions,[11] and, eventually, we learn to consider the complexity of our own actions, to account for our motivations and to value our actions as adequate or inadequate.[12] Regarding our ends,[13] we learn to be able to say *I did well or I was wrong*.[14]

So how is an action known? What is perceived of human actions? And if what is perceived by the senses is not the total action, what other resources do we have to consider it? Is there an intellectual knowledge of the action? How do you get to it and what reach do you have?

We want to put on the table the fact that the knowledge of actions is problematic and that an approach of particular interest can be found in aesthetics. Indeed, Aristotle—and others after him—recognize in a certain type of mimetic-artistic works the ability to put the entire action in sight as a whole and, through its fictional representation, improve man's understanding of his own act. Ultimately, that is the function that *mythos* has in the structure of the work according to Aristotle himself in *Poetics*.[15]

Dramatic mimesis has the quality of placing the complexity of human actions in the sight of the spectators.[16] We are not just talking about establishing

---

I must go," and I would justify everything, even if it were likely that he was telling me a lie. His declaration is thus stronger than my assumption.

9   *Nicomachean Ethics*, II-2, 1104a 1–5; 4, 1105a 18-b18.

10   *Poetics*, 4, 1148b 5.

11   *Prior Analytics*, I-30, 46a 27–28.

12   See William W. Fortenbaugh, *Aristotle on Emotion*, London: Duckworth 2002, pp. 75–6.

13   *Nicomachean Ethics*, III-3, 1112a 31-b12.

14   *Rhetoric*, I-12,1372a 5–10; 1372b 13–23; 13, 1373b 1-1374b 24.

15   *Poetics*, 6, 1450a 3–6; 15–24. "The plot [μῦθος], in our present sense of the term, is simply this, the combination of the incidents, or things done in the story [μῦθον]; whereas character [πραγμάτων] is what makes us ascribe certain qualities to the agents [πράττοντας] … The most important of the six is the combination of the incidents [σύστασις] of the story. Tragedy is essentially an imitation not of persons but of action and life. All human happiness or misery takes the form of action; the end for which we live is a certain kind of activity, not a quality. Character gives us qualities, but it is in our actions that we are happy or the reverse. In a play accordingly they do not act in order to portray the characters; they include the characters for the sake of the action. So that it is the action in it, i.e. its plot, that is the end and purpose of the tragedy; and the end is everywhere the chief thing."

16   We found this conviction on two sources: on the one hand, philosophical reflection, see Cecilia Sabido, "Mito y estructuración en la *Poética* de Aristóteles," *Iztapalapa*, no. 58, 2005, pp. 63–87; Cecilia Sabido, "Poética y ficción en Aristóteles," *Estudios: filosofía, historia, letras*, no. 101, 2012, pp. 151–63; Cecilia Sabido, "Ritmo, mimesis y temporalidad en el

a theory of moral formation, although this could be derived and is a recurring theme in some authors,[17] but about considering a *theory of action* in general. For this, we will specifically consider some elements that are present in the Aristotelian *corpus*.

We must justify, first, the reason for using Aristotle as a starting point. It seems to us that, as one of the first theorists of poetic action, he leaves clues throughout his works that shed light on the scope of dramatic art in particular and artistic activity in general. The principles of *mimesis, techne, poetry* and *praxis* are current concepts, and, considering the evolution that they have experienced, both conceptually and in the field of artistic practice, they are still parameters to examine the artistic fact.[18] On the other hand, we must clarify that we do not intend to make an exhaustive exposition of an Aristotelian theory here, or attribute the ideas we present here to the Stagirite himself, but to highlight a series of aesthetic qualities as a result of his work in general and of *Poetics* in particular.

Methodologically, we will stick to the works of Aristotle and consider above all the *Politics*, the *Nicomachean Ethics*, *Problems*, *Rhetoric* and, of course, the *Poetics*. We will try to determine first, and briefly, what value the exemplary quality of the actions has in Greek moral formation in general and for Aristotle in particular. Secondly, we will consider the aspects of the perception of the action, specifically those related to hearing and sight. Third, we will consider the structuring of the facts as a mimetic resource that enables a different form of *vision*, that is, an intellectual interpretation of the actions *perceived* by the viewer. It will be necessary to distinguish the resources of this perception in everyday life and the particular eloquence that, on this fact, gains the mimetic representation of the actions in the dramatic works, finally, to propose that a specific quality of the performing arts in particular and of the art in general is the ability *to put in sight*, in the face of sense perception, "an action that is

---

arte," *Euphyía*, vol. 7, no. 1, 2013, pp. 45–64, to name a few. The second source is the direct experience that Sabido has had over twenty-five years of practice in the performing arts. Of course, there is relevant theoretical and pedagogical dramatic literature, but it will not be cited in this work and will be the subject of further research.

17 Like Martha Nussbaum, *The Fragility of Goodness: Luck and Ethics in Greek Tragedy and Philosophy*, Cambridge: Cambridge University Press 1986; or Carmen Trueba, *Ética y tragedia en Aristóteles*, Barcelona: Anthropos and Universidad Autónoma Metropolitana-Iztapalapa 2004.

18 A clear example of this trajectory, to mention an example, is the work of Wladislaw Tatarkiewicz, *A History of Six Ideas: An Essay in Aesthetics*, The Hague: Martinus Nijhoff 1980.

whole and complete," something that Aristotle refers to in his *Poetics* as the core of representation.[19]

2   The Exemplarity of the Action

Werner Jaeger in his *Paideia* explains that Greek culture based its education on the imitation of the ἀρετή of the Greek heroes, as they were presented in the Homeric poems.[20] Originally the term ἀρετή referred to a force or a quality that distinguished the hero, but the narratives highlighted the aptitudes related to the actions that made them stand out: at first it was their strength and ability, and later it was their sense of duty. The stories were attractive because they showed the hero's constant effort to preserve his or her superiority. Whoever listened to these stories longed to appropriate the peculiar moral beauty that the heroes achieved through their actions. From the introductory pages of Jaeger's study, we highlight in particular the relationship between the eloquence of poems to refer to the vitality of heroic actions and the desire to "appropriate the beauty of heroes" by imitating them.[21]

In his *Politics*, Aristotle focuses his attention on two educational resources related to imitation: game and music. In the game he distinguishes how it entertains and serves as a rest for the adult; for the child, however, it is also a way of access to knowledge, so it should be used to prepare him or her for life.[22] He also affirms that music contributes to the formation and character of the soul because it has the capacity to imitate passions and form in young people an adequate judgment of good dispositions and honorable actions.[23] When he categorizes the types of music, he distinguishes them by qualities related to actions: ethical, practical and enthusiastic, as they serve for education, distraction or purification.[24]

---

19   *Poetics,* 7, 1450b 25–28. "We have laid it down that a tragedy is an imitation of an action that is complete in itself, as a whole of some magnitude; for a whole may be of no magnitude to speak of. Now a whole is that which has beginning, middle, and end."

20   Werner Jaeger, *Paideia, The Ideals of Greek Culture,* trans. by Gilbert Highet, Oxford: Oxford University Press 1945, p. 21.

21   Jaeger, *Paideia,* p. 23.

22   *Politics,* VII-17, 1136a 4–1136b 11.

23   *Politics,* VIII-5, 1340a 5–30.

24   *Politics,* VIII-7, 1341b 35. See Myles F. Burnyeat, "Aristotle on Learning to Be Good," in *Aristotle's Ethics: Critical Essays,* ed. by Nancy Sherman, Lanham: Bowman & Littlefield 1999, p. 217.

From these mentioned characteristics about entertainment and access to knowledge of the game, plus the formation of character by music and its function for education, distraction and purification, two elements can be extracted: (1) On the one hand, if there is the possibility of representing actions and qualities related to the action, the child can perceive these representations as a spectator and learn from them in auditory but also visual ways. (2) However, you can also learn by participating directly in imitation, whether you play—that is, you perform actions for recreational purposes, in fictional settings—or perform the music yourself as an interpreter.

Imitation is not just a way of knowing, but also the first way of learning. In fact, Aristotle claims in *Poetics* that men acquire their first knowledge through imitation, and recognizes that it is a natural and distinctive characteristic of man and also causes pleasure.[25] We also know that Aristotle considers many types of imitations and categorizes them by their means and their ways, but restricts imitation, above all, to actions. This is especially interesting. To the Stagirite those who imitate, imitate men acting: "The objects the imitator represents are actions."[26] Much has been studied and written about the entire categorization of imitations from these first chapters of the *Poetics*, but we want to focus especially on this simple statement, which essentially implies two things: those actions are representable, imitable, and that, at least for Aristotle, imitation [μίμησις] implies an action [πρᾶξις].[27]

Now, it is necessary to distinguish what is *action* for Aristotle in this context. The term "action" implies some kind of process, some kind of change or movement, both kinetic and metabolic.[28] When dealing with human action, the process implies a new specific complexity: the intrinsic principle that makes it voluntary and intentional.[29] Thus, every human action is a process that implies a change and a practical reasoning, an intention and an execution that reaches, or not, an end to which it tends.[30] Human action, therefore, is a type of process that refers to a term of ethical relevance: πρᾶξις.

---

25   *Poetics*, 4, 1448b 4–9.

26   *Poetics*, 2, 1448a 1.

27   To deepen these ideas, see two essays collected in *Essays on Aristotle's Poetics*, ed. by Amelie Oskenberg Rorty, Princeton: Princeton University Press 1992: Rudiger Bittner, "One Action," pp. 97–110; and Cynthia Freeland, "Plot Imitates Action," pp. 111–32.

28   *Physics*, III, 1–3. 200b-202b 30.

29   Ana Marta González, "Action in a Narrow and in a Broad Sense," in *Practical Rationality: Scope and Structures of Human Agency*, ed. by Ana Marta González and Alejandro G. Vigo, Hildesheim: Georg Olms Verlag 2010, pp. 123–68.

30   David Charles, *Aristotle's Philosophy of Action*, London: Duckworth 1984.

Music imitates action better than painting, because melody and rhythm imply movement, while drawing is limited to presenting figures and colors.[31] We will see that the action is seen in a different way, different from how the mere elements of sense are perceived, but it should be noted, in the last instance, that imitation for Aristotle eminently implies the complexity and dynamism of any process. That is what happens, for example, in *Physics* II-8, 199a 15–33 and *Metaphysics* VII-7, 1032a 11-a 9, 1034b19, where Aristotle explains how art imitates nature or contributes to it in terms of generation as a teleological process.[32]

Now, in the *Poetics* Aristotle also admits that imitations involve characters, passions and actions.[33] All of them are relative to the action: the personality is the moral style of the characters, the passions are their affections, which they experience as motives and consequences of their actions. In short, for Aristotle, imitations always involve actions and what is related to them.

The problem that now emerges is to understand how the viewer "perceives" an action. Because it is a fact that there must be a reception of the senses, if not of the whole action, at least of some of its parts, from which one can know and judge it. And, as we have already noted, it will be necessary to consider whether it is necessary to distinguish between the perception of the real and the imitated action, because it is a fact that the poet intervenes in the composition of the elements and must present them to the viewer: "At the time when he is constructing his plots, and engaged in the diction in which they are worked out, the poet should remember to put the actual scenes as far as possible before his eyes. In this way, seeing everything with the vividness (ἐνα ργέστατα) of an eye-witness as it were, he will devise what is appropriate, and be least likely to overlook incongruities."[34] However, the perception of real and everyday events and, especially, of whole actions, does not seem to be something entirely clear.

---

31 *Problems*, XIX-29, 920a 4–7.

32 *Physics*, II-8, 199a 15–33. Charlotte Witt, "In Defense of the Craft Analogy: Artifacts and Natural Teleology," in *Aristotle's Physics: A Critical Guide*, ed. by Mariska Leunissen, Cambridge: Cambridge University Press 2015, pp. 109–10.

33 *Poetics*, 1, 1447a 25.

34 *Poetics*, 17, 1455a 23–25.

3   The Perception of Movement and Human Actions

As we have said, the problem that arises now is the way of perceiving actions according to Aristotle and if real actions are perceived differently from their imitations. First, we will comment on some passages from Aristotle that refer to the sense perception of the actions or their elements. In *Politics* VIII he notices the ear's ability to capture moral states as opposed to other external senses:

> The objects of no other sense, such as taste or touch, have any resemblance to moral qualities; in visible objects there is only a little, for there are figures which are of a moral character, but only to a slight extent, and all do not participate in the feeling about them. Again, figures and colours are not imitations, but signs, of character, indications which the body gives of states of feeling ... even in mere melodies there is an imitation of character, for the musical modes differ essentially from one another, and those who hear them are differently affected by each.[35]

In the passage quoted, Aristotle refers to the perception of elements related to action and not to the action itself: moral states, characters and bodily signs thereof. As such, these signs are only useful references that should be interpreted. It is interesting to point out that the representative qualities of the action seem to belong eminently to the auditory stimuli, while the visual ones appear subject to the symbolic function so that their interpretation is not immediate.

In the *Problems*, Aristotle considers this subject frequently, adding nuances that may be of great interest and whose resonances appear vaguely cited in other treaties, such as the *Politics* or the *Rhetoric*, and very rarely in the *Nicomachean Ethics*. For example, in section XIX-27 he asks:

> Why is it that of all things which are perceived by the senses that which is heard alone possesses character? For music, even if it is unaccompanied by words, yet has character; whereas a colour and an odour and a savour have not. Is it because that which is heard alone has movement, not, however, the movement in us to which the sound gives rise (for such movement exists also in the other things which affect our senses, for colour also moves our sight), but we perceive the movement which follows such and

---

35   *Politics*, VIII, 1340a 29–43.

such a sound? This movement resembles character both in the rhythms and in the melodic disposition of the high and low notes, but not in their commingling; for symphony does possess character. This does not occur in the other objects of sense-perception. Now these movements are connected with action, and actions are indicative of character.[36]

As we have said before, Aristotle relates sound to *movement,* and he does not refer so much to a physical movement (which is compared in the example with the effect of color in sight, or the mixture of sounds in consonance), but in the mood, and it refers to *action* and *character.* In addition, a few lines later he adds:

> Why do rhythms and tunes, which after all are only voice, resemble characters, whereas savours do not, nor yet colours and odours? Is it because they are movements, as actions also are? Now activity possesses and instils character, but savours and colours have no similar effect.[37]

This text also connects rhythms and melodies, which are expressions of compound sounds, to passions, and in this manner describes them as "actions," establishing thus the relation between actions and character.

However, does Aristotle refer to imitations of actions or to human actions themselves? Is there a principle of comparison that allows imitation? What does it consist of? In section VII-1, Aristotle addresses the problem of sympathy, both physical and emotional, and wonders if there is a certain mutual influence among all that exists. He gives yawns as an example of this and proposes that *the sight causes the memory,* and this, in turn, puts the impulse into action. Something similar happens with sexual pleasure and food.[38] Later, he

---

36 *Problems,* XIX-27, 919b 26–36. On this topic see Stephen Halliwell, "Music and the Limits of Mimesis," in his *The Aesthetics of Mimesis,* Princeton: Princeton University Press 2002, pp. 237–49.

37 *Problems,* XIX-29, 920a 7-1434.

38 Consider the following passages: "Why do men generally themselves yawn when they see others yawn? Is it because, if they are reminded of it when they feel a desire to perform any function, they then put it into execution, particularly where the desire is easily stirred, for example, that of passing urine? Now a yawn is a breath and a movement of moisture; it is therefore easy of performance, if only one sees someone else yawning; for the yawn is always ready to come. ... Why is it that, although we do not imitate the action if we see a man stretching out his hand or foot or doing anything else of the kind, yet we ourselves yawn if we see someone else doing so? Or, does this not always occur, but only when the body happens to feel a desire and is in such a condition that its moisture becomes heated? For then it is recollection which gives the impulse, as also in sexual desire and hunger; for it is that which causes recollection to exist that provides the stimulus towards

adds that for men, due to the fact that they are more attuned to the senses, the movement and memory come over immediately. To him, the memory is what contains an impulse towards the imagined sensation.[39]

First, sight seems to be associated with internal sense, in particular, memory and imagination. On the other hand, it should be noted that sympathy seems to work in a way analogous to the senses, oriented to the internal sense; that is to say that sense stimuli seem to move the sense not only towards the present perceptions, but also to previous or concomitant ones. Especially concerning empathy—understood as the ability to feel or be moved by the affections of another—Aristotle asks in the following paragraph:

> Why is it that when we see any one cut or burned or tortured or undergo-
> ing any other painful suffering, we share mentally in his pain? Is it because
> nature is common to us all, and it is this which shares in the sufferer's pain,
> when we see one of these things happening to him, through kinship with
> him? Or is it because, just as the nose and hearing according to their partic-
> ular faculties receive certain emanations, so also the sight does the same as
> the result of things pleasant and painful?[40]

The text suggests a relationship between what is sensibly perceived and an affective assessment, related to pain or pleasure. This implies that the entire sensibility—external and internal—is compromised in what we might call a *sense perception* of the actions or those related to them.[41] Aristotle does affirm

---

the condition observed in another person." *Problems*, VII-1, 2 and 6, 886a 25–35. Another passage is this: "Why is yawning caused by the sight of others yawning, and so also the passing of urine, particularly in beasts of burden? Is it due to recollection? For when rec-ollection occurs the part of the body concerned is stimulated. In men then, because their sensations are finer, when they see something stimulation and recollection occur simul-taneously. But in the beasts the sight is not sufficient by itself, but they require another sense to be called into activity; so the sense of smell must also be employed, this being a more easily stimulated sense in unreasoning animals. So the other animals always pass urine in the same spot as the first one; for the stimulus is most acute when the sense of smell is employed; and the sense of smell is called into play when they are near the spot." *Problems*, VII-2, 887a 4–14.

39 *Problems*, VII-2, 886a 29–35. "For then it is recollection what gives the impulse, as also in sexual desire and hunger; for it is that which causes recollection to exist that provides the stimulus towards the condition observed in another person." About this see Stephen Halliwell, *The Aesthetic of Mimesis*, p. 182.

40 *Problems*, VII-7, 887a 15–21.

41 Fortenbaugh, *Aristotle on Emotion*, pp. 18–22. This sense perception is related to Fortenbaugh's "emotional response" which is never only a matter of emotion but "complex phenomena involving thoughts as well as physiological changes." Fortenbaugh, *Aristotle*

in the *Nicomachean Ethics* the intervention of the perception in the acquisition of virtues and considers that this is the faculty that apprehends "the particular," information that is necessary to deliberate properly on the means and discern what is convenient in each case.[42]

It can be said, therefore, that the resources of the perception of actions in general—and of what has to do with them—involve complex elements both in real actions and in what can be represented by imitation. With regard to sight as perception of images we must not forget what Aristotle affirms in the *Poetics*:

> the reason of the delight in seeing the picture is that one is at the same time learning—gathering the meaning of things, e.g. that the man there is so-and-so; for if one has not seen the thing before, one's pleasure will not be in the picture as an imitation of it, but will be due to the execution or colouring or some similar cause.[43]

Just as the ear has been referred to as the moral sense in the *Politics*, so also here sight is the sense that stands out to perceive the products of imitation.

In sum, concerning the elements of sense that human beings perceive in relation to actions, the following can be said: (a) They are captured by *sight* and *hearing*, where what is captured by the ear refers above all to emotions and moral character, while the visible makes it possible to compare and distinguish similarities and differences of a formal nature more clearly than in auditory contrasts. (b) The senses that relate *to human actions* allude to some kind of movement or process. (c) In both cases, perception links the viewer with a memory and generates a movement in the viewer that can be sympathetic or empathetic. Ultimately, in all cases there is a relationship with a previous

---

on *Emotion*, p. 18. Sense perception is complex too. It implies emotions and thoughts, which combined by practical reason may produce an idea about an action. Takatura Ando, *Aristotle's Theory of Practical Cognition*, The Hague: Springer 1965, pp. 235–6.

42   In *Nicomachean Ethics* (11-9, 1109b 23) we read: "such things depend on *particular facts* [καθ' ἕκαστα], and the decision rests with perception, and the decision lies with perception." About this, see the work of Eve Rabinoff (*Perception in Aristotle's Ethics*, Evanston: Northwestern University Press 2018) to deepen in the importance of perception as an important path for the acquisition of virtues. The author recalls that understanding is not enough to learn the virtue: discernment in virtuous action also requires perception. As part of the problem, she suggests the following passages where Aristotle develops this idea: *Nicomachean Ethics* 1113a 1–2; 1126b 4; 1142a 27; 1143b 6; 1147a 27; 1147b 18. *De anima*, 11-5, 417b 21–29.

43   *Poetics*, 4, 1448b 15–20.

experience with which the perceived is linked, already as an impulse, as a memory, and as a comparison.

Thus, in the perception of the actions—both real and fictitious—there is a capacity for comparison, so that to the physical capture of the movement that is part of an action interpretative stimuli, sounds and images are added, that, by comparison or relationship, are significant and are integrated into the practical knowledge of the particular.[44]

The central point, the axis of our investigation, is the affirmation that Aristotle makes in the *Poetics* regarding the imitated action, because he states: "We have laid it down that a tragedy is an imitation of an action that is complete in itself, as a whole of some magnitude."[45] To be complete, it must have structural parts, beginning, middle and end, and its magnitude must be ordered and "visible," that is, the *viewer* must not be lost when contemplating his unity.

Beauty consists in magnitude and ordered arrangement. From this it follows that neither a very small creature would be beautiful—for our view [θεωρία] of it is almost instantaneous and therefore confused—nor a very large one, since being unable to view it all at once, we lose the effect of a single whole; for instance, imagine a creature a thousand miles long. Just as creatures and other organic structures must have a certain magnitude and yet be easily taken in by the eye, so too with plots: they must have length, but must be easily taken in by the memory.[46]

The other criterion that Aristotle gives for magnitude is that the transition from fortune to misfortune or vice versa is produced properly, that is, that a certain movement, a process, occurs. In addition, we are again faced with the need for the viewer to contemplate and remember, that is, that he or she can link the story's elements of sense and therefore be affected by them. Of this he warns in the *Rhetoric*:

---

44   *Nicomachean Ethics*, 11-9, 1109b 21–26: "But up to what point and to what extent a man must deviate before he becomes blameworthy it is not easy to determine by reasoning, any more than anything else that is perceived by the senses; such things depend on particular facts, and the decision rests with perception." To deepen this idea see Ando, *Aristotle's Theory of Practical Cognition*, pp. 255f.

45   *Poetics*, 7, 1450b25.

46   *Poetics*, 7 1450b34-1451a6. For "vision" Aristotle uses θεωρία, meaning both sight and the place of the spectator at the theatre or public games. See Henry George Liddell and Robert Scott, *A Greek-English Lexicon*, Oxford: Clarendon Press 1940, voice: θεωρία. It is interesting how he compares here vision and memory.

> Further, pleasure is the consciousness through the senses of a certain kind of emotion; but imagination is a feeble sort of sensation, and there will always be in the mind of a man who remembers or expects something the imagination of what he remembers or expects. If this is so, it is clear that memory and expectation also, being accompanied by sensation, may be accompanied by pleasure. It follows that anything pleasant is either present and perceived, past and remembered, or future and expected, since we perceive present things, remember past ones, and expect future ones.[47]

Later in the text, Aristotle continues to affirm that in most wishes a certain pleasure is followed, and he gives as examples the thirst due to fever or the relationship of lovers who speak and write:

> So also a lover enjoys talking or writing about his loved one, or doing any little thing connected with him; all these things recall him to memory and make him as it were present to the eye of imagination. Indeed, it is always the first sign of love, that besides enjoying some one's presence, we remember him when he is gone; and we love when we actually feel pain because he is there no longer.[48]

Thus, for Aristotle, sense is associated with pleasure and pain, whether present or related to time (past and future), and their participation is essential to discern and guide actions, or to value what is perceived relative to them imitatively. In this way, the entire field of sense intervenes in the process of perceiving actions and what they have of particularity and concreteness. However, the *visibility* to which Aristotle alludes is not only depleted in sense, but it aspires to an intelligibility of the action in order to be "whole and complete." It is a matter of practical knowledge.

4   The Intellectual Vision of Actions

The main problem of the intellectual visibility of actions lies in their concretion. It seems that, properly, we can only have a vision of the complete action from the mimetic representation of it since it is more general, while concrete

---

47   *Rhetoric,* I, 11 1370a 6–8. See also Stephen Halliwell, "Pleasure, Understanding and Emotion," in *Aristotle's Ethics: Critical Essays,* pp. 243–9.

48   *Rhetoric,* I, 11 1370b 11–12.

actions are difficult to understand precisely because of the particular limitations of their concretion. This requires an explanation.

For Aristotle, the main elements that are recognized in human action are the end, the deliberation, the decision, the execution and the results. From the latter, correction and consequences are also followed.[49] In addition, they are executed in a specific and particular context; human action is always a mediated activity, that is, mediated by deliberation and choice.[50] If these elements could be synthesized, one would say that choice is the distinguishing key to human action, and execution is the direct cause of its manifest reality. Therefore, before the "concrete execution" everything that can be said about the action is general, being broader, and not real, but possible. Hence the famous passage in the *Poetics*, Book 9, where Aristotle explains the difference between history and poetry:

> it consists really in this, that the one describes the thing that has been, and the other a kind of thing that might be. Hence poetry is something more philosophic and of graver import than history, since its statements are of the nature rather of universals, whereas those of history are singulars. By a universal statement I mean one as to what such or such a kind of man will probably or necessarily say or do—which is the aim of poetry, though it affixes proper names to the character.[51]

Like everything that can be otherwise, there is a tension between the possibility and the realization of that possibility.[52] Being contingent, human actions are strictly real when they materialize. On the other hand, the imitation of human actions takes shape only in the poetic sphere. Being an object external to the action, the goal of the poetic activity is distinguished from the action itself and not the concrete one because it shows only the possible nature of

---

49   Sarah Broadie, *Ethics with Aristotle*, New York. Oxford University Press 1993, pp. 179–85. See also Ricardo Yepes and Javier Aranguren, *Fundamentos de antropología*, Pamplona: Eunsa 2001, pp. 104–6; and Daniel Westenberg, *Right Practical Reason, Aristotle, Action and Prudence in Aquinas*, New York: Oxford University Press 1994.

50   *Nicomachean Ethics*, 111-3, 1112b 30 - 1113a 13. On the elements of the action, see I-10 (5), 1369a 31-1369b 35, §12–19.

51   *Poetics*, 9, 1451b 4–9. See also Martha Husain, *Ontology and the Art of Tragedy: An Approach to Aristotle's Poetics*, New York: State University of New York Press 2002, p. 65, pp. 89–90.

52   Franz Brentano, *Von der Mannigfachen Bedeutung des Seienden nach Aristoteles*, Charleston: Nabu Press 2014, pp. 29–30: "Something is current if it exists in complete reality. The potential being lacks this reality, although nothing impossible can result if the potential being reaches the actuality of which it is said to be capable."

the action.[53] In this sense, poetic works are more general than history because the realities that come together in it remain open and philosophical. The truth that is discovered in them is a possible truth: it is plausibility. Thus, all the versatility that Aristotle finds in poetic activity has, in its same purpose, a border, a more or less precise circumscription.[54] This statement is surprising when one considers that, for Aristotle, poetry is more universal than history and is therefore more philosophical.

The question we must solve now is why fictitious actions are more eloquent to gain practical knowledge than real actions. Aristotle poses a similar question in *Problems* section XVIII-3:

> Why is it that in rhetorical displays men prefer examples and stories rather than enthymemes? Is it because they like to learn and to learn quickly, and this end is achieved more easily by examples and stories, since these are familiar to them and are of the nature of particulars, whereas enthymemes are proofs based on generalities, with which we are less familiar than with the particular? Further, we attach more credence to any evidence which is supported by several witnesses, and examples and stories resemble evidence, and proofs supported by witnesses are easily obtained. Further, men like to hear of similarities, and examples and stories [μῦθοι] display similarities [παραδειγμα].[55]

This fragment is a treasure. It not only refers to the exemplarity and eloquence of the speeches, but also to the credibility of the testimonies and learning by similarities, which is found both in examples and in myths. This leads us to propose that the kind of vision we should refer to with Aristotle on this subject is not limited or does not merely refer to the sense of sight, but to a more complex composition of perceptions and valuations, to principles of unity and possibility, that they belong to an intelligible level of understanding. A composition that can only occur in practical reasoning.[56] Therefore, Aristotle, speaking of the "vision" of the viewer, refers to an experience more related to testimony and practical judgment than to the ability to see colors or figures.

---

53   *Poetics*, 9, 1451a 35-1451b 11. Especially the statement in 4–9.
54   On the fallacy of believing that, being more universal, poetry is more *scientific* in the *positivist* sense of the word, see Geoffrey Ste. Croix, "Aristotle on History and Poetry," in *Essays on Aristotle's Poetics*, ed. by Amelie Oskenberg Rorty, Princeton: Princeton University Press 1992, pp. 23–32.
55   *Problems*, XVIII, 3, 916b 27–34.
56   Ando, *Aristotle's Theory of Practical Cognition*, pp. 256–8.

It is important to remember that, for Aristotle, this vision is not only a source of knowledge, but also implies some kind of emotion, and when it comes to fictions it also involves pleasure.[57] To this he also refers in *Problems* XVIII, 9 and 10:

> Why do we feel more pleasure in listening to narratives in which the attention is concentrated on a single point than in hearing those which are concerned with many subjects? Is it because we pay more attention to and feel more pleasure in listening to things which are more easily comprehended, and that which is definite is more easily comprehended than that which is indefinite? Now a single thing is definite, but a plurality partakes of the nature of the infinite.
>
> Why do we like to hear of events which are neither very old nor quite new? Is it because we discredit events which occurred long before our time and take no pleasure in events which we discredit, while we can still, as it were, perceive very recent events and so take no pleasure in hearing about them?[58]

If we return to the elements of sense we studied previously, both the elements involved in music and the visual elements are composed in a *mimesis,* that is, an imitation. They correspond to the *means* of imitation mentioned in the *Poetics,*[59] and because of their relevance they contribute eloquence to the decision as a crucial part of an action; however, they are never simple elements. A single sound does not mimic actions but elements of them, like a line of a sketch. They are always in relation to something else, even if that something else is not present.

---

57   Fortenbaugh (*Aristotle on Emotion*, pp. 90–1) recalls the intention in Greek *paideia* to develop good dispositions in the future citizens since childhood through the habituation of the proper emotions, since young people live primarily in accordance with their passions and desires. Practical reason is developed later in life.

58   *Problems,* XVIII, 9–10, 917b 7–16.

59   *Poetics,* 1, 1447a 15–23: "But they differ one from another in three ways: either in using means generically different or in representing different objects or in representing objects not in the same way but in a different manner. For just as by the use both of color and form people represent many objects, making likenesses of them—some having a knowledge of art and some working empirically—and just as others use the human voice; so is it also in the arts which we have mentioned, they all make their representations in rhythm and language and tune, using these means either separately or in combination."

Previous experiences allow the artist—and also the viewer—to complete what is missing. This, in part, is due to practical cognition, and it becomes a practice that develops and improves its criteria.

That which in the realm of everyday reality is perceived only superficially and is judged through assumptions and hypotheses, through an exercise in fiction is presented to the viewer's intelligence as a "whole and complete" action, with all its complexity. What we would normally have to assume, is represented through a series of equally complex elements that include physical movement, psychological movements and discourses.

5   About Mimesis as Visibility of the Action

It remains to be considered why it is possible to achieve full visibility of the action through poetic imitation. There is something in the production that mimics practical actions that, in its general nature and in the structure of its composition, allows the full dimension of *praxis* [πρᾶξις] to be revealed. For this, it is necessary to consider what mimesis is, its fictitious dimension and its structure and its specific ability to achieve the visibility of the practical.

Mimesis or imitation [μίμησις] is a complex concept with several analogical meanings in Aristotelian philosophy. It involves the simple idea of a copy, but can also refer to performance or representation. It may also refer to the action or the product obtained through the action, although the main sense tends to refer to the active representation.[60] One of these meanings can be glossed as the tendency to "learn by doing." This doing seems to be carried out just as things and facts are normally done, detached from the express intention to learn. Thus, it is not the same to speak to communicate something than to speak to learn to speak, or to speak in order to learn to speak well; although in all cases the action is mechanically similar.

Understanding this sense of Aristotelian mimesis requires considering its dual purpose: a) learning, b) doing/acting. It is required to do something to learn it and thus understand it [μανθάνω].[61] The question here is what kind of

---

60   Many authors have considered this problem, like the aforementioned Stephen Halliwell in *The Aesthetics of Mimesis* and Martha Husain in *Ontology and the Art of Tragedy: An Approach to Aristotle's Poetics*. See also Claudio W. Veloso, *Aristóteles mimético*, Sao Paulo: Discurso 2004; Viviana Suñol, *Más allá del arte. Mímesis en Aristóteles*, Buenos Aires: Universidad Nacional de la Plata 2012.

61   See Halliwell, *The Aesthetics of Mimesis*, p. 179.

realities can be learned in this way: mainly, those that carry a practical truth, that is, those in which good or perfection depend on our actions.

The fictional aspect of mimesis as a tendency is not an independent operation, but an opening of the soul.[62] In its concrete operation, mimesis is general and abstract. In it, only certain traits of reality are taken: those necessary for production. It is *techne* (the productive habit or art) that makes it possible to specify the selection criteria in each case with their respective degree of particularity.[63] That is why it is different to speak of a single improvisation than to treat a representation with ordered parts, and such a difference gives rise to the birth of "arts" in the *Poetics*.[64]

The truth of mimesis consists, for this reason, in the relationship of the process to its purpose. It rests not in the adequacy of the contents of the antecedent (the song of the bird) and the consequent (the whistle) as a simple copy. It is, instead, the adequacy of the efficient principle with its purpose. If this rightness is achieved, it results in multiple outcomes that are expressed in learning, in the understanding of the so-called "human affairs" [ανθρώπινα], in the end *par excellence* that is the activity itself, and in the pleasure that follows the activity. Losing sight of this unifying and permanent value of mimesis within the activity is equivalent to losing the beginning and substance of the activity itself. Mimesis is for Aristotle a principle of fertile wisdom: as an activity involves a production *per se* (that is, something external to the activity) in its exercise, but its end is none other than the activity itself.[65]

The activity of mimetic production is aimed at finding the principle of activities, mainly those actions of practical life (ethical and civic) related to

---

62   What is said about it in general can also be applied to the Aristotelian examples of the doctor who represents the proceeding of nature to obtain the health of his patient or the navigator who manages the forces of wind and waves to get the ship to advance. Aristotle refers to this when he affirms that art imitates nature in the *Physics*, 11-8, 199a 15.

63   By guiding the production process according to the "true reason," τέχνη or technique gives a principle of *unity* to what is produced. As what is produced is a compound reality, the result of a process, its unity is manifested as a "structure" [σύστασης] where each of the parts makes sense *in* and *through* the "whole." A productive activity perfected by the τέχνη habit results in a *solid*, well-hatched product, because the *generation* process has been oriented in such a way that the parties have a convenient proportion to each other and according to the purpose of production. This relationship between σύστασης and τέχνη is the point that has received the most attention in the criticism of the *Poetics* in recent years due to the importance of language, logic and structuring in contemporary philosophical topics and has great relevance in research on the *mythos*. Freeland, "Plot Imitates Action," pp. 111–32.

64   *Poetics*, 4, 1448b 21 and 1449a 10–15.

65   See Paul Woodruff, "Aristotle on Mimesis," in *Essays on Aristotle's Poetics,* pp. 91–4.

the human good.[66] The human soul—encouraged to "become one" with all reality—has to be versatile, to reveal a principle as unattainable as the one that underlies the activities of free beings. If this is certainly the background of Aristotelian mimesis, it should not be taken as a formal intellection, but as a vital *praxis*.

The link between *mimesis* and practical truth discovers its suitability as a source of learning in human realities because the human soul has its own faculties and actions that allow the realization of life in this free condition by the possible and determinable. The productive activity, *poíesis* [ποίησιζ], and art as perfection of this activity [τέχνη], are part of this open field, not defined beforehand, that imitation can nourish as an efficient cause of an artistic production and as a source of truth.

As we have seen, mimesis, in order to be considered a positive source of knowledge, requires the fictitious statement that derives from the concrete object of poetics, which are practical actions or "human affairs." This is due to the characteristics of freedom, possibility and contingency of the actions that mimesis puts into action in poetic activity. This activity is concretized by the efficiency of the poíesis in a material context, in a formalization that mimesis inspires and moves as a source, as *techne* guides the process with excellence. In order to better understand the perspective of Aristotle's *Poetics*, it is crucial to understand the three terms, *poetry*, *techne* and *mimesis*, in relation with each other and not separately.

Aristotle warns in the *Nicomachean Ethics* that production and action are different activities, both in their aims and in their virtues.[67] However, the *Poetics* begins with the possibility of producing an action. Mimesis, by enduring the tension between both activities, opens a peculiar context that will be called "fiction" in this context.[68]

Fiction may be considered as the *site* of an action, a supposed terrain that allows establishing the constructive possibilities of production and, at the same time, enables the execution of an action which is "whole and complete," as Aristotle states the poetic work should be. Fiction constitutes the poetic reality, that is, the hypothetical space in which the action produced is verified. When talking about fiction, it is not possible to avoid the problem of the

---

66   See Göran Sörbom, *Mimesis and Art, Studies in the Origin and the Early Development of an Aesthetic Vocabulary*, Stockholm: Svenska Bokförlaget 1966, pp. 158–60.

67   *Nicomachean Ethics*, VI-4, 1140a 1–7; 15–17.

68   The use of this word, which is not properly Aristotelian, has been taken by many scholars nowadays. For example, Sarah Worth, "Aristotle, Thought and Mimesis: Our Responses to Fiction," *The Journal of Aesthetics and Art Criticism*, vol. 58, no. 4, 2000, pp. 333–9.

relationship between poetic action and reality. One might think that poetry is unreal, given the hypothetical space in which it develops. But, as stated in the previous paragraph, mimesis is based on reality itself and fiction contributes to quote reality as a possibility. Thus, what poetry presents in fiction not only has reality in a small hypothetical field, but also has the vocation to illuminate the possibilities of real life. This makes poetry an eloquent activity towards the discovery of reality, especially in human life.

Considering the relationship between fiction and reality, one must also take into account the truth of poetry in two categories, one intrinsic and the other manifest. The work of art itself demands a logical coherence, an economy of parts and an intrinsic unity. But what is true *ad intra* has a vocation towards reality as plausibility, as the possibility of the true. Fiction allows us to contemplate what can be true in movement or composition (which is the most appropriate way to contemplate practical truth).[69] Through fiction, poetics allows us to know that truth that becomes true in action.

Now, in its being "one and whole," the poetic cannot—nor should it—encompass the totality of the real. First, because it would be impossible, since reality and its relations are inexhaustible; and second, because such a work would not give rise to any visibility. On the other hand, what could motivate the poet to transcribe or cite historical facts in his work? According to Aristotle, such a reference would take place only insofar as the real thing is plausible because it has already happened, and its possibility is proven, so to speak.[70]

By maintaining the aspect of "possibility," mimesis referring to free action is never a copy. It is a re-production because each action, being re-presented, truly presents an action that is performed at that moment, that is, it is a real action, but its context is fictitious.[71] The intentionality of the action is fictitious and has its starting point, its development and its end within that context.

---

69   Recognizing this feature of reality *put in observation* in a fictional context implies a practical dimension and not only one manufactured by the poet. Aristotle comes to consider in Book VIII of *Politics* the incidence of music and art in the education of citizens, so that the art of political life cannot be subtracted (*Politics*, VIII-6, 1340b 20–25). It is not about proposing a state art, but recognizing a practical dimension of art where the artist has a personal impact on society: his work is, in addition to a specific object, a *political* action.

70   *Poetics*, 9, 1451b 29–32: "Even supposing he represents what has actually happened, he is none the less a poet, for there is nothing to prevent some actual occurrences being the sort of thing that would probably or inevitably happen, and it is in virtue of that that he is their *maker*."

71   Lamarque proposes that the *imaginary worlds* maintain a double perspective: one internal and one external. He points to a lucky example: Who created Frankenstein, the monster? Dr. Victor Frankenstein, of course. That is the answer from the internal perspective. From the external perspective it would be necessary to answer: Mary Shelley. Peter

The "fictional" dimension radically distinguishes poetic actions from actions in the real or natural context of human life. At the same time fiction allows contemplation of the development of the action. In fact, making the process that involves an action visible is already, in itself, a quality that the real action does not possess. It is fiction that manages to put this dimension in view. Woodruff points out that the fictional context is an unavoidable characteristic of mimesis.[72]

This perspective of fiction is more obvious in arts such as theater, cinema, dance, where the viewer is usually more aware of the fictional context that he contemplates. In the constructive and plastic arts, the reference to the sense of mimesis as a real action is blurred because the first thing that is put "in sight" is its work aspect in the sense of ergon: the produced.[73]

What this fictitious dimension shows is the dynamic aspect of poetic imitation related to actions. On the one hand, the action is renewed. On the other hand, it does so in a general and not a particular way, so that it cannot be simply a human praxis. The tension between practical and poetic action can be checked by remembering two Aristotelian texts: first, Aristotle said in the *Nicomachean Ethics* that the action is truer when it is particular, and that everything that is said about the action has a general meaning.[74]

However, in the *Poetics,* as just noted, he says that poetry is more philosophical because it is general.[75] In fact, it is hardly intended to deceive the spectator. However realistic or *hyperrealistic* a work may be, it has at least the intention of surprising, of highlighting something of reality, of framing it,[76] so that the whole work is configured in this understanding.[77]

Lamarque, "In and Out of Imaginary Worlds," in *Virtue and Taste, Essays on Politics, Ethics and Aesthetics*, Hoboken: Blackwell 1993, p. 145.

72   Woodruf, "Aristotle on *Mimēsis*," p. 84: "The audience does know that nothing truly painful or destructive is taking place in stage; otherwise they could not take pleasure in the performance."

73   Here, the idea of mimesis as depiction of a form is more relevant and pleasant to the eye. It is another aspect of mimesis as we previously considered.

74   *Nicomachean Ethics*, 11-7, 1107a, 27–31. What is said about the action is not the same as doing an action. What has been said about the action does not have the concreteness of the action taken.

75   *Poetics*, 9, 1451b 5–8: "For this reason, poetry is something more scientific and serious than history, because poetry tends to give general [καθόλου] truths while history gives particular facts."

76   In this regard, what Danto proposes with the *ready-made* can be considered as a "taking out of reality" and renewal of the everyday. See Arthur Danto, *The Transfiguration of the Commonplace*, Cambridge: Harvard University Press 1981, pp. 90–5.

77   See Emmanuel Lévinas, "Reality and its Shadow," in *Collected Philosophical Papers*, trans. by Alphonso Lingis, Dordrecht: Martinus Nijhoff 1986, pp. 1–13. Levinas proposes that

Levinas' explanation about the relationship and movement of action within "parentheses" agrees in some way with what can be said about fiction from Aristotle's *Poetics*, where fiction is, so to speak, the hypothesis of an action in action. Space is presupposed; it is a projected scenario, but the process that occurs in it—the movement [μεταβολή]—is real. In addition, the rational content of fiction, as a hypothesis, can be true or false, just like any other syllogism in terms of its formal value, even if its subject consists not only of intellectual elements, but of sense and emotional as well.

The Aristotelian term closest to this purpose described as "fiction" is *hypothesis* in the sense of assumption.[78] In the Aristotelian logical works, the *hypothesis* belongs more closely to the scope of the dialectic, the mode of logic itself for things that may be otherwise. It is applied especially in the *Rhetoric*, but in its dialectical character it is also valid for the *Poetics*.[79] For Aristotle, the hypothesis is a supposed premise that will serve to show or make evident (that is, expose) something that has no rational demonstration.[80] One of the most relevant features of the hypothetical syllogism is the fact that there is a convention between the parties they discuss, that is, that they have agreed to take a proposition as if it were true, even if it is not so in a clear manner.[81] Due to the difficulty of the problem being discussed (not being able to be demonstrated, as with all realities that may be otherwise), those who participate in the discussion are guided by plausibility.[82]

---

art *is the shadow* or trace of reality, which shows reality in a "between-time" and as in parentheses. At the same time that the image is suspended—unlike the always transitive everyday reality—it is the result of a real movement *that generates the image*. This real movement is the relationship, according to Lévinas, between reality and its image. Contemporary authors such as Lévinas and Ricoeur show the relevance of this problem in the contemporary sphere.

78 Liddell and Scott place it as the third meaning of the word. In addition, the fourth meaning of *presupposition* that is characterized from ὑποκείμενον, as the presupposition of an action, as proposed before starting and, in syllogism, as the preliminary statement of a fact corresponds better to the explanation of poetics. See H.G. Liddell and R. Scott, *A Greek-English Lexicon*, voices: ὑπόθεσις, ὑποτίθημι and ὑποκείμενον.

79 Cf. *Poetics*, 16, 1455a 13–16.

80 *Prior Analytics*, I-30, 46a 27–28.

81 *Prior Analytics*, I-44, 50a 19, 32–33. Aristotle claims in this chapter that he will explain later the arguments that conclude by hypothesis, but unfortunately he does not give this explanation anywhere.

82 Such is the example of the aforementioned *Poetics*, where the spectators make a paralogism accepting the fact that no one else has stretched the bow before Odysseus, without having verified this. "There is also a kind of fictitious discovery [ἀναγνώρισις] which depends on a false inference on the part of the audience, for instance in *Odysseus the False Messenger*, he said he would recognize the bow, which as a matter of fact he had not

In this way, the statute of fiction, from the mere fact of being posed as a hypothesis, announces a communicative vocation that establishes relationships between the real and the possible, so that the possibilities can be shared in the same terms in which the reality is. The hypothetical formulation of actions is a way of contemplation on human action, on the way in which man relates to realities, intellectually, volitionally and emotionally. This is one of the main reasons why fictions are educational means for the formation of the individual, precisely in those fields of existence that cannot be simply memorized or deductively resolved.[83]

Fiction becomes a mimesis, a departure from the nature of praxis and from it, from its way of proceeding, act in such a way that the truth is revealed in it. The truth thus revealed is a practical truth; it is the experience of an authentic praxis *teleia*, whose only distance from the real is its fictional quality.[84] To maintain the sincerity of such distance, poetic mimesis recognizes its origin in its character of supposition, of convention.[85] What is shown in fiction is not less true or less good or less beautiful because it is fictitious: it is the truth displayed, sought without pretense of deception, by the sharing of the faculties. Thus, the formula "as if" of the hypothesis is the recognition of mimesis as an imitator of the natural process of action that, to be true and real, has to be acted upon, performed and not only thought.[86]

It must be considered that, despite being a commitment to human action, fiction or the poetic hypothesis is not a moral proposal nor is it determined by a specific doctrine. What follows from the nature of art itself, thus considered, appeals to open and free reality, because in this way it corresponds to the nature of human actions. The poetic hypothesis observes a developing conflict. What is presented in it cannot be taken as a definitive conclusion. In fact, with regard to poetics, it is dangerous to opt for a purely moral pedagogy because, for Aristotle, poetry is not a school for spectators, but a

---

seen, but to assume that he really would reveal himself by this means is a false inference." *Poetics*, 16, 1455a 13–18.

83   See Adam Seligman and Robert P. Weller, *How Things Count as the Same: Memory, Mimesis and Metaphor*, Oxford: Oxford University Press 2018, pp. 53–62. Alfonso López, *Cómo formarse en ética a través de la literatura*, Madrid: Rialp 1994, pp. 27–31.

84   See Kenneth McLeish, *Aristotle: Aristotle's Poetics*, London: Phoenix 1998, pp. 15–6.

85   See Gregory Currie, *The Nature of Fiction*, Cambridge: Cambridge University Press 2008, pp. 49–51.

86   Cynthia Freeland ("Plot Imitates Action," p. 113) proposes that, for Aristotle, much of the pleasure that is obtained by imitation consists precisely in recognizing that *it is an imitation*.

field of life.[87] In art it is possible to contemplate praxis, *bouletiké*, through fiction.[88]

Fiction, then, according to the purpose of Aristotelian poetics, is not a hoax but a hypothesis that poses a paradigm. The exemplarity is not in the represented elements of sense or in the concrete facts, as they are cited, but in the energy of the action represented by these means.[89] This is why the paradigm is not the anecdote or the theme of a work, but *the action that moves* in that anecdote. The dramatic resources that Aristotle proposes in the construction of the tragedy, for example, in the *Poetics* account for the exercise of the fictitious construction of a process that must be put in sight, such as a change, a deliberation and its consequences. This implies the περιπέτεια, the ἀναγνώρισις and the pathetic consequence that constitute the nucleus of the structuring.[90]

In poetic fiction the viewer is not intended to act after the show or as a consequence of it, but rather to act with the show, to see with and in the play, to think with and in it, to make it his or her own, as the magnetic circles whose strength unites the entire stadium.

6   Conclusion

To sum up our previous arguments we can affirm: 1. Aristotle considers knowledge of external human action important because it contributes to the formation of the young person and the moral orientation of the citizen. 2. There is access via the senses or knowledge of the actions performed by other people, according to Aristotelian philosophy. 3. This sense knowledge provides specific data of elements related to the action according to the so-called "superior

---

87   See John S. Marshall, "Art and Aesthetic in Aristotle," *The Journal of Aesthetics and Art Criticism,* vol. 12, no. 2, 1953, pp. 228–31; López, *Cómo formarse en ética a través de la literatura,* p. 31.

88   See Freeland, "Plot Imitates Action," pp. 115–6.

89   In this regard, the following text by Emmanuel Lévinas is revealing: "The conflict between freedom and necessity in human action appears in reflection: when action is already sinking into the past, man discovers the motifs that necessitated it. But an antimony is not a tragedy. In the instant of a statue, in its eternally suspended future, the tragic, simultaneity of necessity and liberty, can come to pass: the power of freedom congeals into impotence. And here too we should compare art with dreams: the instant of a statue is a nightmare. Not that the artist represents beings crushed by fate—beings enter their fate because they are represented. They are enclosed in their fate but just this is the artwork, an event of darkening of being, parallel with its revelation, its truth." Lévinas, "Reality and its Shadow," p. 9.

90   *Poetics,* 11, 1452a 22-1452b 13.

external senses," that is, hearing and sight. A. Specifically, sound provides information regarding moral character. It is important to note that it is perceived as such since it has some kind of movement that is not only physical but is also related to a practical "process." B. Meanwhile, sight makes possible the acquisition of relative knowledge. This allows both the development of biological sympathy (yawning) and emotional empathy (sadness).

4. The knowledge of human actions has an intelligible level that allows us to know the complexity of human action since it is a complex reality, a process composed of parts, e.g., intention, deliberation, choice of means and performance. A. The single perception does not allow the knowledge of the action as "one and whole." Practical reason is needed to understand its meaning. B. Practical reason uses assumptions to fill in the missing information in the actual event as it has been perceived. C. Since it is the knowledge of particular realities, Aristotle refers to this knowledge as "visibility," but does not refer to the knowledge of sight but, by analogy, of a certain "intelligible vision" of action. D. Since these are contingent realities, they cannot be discussed in a concrete way other than in the action taken. For this reason, poetry represents human actions in a general "particularized" sense, unlike history, which refers to particular and concrete actions.

5. In view of the complexity of human actions, there are differences between the knowledge of real human actions and their fictitious representations. A. The perception of real actions only provides fragments of perceptions. B. Actions represented by fiction are presented to knowledge as actions with "unity and wholeness." C. Mimesis, in its poetic dimension, is capable of representing actions in a "credible" way, in a general, coherent and possible sense. This is because mimesis opens a fictional environment based on a hypothesis.

6. The actions represented by imitation or mimesis, to be truly visible to the viewer, must represent an action that is "one and whole." A. *Mimesis* or imitation should be understood as a productive activity [ποίησιζ] that mimics the practical processes of actions [πρᾶξις] through technical excellence [τέχνη]. B. The axis of technical excellence in the mimesis of human actions lies in the composition of the plot or μῦθος. C. The myth contributes to the visibility of the action by the coherence between its parts, which are περιπέτεια or change, ἀναγνώρισις or recognition, and pathetic consequence or outcome.

7. In this way, the action put "in sight" of the spectators is able to reproduce the actions in all their complexity and with all its parts, so that: (a) The narration of the events in the epics may contribute to the moral and practical formation of young people; (b) the scenic representation contributes to the formation of the moral orientation of the citizens who come as spectators to the theater. A. When they see the work of art, they not only contemplate the action represented, but, by virtue of what they see and hear in it, they develop

their emotionality and their empathy. In addition, they recognize their own processes as agents of moral action.

Translated by Carlos Rafael Domínguez

Bibliography

Ando, Takatura, *Aristotle's Theory of Practical Cognition*, The Hague: Springer Netherlands 1965.

[Aristotle], *The Complete Works of Aristotle*, ed. by Jonathan Barnes, Princeton: Princeton University Press 1991.

Bittner, Rudiger, "One Action," in *Essays on Aristotle's Poetics*, ed. by Amelie Oskenberg Rorty, Princeton: Princeton University Press 1992, pp. 97–110.

Brentano, Franz, *Von der mannigfachen Bedeutung des Seienden nach Aristoteles*, Charleston: Nabu Press 2014.

Broadie, Sarah, *Ethics with Aristotle*, New York: Oxford University Press 1993.

Burnyeat, Myles F., "Aristotle on Learning to Be Good," in *Aristotle's Ethics: Critical Essays*, ed. by Nancy Sherman, Lanham: Bowman & Littlefield 1999, pp. 205–30.

Charles, David, *Aristotle's Philosophy of Action*, London: Duckworth 1984.

Currie, Gregory, *The Nature of Fiction*, Cambridge: Cambridge University Press 2008.

Danto, Arthur, *The Transfiguration of the Commonplace*, Cambridge: Harvard University Press 1981.

Fortenbaugh, William W., *Aristotle on Emotion*, London: Duckworth 2002.

Freeland, Cynthia, "Plot Imitates Action," in *Essays on Aristotle's Poetics*, ed. by Amelie Oskenberg Rorty, Princeton: Princeton University Press 1992, pp. 111–32.

González, Ana Marta, "Action in a Narrow and in a Broad sense," in *Practical Rationality: Scope and Structures of Human Agency*, ed. by Ana Marta González and Alejandro G. Vigo, Hildesheim: Georg Olms Verlag 2010, pp. 123–68.

Halliwell, Stephen, "Music and the Limits of Mimesis," in his *The Aesthetics of Mimesis*, Princeton: Princeton University Press 2002.

Halliwell, Stephen, "Pleasure, Understanding and Emotion," in *Aristotle's Ethics: Critical Essays*, ed. by Nancy Sherman, Maryland: Bowman & Littlefield 1999, pp. 241–60.

Husain, Martha, *Ontology and the Art of Tragedy: An Approach to Aristotle's Poetics*, New York: State University of New York Press 2002.

Jaeger, Werner, *Paideia, The Ideals of Greek Culture*, trans. by Gilbert Highet, Oxford: Oxford University Press 1945.

Lamarque, Peter, "In and Out of Imaginary Worlds," in *Virtue and Taste, Essays on Politics, Ethics and Aesthetics*, ed. by Dudley Knowles and John Skorupsi, Hoboken: Blackwell 1993.

Leunissen, Mariska (ed.), *Aristotle's Physics: A Critical Guide*, Cambridge: Cambridge University Press 2015.

Lévinas Emanuel, "Reality and its Shadow," in his *Collected Philosophical Papers*, trans. by Alphonso Lingis, Dordrecht: Martinus Nijhoff 1986, pp. 1–13. (Originally published as "La réalité et son ombre," *Les Temps Modernes*, vol. 38, 1948, pp. 771–89.)

Liddell, Henry George and Scott, Robert, *A Greek-English Lexicon*, Oxford: Clarendon Press 1940.

Lledó, Emilio, "Introducción a las éticas," in Aristóteles, *Ética nicomáquea, Ética eudemia*, Madrid: Gredos 1998.

López, Alfonso, *Cómo formarse en ética a través de la literatura*, Madrid: Rialp 1994.

Marshall, John S., "Art and Aesthetic in Aristotle," *The Journal of Aesthetics and Art Criticism*, vol. 12, no. 2, 1953, pp. 228–31.

McLeish, Kenneth, *Aristotle: Aristotle's Poetics*, London: Phoenix 1998.

Nussbaum, Martha, *The Fragility of Goodness: Luck and Ethics in Greek Tragedy and Philosophy*, Cambridge: Cambridge University Press 1986.

Rabinoff, Eve, *Perception in Aristotle's Ethics*, Evanston: Northwestern University Press 2018.

Sabido, Cecilia, "Mito y estructuración en la *Poética* de Aristóteles," *Iztapalapa. Revista de Ciencias Sociales y Humanidades*, vol. 58, 2005, pp. 63–87.

Sabido, Cecilia, "Poética y ficción en Aristóteles," *Estudios: filosofía, historia, letras,* vol. 101, 2012, pp. 151–63.

Sabido, Cecilia, "Ritmo, mimesis y temporalidad en el arte," *Euphyía*, vol. 7, no. 12, 2013, pp. 45–64.

Seligman, Adam and Weller, Robert P., *How Things Count as the Same. Memory, Mimesis and Metaphor*, Oxford: Oxford University Press 2018.

Sherman, Nancy, "The Habituation of Character," in, *Aristotle's Ethics: Critical Essays*, ed. by Nancy Sherman, Maryland: Rowman & Littlefield 1999, pp. 231–60.

Sörbom, Güron, *Mimesis and Art: Studies in the Origin and the Early Development of an Aesthetic Vocabulary*, Stockholm: Svenska Bokförlaget 1966.

Ste. Croix, Geoffrey E., "Aristotle on History and Poetry," in *Essays on Aristotle's Poetics*, ed. by Amelie Oskenberg Rorty, Princeton: Princeton University Press 1992, pp. 23–32.

Suñol, Viviana, *Más allá del arte. Mímesis en Aristóteles*, Buenos Aires: Universidad Nacional de la Plata 2012.

Tatarkiewicz, Wladislaw, *A History of Six Ideas: An Essay in Aesthetics*, Warsaw: Martinus Nijhoff 1980.

Trueba, Carmen, *Ética y tragedia en Aristóteles*, Barcelona: Anthropos and Universidad Autónoma Metropolitana-Iztapalapa 2004.

Veloso, Claudio W., *Aristóteles mimético*, Sao Paulo: Discurso 2004.

Westenberg, Daniel, *Right Practical Reason, Aristotle, Action and Prudence in Aquinas*, New York: Oxford University Press 1994.

Witt, Charlotte, "In Defense of the Craft Analogy: Artifacts and Natural Teleology," in *Aristotle's Physics: A Critical Guide*, ed. by Mariska Leunissen, Cambridge: Cambridge University Press 2015, pp. 107–20.

Woodruff, Paul, "Aristotle on *Mimēsis*," in *Essays on Aristotle's Poetics*, ed. by Amelie Oskenberg Rorty, Princeton: Princeton University Press 1992, pp. 73–96.

Worth, Sarah, "Aristotle, Thought and Mimesis: Our Responses to Fiction," *The Journal of Aesthetics and Art Criticism,* vol. 58, no. 4, 2000, pp. 333–9.

Yepes, Ricardo and Aranguren, Javier, *Fundamentos de antropología*, Pamplona: Eunsa 2001.

The Philosopher Is Somehow a Lover of Metaphors

Enrique Martínez

Abstract

The aim of this article is to explain the approach of Saint Thomas Aquinas in relation to the language that man uses to speak of God, in particular metaphorical language. Thus, it is a question of responding in this way to the apophatic problem. It begins with the claim of Aquinas, commenting on Aristotle's *Metaphysics*: "The philosopher is, in a sense, a philo-myth, i.e., a lover of myth." Aristotle's position regarding myth is explained first; then I discuss the place of metaphor in the epistemological doctrine of Saint Thomas, following the perspective of the Thomistic School of Barcelona. I conclude that human language, including metaphorical language, can really express divine perfections, but without reaching the knowledge of the essence of God. Finally, I explain how God helped the cognitive weakness of man through Revelation, using metaphors to adapt to man's way of knowing, which reaches the intelligible through the sensible.

1 Introduction

When St. John of the Cross introduces his statements to the two versions of the *Cántico Espiritual* (*Spiritual Canticle*), he states that the mystical experience of God cannot be explained in words understandable to human intellect, for the divine mysteries overflow its capacity.[1] That is why man must resort to "figures, comparisons and similarities,"[2] imitating the way of acting of the Holy Spirit, who, as St. Paul teaches, "asks for us with ineffable groans what we cannot well know nor understand to manifest."[3] That is why the Carmelite saint goes on to say that "the holy doctors, although much they say and say even more, can never end by declaring it by words, just as by words it could not be said. And so, what is declared of it, ordinarily it is the least it contains in itself."[4]

---

1 Juan de la Cruz, "Cántico espiritual," in *Obras Completas*, Madrid: Editorial de Espiritualidad 1980, pp. 677–9.
2 Ibid., p. 677.
3 Ibid.
4 Ibid., p. 678.

© ENRIQUE MARTÍNEZ, 2021 | DOI:10.1163/9789004448674_005

The most prominent of these holy doctors of the Church is St. Thomas Aquinas, whom St. John of the Cross knew well after his training at the University of Salamanca, and whom he venerated receiving him as a magisterial authority.[5] Starting from the statement of the Carmelite at the beginning of the *Cántico* about the limitation of human language regarding God and the reference to the teaching of theologians, we can ask ourselves what is the approach of St. Thomas Aquinas regarding the language used by men to talk about God and to God, and in particular those who use "figures, comparisons and similarities," that is, metaphorical language. Such is the purpose of this paper.

2   "Philosophus est aliquater philomythes"

We will begin our reflection with the statement made by Aquinas when commenting on Aristotle's *Metaphysics*: "The philosopher is, in a sense, a philomyther, i.e., a lover of myth."[6] The ruling of the Dominican master will certainly not solve the question raised, but it will help us to guide it; it is a method similar to the one he used daily in his academic life, in which the *lectio* gave rise to the approach of the various *quaestiones* to be disputed.

To understand the meaning of this statement, it is convenient to contextualize it by putting it in relation to what Aristotle said, of which it is a comment. Let us first read the text of the Stagirite:

> It is through wonder that men now begin and originally began to philosophize; wondering in the first place at obvious perplexities, and then by gradual progression raising questions about the greater matters too, e.g. about the changes of the moon and of the sun, about the stars and about the origin of the universe. Now he who wonders and is perplexed feels that he is ignorant (thus the myth-lover is in a sense a philosopher, since myths are composed of wonders).[7]

---

5   Marcelo del Niño Jesús, *El tomismo de San Juan de la Cruz*, Burgos: Tipografía de El Monte Carmelo 1930, pp. 63–71. Juan González Arintero, *La influencia de santo Tomás en la mística de san Juan de la Cruz y santa Teresa*, Salamanca: Convento de San Esteban 1924, pp. 5–41.

6   Thomas Aquinas, *In Met. In duodecim libros Metaphysicorum Aristotelis expositio*, Rome: Marietti 1950, I, lect.3, n.4.

7   Aristotle, *Metaphysics*, ed. by W.D. Ross Oxford: Clarendon Press 1924,. I, 2, 982b 11–19.

Aristotle is arguing in favor of wisdom as a speculative and non-productive science. He suggests that the admiration was what moved the first philosophers, and not the utility; thus, admired by changes in the natural things that surprised them, they sought to flee from ignorance and ask themselves about their causes. Aristotle highlights in the philosopher both his desire to know the truth and the recognition of his ignorance of what surprises him. This leads him to add an accidental statement to his argumentation, but of notable interest: the philomyther or lover of myths [φιλόμυθος] is in a way a philosopher [φιλόσοφός], because he also admires the surprising. What links the philosopher and the philomyther is not, therefore, the way to respond to their admiration, but what is the beginning of the work of both.

It is true that in some places Aristotle underestimates myths. Suffice it to recall his well-known expression "empty words and poetic metaphors" referring to Plato's theory of Ideas: "To say that the Forms are patterns, and that other things participate in them, is to use empty phrases and poetical metaphors."[8] Or also how he considers unnecessary to investigate the meaning of myths: "However, it is not worthwhile to seriously consider the subtleties of mythologists."[9] But there are also times when he praises them; and not only as a resource of poetic art, but for the truth that they contain.[10] Thus, for example, in Book XII of *Metaphysics:*

> A tradition has been handed down by the ancient thinkers of very early times, and bequeathed to posterity in the form of a myth, to the effect that these heavenly bodies are gods, and that the Divine pervades the whole of nature. The rest of their tradition has been added later in a mythological form to influence the vulgar and as a constitutional and utilitarian expedient; they say that these gods are human in shape or are like certain other animals, and make other statements consequent upon and similar to those which we have mentioned. Now if we separate these statements and accept only the first, that they supposed the primary substances to be gods, we must regard it as an inspired saying and reflect that whereas every art and philosophy has probably been repeatedly developed to the utmost and has perished again, these beliefs of theirs have been preserved as a relic of former knowledge. To this extent only, then, are the views of our forefathers and of the earliest thinkers intelligible to us.[11]

---

8   Ibid., I, 9, 991a 20–22.
9   Ibid., III, 4, 1000a 19.
10   To deepen in these ideas see Héctor Zagal, "Metáfora y analogía en Santo Tomás," *Medievalia*, vols. 29–30, 1999, p. 110.
11   Aristotle, *Metaphysics*, XII, 8, 1074b 1–14.

We see here the difference established by the Stagirite between the primitive elements and the later additions that can be discovered in the myths. Those who have been incorporated seek to persuade the people in order to what is convenient for political life, making the divine closest to the people through anthropomorphic descriptions. But the primitive elements of the myths state that the first entities that move the celestial spheres are intelligent and immutable gods, and that is why it can be said that the philosophers expressed themselves "divinely."

On the other hand, in the *Poetics* Aristotle also states that poetic metaphors serve two purposes: to please the listener, which is characteristic of poetry, but also to manifest the truth in some way and thus to be able to learn, which is characteristic of philosophy:

> Speaking generally, poetry seems to owe its origin to two particular causes, both natural. From childhood men have an instinct for representation, and in this respect, differs from the other animals that he is far more imitative and learns his first lessons by representing things. And then there is the enjoyment people always get from representations. What happens in actual experience proves this, for we enjoy looking at accurate likenesses of things which are themselves painful to see, obscene beasts, for instance, and corpses. The reason is this: Learning things gives great pleasure not only to philosophers but also in the same way to all other men, though they share this pleasure only to a small degree. The reason why we enjoy seeing likenesses is that, as we look, we learn and infer what each is, for instance, that is so and so.[12]

This positive attitude of Aristotle, although punctual, towards myths seems to maintain what he had in his Academy period manifested in the youth dialogue *On Philosophy*.[13] In any case, the cited texts of *Metaphysics* and *Poetics* show that myth not only serves to please and for usefulness in political life, but also to achieve a certain theological knowledge, although it may be veiled by sensitive images.

12   Aristotle, *Ars Poetica*, ed. by R. Kassel, Oxford: Clarendon Press 1966, 1448b, 4–18. Daniel Vázquez, "Metáfora y analogía en Aristóteles: Su distinción y uso en la ciencia y la filosofía," *Tópicos*, vol. 38, 2010, pp. 85–116.

13   See M. Isabel Méndez, "Consideraciones sobre el mito en Platón y Aristóteles," *Teoría/ Crítica*, vol. 6, 1999, p. 13.

Let us now turn to the comment of St. Thomas Aquinas on the passage of Aristotle in which he states that the philomyther is somewhat a philosopher. He says the following:

> And since wonder was the motive which led men to philosophy, it is evident that the philosopher is, in a sense, a philo-myth, i.e., a lover of myth, as is characteristic of the poets. Hence, the first men to deal with the principles of things in a mythical way, such as Perseus and certain others who were the seven sages, were called the theologizing poets. Now the reason why the philosopher is compared to the poet is that both are concerned with wonders.[14]

We can make several considerations about this passage. On the one hand, and following the Aristotelian approach, Aquinas affirms that the cause for which the philosopher and the poet are similar is in the principle from which both start: admiration for what surprises; neither the way they speak nor what they say equate them. It is true that there is a difference between the commented text and the commentary: Aristotle says that it is the philomyther is somewhat a philosopher, while Saint Thomas points out that it is the philosopher who is in some way a philomyther; but it does not seem from the context that this implies any modification in the sense of the sentence.

On the other hand, he defines the philomyther as a lover of fables; indeed, *fabula* is the usual Latin translation of the Greek μῦθος.[15] He adds that, therefore, the philomyther is a kind of poet, because they love fables. Consequently, when St. Thomas speaks of fables, it must be understood that he refers to a story in poetic language, or more specifically to something proper to that language, that is, the metaphor, as he makes it very clear here: "And Plato's opinion about the materiality of natural species he calls a parable, because it is similar to fables, which are devised for the purpose of conveying some opinion by means of a metaphor."[16] That is why from now on we will no longer use the expression "fable" but "metaphor."

But when this poet deals with the principles of all things, that is, with God, then he is called a "theologizing poet," designating with these words what Aristotle simply calls "theologians." The expressions "theologizing poet" and

---

14   Thomas, *In Met. In duodecim libros Metaphysicorum Aristotelis expositio*, I, lect.3, n.4.

15   See Alfred Ernout and Antoine Meillet, *Dictionnaire Étymologique de la Langue Latine. Histoire des mots*, Paris: Éditions Klincksieck 2001, p. 245.

16   Thomas Aquinas, *In Met.*, VII, lect.11, n.18.

"theologian poet" are used by Aquinas on more occasions than "philomyther," which appears only once in all his work. In this way he resorts to an expression that is present in the patristic tradition. St. Augustine, for example, refers to theological poets with these words: "During the same period of time arose the poets, who were also called *theologues*, because they made hymns about the gods."[17]

We saw that for Aristotle on the one hand it is not worth scrutinizing the meaning of myths, but on the other hand he goes so far as to say that they are useful for political life and even to reach a certain knowledge of God, although in a veiled manner. Is this also true in St. Thomas? The text with which we have begun our reflection does not solve it, so we will have to delve into his thinking. First I will expose the place of the metaphor in the epistemological doctrine of Aquinas in general, and then, more particularly, the relationship of the meta phor with the knowledge of God.

3   The Living Insofar as He Has Word

"A man lives by reason,"[18] St. Thomas states, following Aristotle. And what is proper to reason is the knowledge of the truth, as he himself points out when relating the natural inclinations of man: "Thirdly, there is in man an inclination to good, according to the nature of his reason, which nature is proper to him: thus man has a natural inclination to know the truth about God."[19]

But what is knowing the truth? Any entity is true when it has its proper form, thus being intelligible. And so, the understanding is true when it has the form that corresponds to it, which is the similarity of the intelligible form of the entity:

> Now since everything is true according as it has the form proper to its nature, the intellect, in so far as it is knowing, must be true, so far as it has the likeness of the thing known, this being its form, as knowing. For this reason truth is defined by the conformity of intellect and thing.[20]

17   Augustine of Hippo, *De Civitate Dei libri XXII*, Paris: J.P. Migne 1900, XVIII, 14.
18   Thomas Aquinas, SCG. *Liber de veritate catholicae Fidei contra errores infidelium seu Summa contra Gentiles*, Rome: Marietti 1961, III, c.122, n.8.
19   Thomas Aquinas. *S.Th. Summa Theologiae*, Rome: S. C. de Propaganda Fide 1888–1906, I-II, q.94, a.2 in c.
20   Ibid., I, q.16, a.2 in c.

To apprehend this intelligible form of the entity is to be in the act of understanding, so that it goes on to say that "the intellect in act and the intelligible
in act are one."[21] This immaterial union with the intelligible becomes fruitful
from its perfection in act, forming that similarity of the known, which is the
mental word. This formation of the word arises, therefore, from the fullness
of knowledge, and not so much from its destitution, and must be affirmed as
belonging to the very nature of knowledge as such;[22] the *verbum mentis* is an
act that emanates from the act, and that Aquinas compares to the splendor
coming from the light:

> In like manner, too, the word conceived by our intellect does not pro-
> ceed from potency to act except in so far as the intellect proceeds from
> potency to act. For all that, the word does not arise in our intellect except
> as it exists in act; rather, simultaneously with its existence in act, there is
> a word conceived therein (...) Therefore, the generation of the word itself
> is not like the process from potency to act, rather it is like the origin of
> act from act, as is brilliance from light and an understanding understood
> from an understanding in act.[23]

As the mental word pronounced by the intellect is by nature a similarity of the
thing, it must be said that the very thing of the understanding is to know the
adequacy between the mental word and the thing. That is why "true" is said
mainly of the judgment by which the correspondence of the concept with the
being of the thing is affirmed:

> But the intellect can know its own conformity with the intelligible thing;
> yet it does not apprehend it by knowing of a thing "what a thing is."
> When, however, it judges that a thing corresponds to the form which it
> apprehends about that thing, then first it knows and expresses truth.[24]

Therefore, it must be affirmed with the Dominican master that the purpose
of every word is to manifest the known, which is nothing but what the thing

---

21   Thomas Aquinas, SCG II, c.55, n.11; Enrique Martínez, "Ser, conocimiento y amor," *Sobre los
     tipos y grados de conocimiento: Cognoscens in actu est ipsum cognitum in actu*, ed. by C.A.
     Casanova and I. Serrano del Pozo, Santiago de Chile: RIL–Centro de Estudios Tomistas
     2018, pp. 63–91.

22   Francisco Canals, *Sobre la esencia del conocimiento*, Barcelona: PPU 1987, pp. 272–5.

23   Thomas Aquinas, SCG IV, c.14, n.3.

24   Thomas Aquinas, *S.Th.*, I, q.16, a.2 in c.

is, its truth: "But the true that is in things is convertible with being as to substance; while the true that is in the intellect is convertible with being, as the manifestation with the manifested; for this belongs to the nature of truth."[25] And hence, if we said that the nature of man is to live by reason, we could now more adequately express the Aristotelian definition of man as "living as he has a word." This is how Francisco Canals, the maximum representative of the so-called "Tomist School of Barcelona," develops this thesis:

> Speaking *significantly* belongs to the essence of the human as such. The coined formula that defines it as a *rational animal* originally had the meaning, not to mean it with the generic character of animality, as a sensitive organic corporeity, to specifically differentiate it by rationality, as a qualifier of the what of his substance, but it directly referred to human life, naming the man with the participial term of the verb to live: *living*, or what is the same, as *someone who lives*, to specify that he exercises his life by possessing the word endowed with *intelligible* meaning; *living in so far as he has a word* would be a deeper version of the Aristotelian definition.[26]

Consequently, it must be concluded that man's inherent characteristic is to speak meaningfully or intelligibly, that is, manifesting with his words the truth of things.

4   The Metaphor as a Manifestation of the Truth

Assuming these metaphysical, epistemological and anthropological principles, and returning to our purpose, we must now ask ourselves whether the metaphor is also a manifestative word of the truth of things, thus adapting to the natural inclination of man. For this, we must approach one of the ways of saying the entity that is the analogy.[27] It is certainly not the time to explain this admirable Aristotelian metaphysical method, assumed by St. Thomas and

25   Ibid., I, q.16, a.3 ad 1.

26   Canals, *Sobre la esencia del conocimiento*, pp. 79–80.

27   See Ralph McInerny, *Studies in Analogy*, The Hague: Martinus Nijhoff 1968; Lucero González, "La doctrina de Tomás de Aquino sobre la analogía como recurso para el conocimiento natural de Dios. Una meditación filosófica sobre sus límites y alcances," *Revista Perseitas*, vol. 3, no. 2, 2015, pp. 154–74; José I. Saranyana, "Tomás de Aquino: significante, significado y palabras fundamentales," *Scripta Theologica*, vol. 11, 1979, pp. 187–95.

developed, among others, by Cardinal Tomás de Vío "Cayetano" in his work *De nominum analogia*, or by Santiago Ramírez in *De analogia*.[28] Nevertheless, it should be remembered with Canals that the analogy is the synthetic way of saying reality, allowing:

> To put together harmoniously, without contradiction, the one and the multiple, the current and permanent with the changing and mutable, the material singularity and the essential universality, the subsistence of the personal spirit and its infinite openness to the universe and God (...) It is also the path for making visible the gradation of perfections in the plural reality of the universe and the presence, in every entity, of the ontological dimensions that explain its activities and its inclinations and make it possible to discover teleology, present in the order of the universe, ordered, as a cause of the causes, to the infinite and divine good, whose love moves the sun and the stars.[29]

One of those synthetic ways of saying reality is the metaphorical analogy.[30] It is not an attribution analogy; in this, the form signified by the analogous term occurs only in one of the subjects of which it is preached—first analogous—but not in the others, of which it is predicated only by a certain relationship with the first analogous. Thus, when I say "military," I refer properly to the people who are dedicated to the defense of the homeland, but secondarily to the uniforms, weapons, buildings, etc., because of the relationship they have with those people.

On the contrary, the metaphoric is a kind of analogy of proportionality; in this, the relation signified by the analogous term occurs properly in the subjects of which it is predicated, but not in the same way, but proportionally. Thus, when I say "knowledge" I mean both the relationship between the senses and the sensitive objects, as well as the relationship between the understanding and the intelligible objects, but according to a different proportion of immaterial apprehension in each case.

What happens in the metaphorical analogy is that the relationship occurs properly only in one of the analogous, but the other is said as if it was given properly, moving—which is what etymologically means "metaphor"—the

---

28   See José M. Gambra, *La analogía en general: síntesis tomista de Santiago M. Ramírez*, Pamplona: EUNSA 2002.

29   Canals, *Sobre la esencia del conocimiento*, pp. 232–233.

30   Victorino Rodríguez, "Peculiaridades de la analogía metafórica," *Analogía*, vol. 3, no. 2, 1989, pp. 3–11.

meaning in a relationship to the other.[31] Thus, when I say that old age is the sunset of life, the "sunset" occurs properly in the day in relation to the concealment of the sun, but I predicate it metaphorically to the life of man when he ages. This metaphor is what allows St. John of the Cross to affirm in the number 64 of *Dichos de luz y amor* (*Sayings of Light and Love*) that "in the sunset they will examine you in love."[32]

St. Thomas clearly explains the difference between the analogy of proportionality and that of metaphorical proportionality—which he calls "by similarity"—, giving as an example of this the lion character that a man can have:

> A name is communicable in two ways: properly, and by similitude. It is properly communicable in the sense that its whole signification can be given to many; by similitude, it is communicable according to some part of the signification of the name. For instance this name "lion" is properly communicable to all things of the same nature as "lion;" by similitude it is communicable to those who participate in the nature of a lion, as for instance by courage, or strength, and those who thus participate are called lions metaphorically.[33]

This translation is possible, however, because the meaning of the analogous term occurs in some way in the subject of which it is metaphorically preached, although not according to all the significance it has in the subject of which it is properly predicated. He exemplifies it with the metaphor of the lion, so that the nature of the lion certainly does not occur in man, but a boldness and strength that allows one to say that he is "a lion:"

> Moreover, with regard to words used in a transferred sense, a metaphor is not to be understood as indicating complete resemblance, but only some agreement in a characteristic belonging to the nature of the thing whose name is being applied. For example, the word lion is applied to God, not because of a resemblance between two natures possessing sensation, but because of a resemblance based on one property of the lion.[34]

31   See Santiago Ramírez, *De analogía*, Madrid: CSIC 1972, vol. IV, p. 1777; Jesús García-López, "La analogía en general," *Anuario Filosófico*, vol. 7, 1974, pp. 200–3.

32   "A la tarde te examinarán en el amor." Juan de la Cruz, "Dichos de luz y amor," in his *Obras Completas*, Madrid: Editorial de Espiritualidad 1980, p. 119.

33   Thomas Aquinas, *S.Th.* I, q.13, a.9 in c.

34   Thomas Aquinas, *De Veritate. Quaestiones disputatae de veritate*, Rome: Editori di San Tommaso 1976, q. 7, a. 2 in c.

Santiago Ramírez states that this translation is made not so much by a similarity of the essence or nature, but of the operations or their effects: "This [the metaphorical proportionality analogy] is only given according to the similarity of the operation or of the effect, not according to the similarity of essence or nature."[35] In this way, the metaphorical analogy expresses something that really occurs in the subject, even if it is through a term that does not manifest it properly but from a relationship better known to us. And that is why the metaphor always relies on concepts obtained from sensitive knowledge, as Aquinas teaches: "The metaphor is taken from those things that are manifest to the senses;"[36] thus, we can metaphorically translate the meaning behind the terms "lion," "face," "laugh," "sunset," etc., but not the meaning behind the terms "being," "essence," "truth," etc.

Why do we use the metaphorical analogy? We can identify the two reasons we saw earlier in the text of Aristotle's *Poetics*. In the first place, the metaphor is used by the poet to express himself in a pleasant way, as indicated by the Dominican in the first question of the *Summa Theologiae*: "Poetry makes use of metaphors to produce a representation, for it is natural to man to be pleased with representations."[37]

Second, the philosopher uses the metaphor to express the truth of things and for others to learn; but given the limitation of our understanding to do it properly, he then resorts to a similarity based on the sensitivity that comes to his aid. It is true that the metaphor veils the meant reality, as he recalls in the same place: "But by such similarities truth is obscured."[38] But this does not mean that it is a false judgment: "In metaphorical expressions there is no falsehood."[39] This concealment of the truth leads him to recognize, commenting Aristotle, that metaphors are more typical of poets than of philosophers. Thus, that the salinity of the sea is explained by Empedocles as the sweat of the earth is fine in a poem, but not in a philosophical argument, because it does not give a reason for the true cause:

> This perhaps satisfies the demands of metaphorical utterances according to the manner of poets—for to speak in metaphors pertains to poets, and it is probable that Empedocles, who wrote in meter, so they say, uttered

---

35   Ramírez, *De analogía*, vol. IV, p. 1777.

36   Thomas Aquinas, *In Sent. Commentum in quartum librum Sententiarum magistri Petri Lombardi*, Parma: Pietro Fiaccadori 1856–1858, I, d.34, q.3, a .2 ad 3.

37   Thomas Aquinas, *S.Th.*, I, q.1, a.9 ad 1.

38   Ibid., I q.1, a.9 obi. 2.

39   Thomas Aquinas, *Sent.*, II, d.8, q.1, a.3 ad 1.

many things metaphorically. But such a manner of speaking is not sufficient for knowing the nature of a thing; because a natural thing is not
revealed by the comparisons employed in a metaphor (...) But what it is
that can in like manner produce salt in the sea Empedocles has yet to say,
since this is not manifest. And so it is plain that Empedocles sinned in
this: that he did not clearly indicate the cause.[40]

But this does not mean that one cannot learn to a certain extent through metaphors. The clearest example is found in the Divine Revelation; indeed, St.
Thomas teaches that God uses metaphors so man can approach the knowledge, although in a veiled manner, of those truths that exceed his capacity:

> It is befitting Holy Writ to put forward divine and spiritual truths by
> means of comparisons with material things. For God provides for every-
> thing according to the capacity of its nature. Now it is natural to man
> to attain to intellectual truths through sensible objects, because all our
> knowledge originates from sense. Hence in Holy Writ, spiritual truths
> are fittingly taught under the likeness of material things. This is what
> Dionysius says (Coel. Hier. i): *We cannot be enlightened by the divine rays
> except they be hidden within the covering of many sacred veils.*[41]

There is also a reason worth highlighting that unites the two purposes of the
metaphor: to please and to teach. This reason is that the beauty that pleases to
contemplate it, moves the appetite towards good. This is explained by Aquinas,
following Dionysius:

> The object that moves the appetite is an apprehended good. Now if a
> thing is perceived to be beautiful as soon as it is apprehended, it is taken
> to be something becoming and good. Hence Dionysius says (*Div. Nom.* iv)
> that *the beautiful and the good are beloved by all*. Wherefore the honest,
> inasmuch as it implies spiritual beauty, is an object of desire.[42]

Therefore, that decorum or spiritual radiance of beauty precedes the appetite
of good. Francisco Canals insists in this way in this little known thesis of the
Common Doctor, inherited from Dionysius and St. Albert the Great:

---

40   Thomas Aquinas, *In Metereol. In libros Aristotelis Meteorologicorum expositio*,
      Rome: S.C. de Propaganda Fide 1886, II, c.5, n.4.
41   Thomas Aquinas, *S.Th.*, I, q.1, a.9 in c.
42   Ibid., II-II, q.145, a.2 ad 1.

The previous foundation of the effulgence and incandescence of the true. What is the beauty of the true entity is a constitutive condition that we get to apprehend it as good, attractive and naturally desirable. In the attraction of the entity as good, the glowing and incandescent glow of beauty is constitutively present.[43]

Therefore, the beauty of the metaphor can move the appetite to want to know the truth that lies behind it, and to which one is ignorant. That is why the explanation of St. Thomas that links the beauty and appetite of good ends with this quote from Cicero in which he states that this beauty awakens the love of wisdom: "And for this reason Tully says (*De Offic.* I, 5): *Thou perceivest the form and the features, so to speak, of honesty; and were it to be seen with the eye, would, as Plato declares, arouse a wondrous love of wisdom.*"[44] This shock in front of beauty is part of the admiration that was proposed to us at the beginning in the text of *Metaphysics* and its commentary as a starting point for both the work of the poet and that of the philosopher, and hence they can be equated in this. That is why we saw in Aristotle's *Poetics* that the liking for metaphorical similarities naturally moves the desire to learn what things are.

In short, it must be concluded that the metaphor serves the natural inclination of man to know and manifest the truth of things with his words, even if it is from the imperfection of his own way of knowing from the senses, but based on the reality of the compared and on the beauty of the image used. And thus, thanks to the sensitive metaphor we can name the intelligible realities. From the many examples that could be brought up, let us mention these two for their particular beauty: in the first St. Thomas refers to the highest of the judgments of conscience through the sparkle of fire: "Just as the spark is that part of fire which is purer and hovers above the whole fire, so synderesis is that which is supreme in the judgment of conscience. And it is according to this metaphor that synderesis is called a spark of conscience."[45] And in the second example, the Dominican uses the metaphor of light to signify the intelligibility of truth: "By *light*, the *truth* is metaphorically understood."[46]

---

43   Francisco Canals, *Tomás de Aquino, un pensamiento siempre actual y renovador*, Barcelona: Scire 2004, pp. 340–50.

44   Thomas Aquinas, *S.Th.*, II-II, q .145, a.2 ad 1.

45   Thomas Aquinas, *De Veritate*, q.17, a .2 ad 3.

46   Thomas Aquinas, *In De Div. Nom. In librum Beati Dionysii De divinis nominibus expositio*, Rome: Marietti 1950, C.2, lect.4.

5   Know the Truth about God

We must go one step further, and ask ourselves now if man can use adequate words to speak of God, and if among these words we must include metaphors.[47] Let us recall that in the initial text in which the one who claimed that the philosopher is in some ways a philomyther, he was identified as a "theologizing poet."

It is also worth remembering the identification that St. Thomas makes of man's own natural inclination: "Thirdly, there is in man an inclination to good, according to the nature of his reason, which nature is proper to him: thus man has a natural inclination to know the truth about God."[48] Indeed, it is not just a natural inclination to know the truth, but the truth about God.

The goal of a natural inclination must, logically, be attainable by the subject, since otherwise it would lead to deny that very nature. Such a possibility must be affirmed even more if it is the ultimate goal of human life, the one in which one's perfection is reached, which is happiness. St. Thomas starts from the natural desire that exists in man to know the cause of an effect, typical of those who admire what they see; he argues that, if the first cause of all things could not reach the intellect, this natural desire would be disappointed; thus it must be concluded that there is a natural capacity in man's understanding to know God:

> For there resides in every man a natural desire to know the cause of any effect which he sees; and thence arises wonder in men. But if the intellect of the rational creature could not reach so far as to the first cause of things, the natural desire would remain void.[49]

Moreover, as it is about the perfection itself, that the intellect knows God is not only something possible, but it is something due. Therefore, not knowing him should be judged as a guilty ignorance, as explained by Aquinas commenting St. Paul: "So what is notorious of God is for them, who are inexcusable, that is, that they cannot be excused for ignorance."[50]

---

47   Rafael Cúnsulo, "Las metáforas ¿son el único camino para conocer a Dios?," *Studium, Filosofía y Teología*, vol. 39, 2017, pp. 43–53.

48   Thomas Aquinas, *S.Th.*, I-II, q.94, a.2 in c.

49   Ibid., *S.Th.*, I, q.12, a.1 in c.

50   Thomas Aquinas, *In Rom. Super Epistolam ad Romanos lectura*, Turin and Rome: Marietti 1953, c.1, lect.7.

The name given to that knowledge of God is "wisdom," the characteristics of which St. Thomas describes suggestively at the beginning of the *Summa contra Gentiles*: "Among all human pursuits, the pursuit of wisdom is more perfect, nobler, more useful, and fuller of joy."[51] However, he adds that this wisdom occurs in man according to the capacity of his understanding, which is limited by his corporeal condition and, therefore, by sensitive knowledge: "Our natural knowledge begins from sense. Hence our natural knowledge can go as far as it can be led by sensible things."[52] Therefore, it must be said that our understanding cannot reach by its natural forces the knowledge of the divine Essence, to form a similarity to it. It can be said then with St Thomas, who resorts to the Aristotelian comparison that human understanding is to God as the eye of the owl with respect to the sun: "He remarks that Aristotle likewise agrees with this conclusion. He says that *our intellect is related to the prime beings, which are most evident in their nature, as the eye of an owl is related to the sun*."[53]

That is why, when speaking about God, we know more about what he is not than what he is, because his essence is always beyond the reach of the natural capacity of human understanding, a principle that is insistently affirmed by the Dominican: "Now, because we cannot know what God is, but rather what He is not, we have no means for considering how God is, but rather how He is not."[54]

But what then can we know about God? Aquinas teaches that by the principle of causality we can get to know his existence as the ultimate and uncaused cause of all things; from there we deduce some attributes that necessarily belong to him, which we always know in relation to the created, denying how much of creatural we recognize in the effects:

> But because they are His effects and depend on their cause, we can be led from them so far as to know of God whether He exists, and to know of Him what must necessarily belong to Him, as the first cause of all things, exceeding all things caused by Him.[55]

And we must not give up this knowledge, even if it is very poor in comparison to what God is, as he says quoting Aristotle:

---

51   Thomas Aquinas, *SCG*, I, c.2, n.1.
52   Thomas Aquinas, *S.Th.*, I, q.12, a.12 in c.
53   Thomas Aquinas, *SCG*, I, c.3, n.7.
54   Thomas Aquinas, *S.Th.*, I, q.3, pr.
55   Ibid., *S.Th.*, I, q.12, a.12 in c.

Aristotle says that *man should draw himself towards what is immortal and divine as much as he can*. And so he says in the *De animalibus* [I, 5] that, although what we know of the higher substances is very little, yet that little is loved and desired more than all the knowledge that we have about less noble substances. He also says in the *De caelo et mundo* [II, 12] that when questions about the heavenly bodies can be given even a modest and merely plausible solution, he who hears this experiences intense joy. From all these considerations it is clear that even the most imperfect knowledge about the most noble realities brings the greatest perfection to the soul.[56]

This which man knows of God can also be expressed in words, as is characteristic of the nature of knowledge. Now, since human understanding cannot know God but from creatures, recognizing him as the first cause of everything, in the same way the names used to refer to God will necessarily be taken from the same creatures:

> It follows therefore that we can give a name to anything in so far as we can understand it. Now it was shown above that in this life we cannot see the essence of God; but we know God from creatures as their principle, and also by way of excellence and remotion. In this way therefore He can be named by us from creatures, yet not so that the name which signifies Him expresses the divine essence in itself.[57]

He adds in that same place that in the divine names that man expresses, one must distinguish the reality signified and the way of meaning. According to the former, these names may properly mean divine perfections, which occur in a more excellent way in God than in creatures; thus, for example, "being," "good," "living," etc., and according to the latter, these names will always be expressed in the human way of knowing God, that is, very imperfectly, and therefore not appropriate to the way in which God is cognizable in himself:

> Therefore as to the names applied to God—viz. the perfections which they signify, such as goodness, life and the like, and their mode of signification. As regards what is signified by these names, they belong properly to God, and more properly than they belong to creatures, and are applied

---

56   Thomas Aquinas, *SCG*, I, c.5, n.5.
57   Thomas Aquinas, *S.Th.*, I, q.13, a.1 in c.

primarily to Him. But as regards their mode of signification, they do not properly and strictly apply to God; for their mode of signification applies to creatures.[58]

6   The Metaphor as a Manifestation of the Truth about God

And finally we come to the specific object of our study: the use of metaphor in relation to our knowledge of God, which St. Thomas calls "metaphoric," "parabolic" or "symbolic:" "And because, furthermore, these principles are not proportionate to human reason in the condition of the present life, which customarily receives truths from sensitive things, that is why we must be led to knowledge of these principles by sensitive similarities: hence the mode of this science must be metaphorical or symbolic or parabolic."[59]

We find this metaphorical way of meaning from the distinction it makes between the names whose significance only includes the same perfection that is predicated about God, even if it is in the human way, and those that maintain the imperfection of the creature in its meaning. The former are called according to an intelligible mode and the latter according to a metaphorical mode: "He writes *intelligible* unlike those things that are said of God in a symbolic or metaphorical way, whose meanings are sensitive."[60] This is how Aquinas presents this distinction:

> There are some names which signify these perfections flowing from God to creatures in such a way that the imperfect way in which creatures receive the divine perfection is part of the very signification of the name itself as "stone" signifies a material being, and names of this kind can be applied to God only in a metaphorical sense. Other names, however, express these perfections absolutely, without any such mode of participation being part of their signification as the words *being, good, living*, and the like, and such names can be literally applied to God.[61]

But let us not forget what has been said before regarding the use of metaphor: the translation of meaning is possible because it partially includes a perfection that really does occur in God. Thus, when we say of God that he is

58   Ibid., *S.Th.*, I, q.13, a.3 in c.
59   Thomas Aquinas, *In Sent.*, I, q.1, a.5 in c.
60   Thomas Aquinas, *In De Div. Nom.*, C.13, readings 4.
61   Thomas Aquinas, *S.Th.*, I, q.13, a.3 ad 1.

"lion," we are not predicating of him the animal condition of the lion, but the strength, which in God is real and eminently given. Thus Aquinas says: "So the name of *lion* applied to God means only that God manifests strength in His works, as a lion in his."[62] And if we say of God that he is the Sun, it is because the operation by which he communicates the truth is similar to that of the sun that illuminates the corporeal; this is how Santiago Ramírez explains this metaphorical analogy: "God is said to be the Sun because he illuminates everybody as well as illuminates every spirit."[63]

And if both the metaphorical mode and the proper way of naming the divine perfections really express them, it must also be remembered that neither in the metaphorical mode nor in the proper mode is it possible to know the divine Essence, as we have seen previously. This is very clearly stated by Aquinas in the middle of his commentary on Dionysius' *De Divinis Nominibus*:

> However, since every resemblance of the creature with God is flawed and that what God is overcomes everything that is found in the created realities, anything we know in the created realities is removed from God as to his way of being in creatures, in such a way that, after all that our understanding can conceive of God from creatures, this same thing that God is remains hidden and unknown. Indeed, God is not only not a stone or the sun, as they are known by the sense, but he is not also life or essence, as they can be conceived by our understanding and thus, what God is, because that surpasses everything we know, remains ignored by us.[64]

That man uses metaphors to please and teach, as we have seen, is equally applicable to the way of metaphorically naming God. Indeed, on the one hand man uses metaphors to beautifully express the divine perfections, so that the pleasure caused by the contemplation of certain sensitive perfections provides the understanding for the contemplation of the divine Beauty. In this way, sensitive metaphors allow judging intelligible things from sensitive ones, which belongs to the third degree of contemplation of the six established by Richard of Saint Victor, as Aquinas comments:

> These six denote the steps whereby we ascend by means of creatures to the contemplation of God. For the first step consists in the mere consideration of sensible objects; the second step consists in going forward

---

62   Ibid., *S.Th.*, I, q.13, a.6 in c.
63   Ramírez, *De analogía*, vol. IV p. 1777.
64   Thomas Aquinas, *In De Div. Nom., Prooemium.*

from sensible to intelligible objects; the third step is to judge of sensible objects according to intelligible things.[65]

These words also make it possible to address God with praise in the darkness of faith and to teach men in some way the divine perfections. Hence, man cannot only name God, but must do so, both for the obligation of giving God the due worship in external praise and for the usefulness of others, as Aquinas teaches in dealing with the virtue of religion:

> On the other hand we employ words, in speaking to God, not indeed to make known our thoughts to Him who is the searcher of hearts, but that we may bring ourselves and our hearers to reverence Him. Consequently we need to praise God with our lips, not indeed for His sake, but for our own sake; since by praising Him our devotion is aroused towards Him, according to *Ps.* 49:23: *The sacrifice of praise shall glorify Me, and there is the way by which I will show him the salvation of God.*[66]

Given the limitation of human understanding to know and name God, and the same use of sensitive metaphors, it is easy to fall into many serious mistakes, confusing God with creatures. This is what the Common Doctor acknowledges, citing the book of *Wisdom*: "Well, this glory was changed by attributing it to other beings. *So the uncommunicable name was given to wood and stones*, as it is said in the *Wisdom* 14, 21."[67]

For this reason, and because those who would come by their own strength to the knowledge of God would be very few and after a long and difficult exercise of rational argumentation, St. Thomas concludes the desirability of God revealing truths about Him accessible to reason: "Beneficially, therefore, did the divine Mercy provide that it should instruct us to hold by faith even those truths that the human reason is able to investigate. In this way, all men would easily be able to have a share in the knowledge of God, and this without uncertainty and error."[68]

But not only for these reasons, but mainly because God has wanted to elevate man to a supernatural end that exceeds all his nature and his capacity, the Dominican teaches that the revelation of those truths ordered to the salvation of man was necessary:

---

65   Thomas Aquinas, *S.Th.*, II-II, q.180, a.4 ad 3.
66   Ibid., II-II, q.91, a.1 in c.
67   Thomas Aquinas, *In Rom.*, C.1, lect.7.
68   Thomas Aquinas, *SCG*, I, c.4, n.6.

It was necessary for man's salvation that there should be a knowledge revealed by God besides philosophical science built up by human reason. Firstly, indeed, because man is directed to God, as to an end that surpasses the grasp of his reason: *The eye hath not seen, O God, besides Thee, what things Thou hast prepared for them that wait for Thee* (*Is.* 66:4). But the end must first be known by men who are to direct their thoughts and actions to the end. Hence it was necessary for the salvation of man that certain truths which exceed human reason should be made known to him by divine revelation.[69]

And, as we have seen previously, in the Revelation God wanted to use precisely metaphors to adapt Himself to man's way of knowing, which reaches the intelligible through the sensitive.

These metaphors, which keep the divine truth veiled under sensitive images, do not prevent that truth from being achieved, as we have been arguing throughout this paper. He who receives this truth in the darkness of faith may, however, know it, because he explains by speaking of the virtue of faith that the believer does not stay in the means by which he knows but reaches the same meant reality: "Now the act of the believer does not terminate in a proposition, but in a thing. For as in science we do not form propositions, except in order to have knowledge about things through their means, so is it in faith."[70]

Moreover, the divine truths in faith are achieved more perfectly by means of metaphors than by reason, even if it is by metaphysical arguments. This is what the Dominican states: "In many respects faith perceives the invisible things of God in a higher way than natural reason does in proceeding to God from His creatures. Hence it is written (*Eccles.* 3:25): *Many things are shown to thee above the understandings of man*."[71]

That the believer reaches the revealed truth, even when it is in the darkness of faith and of the mediation of sensitive metaphors, allows this truth to be taught to others, as Aquinas explains by relying on Dionysus:

The ray of divine revelation is not extinguished by the sensible imagery wherewith it is veiled, as Dionysius says (*Coel. Hier.* i); and its truth so far remains that it does not allow the minds of those to whom the revelation has been made, to rest in the metaphors, but raises them to the knowledge of truths; and through those to whom the revelation has been made

---

69   Thomas Aquinas, *S. Th.*, I, q.1, a.1 in c.

70   Ibid., II-II, q.1, a.2 ad 2.

71   Ibid., II-II, q.2, a.3 ad 3.

others also may receive instruction in these matters. Hence those things that are taught metaphorically in one part of Scripture, in other parts are taught more openly.[72]

Thomas applies here the ordaining principle of his whole life, according to the spirit of the Order of Preachers: bring to others what has been contemplated: "For even as it is better to enlighten than merely to shine, so is it better to give to others the fruits of one's contemplation than merely to contemplate."[73] In this way, the revealed metaphors mainly serve the utility of man, as expressly indicated in the first question of the *Summa Theologiae:* "Poetry makes use of metaphors to produce a representation, for it is natural to man to be pleased with representations. But sacred doctrine makes use of metaphors as both necessary and useful."[74]

Does this exclude the purpose of pleasing? Not at all. The divine realities manifested to man through sensitive images are certainly beautiful, and it is pleasing to contemplate them. Let us see an example of this in his commentary on *Psalm* 25. He shows us affection for divine worship, which is the result of the contemplation of his beauty, for every man loves beauty. The sensitive images of the book of Numbers—the shops, like numerous valleys and like irrigated gardens—lead us to superior intelligible realities—good deeds, divine gifts and saints themselves. The contemplation of the beauty of the first disposes us to the contemplation of the beauty of the superiors and, finally, to the contemplation of the Beauty of God himself, who manifests his glory or clarity in his works:

> Here he shows his disposition to divine worship, which, as befits, must be a feeling of love. That's why he says: *Lord, I loved the beauty of your house.* And as Dionysius says: *The good and the beautiful are an object of love for all beings.* This is why every man loves the beautiful: the carnals love the carnal beauty, the spiritual ones love the spiritual beauty, and that is the beauty of the house of God. (*Num.* 24: 5-6): *How beautiful are your tents, Jacob, your dwelling places, Israel! Like valleys they spread out, like gardens beside a river, like aloes planted by the Lord.* Now this beauty is made of good works, or of divine gifts, or saints themselves, for all things are like a beauty of the house of God. Now all these things, I have loved them, that they may make me able to adorn the house of God. Thus is

---

72   Ibid., I, q.1, a.9 ad 2.
73   Ibid., II-II, q.188, a.6 in c.
74   Ibid., I, q.1, a.9 ad 1.

manifested his disposition, which is made of love, beauty and grace. But it must be known that this beauty is due to the habitation of God, as a house is beautiful only to the extent that it is inhabited; so I loved her so that you may live in me, or I have loved the country in order to live there, or to tend towards it. And that is why he says: *and the place where your glory dwells.* And all these things, that is, the good works, the gifts of God, and the saints themselves, are the beauty of the house of God, as shines upon them the divine grace which embellishes as the light, as Ambrose says, because without light all things are ugly: *The majesty of the Lord entered the temple by the door which looked east.*[75]

We must not forget that the ultimate purpose of the Revelation is, according to St. Thomas, to contemplate God by the light of glory, all mediation of sensitive images and intellectual species having disappeared:

Therefore it must be said that to see the essence of God, there is required some similitude in the visual faculty, namely, the light of glory strengthening the intellect to see God, which is spoken of in the Ps. 35:10, *In Thy light we shall see light.* The essence of God, however, cannot be seen by any created similitude representing the divine essence itself as it really is.[76]

That is why theology is both a speculative and a practical science, as he teaches at the beginning of the *Summa Theologiae,* although it needs to be more speculative than practical, when dealing mainly with God and not with human acts: "Still, it is speculative rather than practical because it is more concerned with divine things than with human acts; though it does treat even of these latter, inasmuch as man is ordained by them to the perfect knowledge of God in which consists eternal bliss."[77]

Together with the contemplative purpose, the manifestation of divine truths and their contemplation also has a practical purpose, which is one's own salvation and that of other men. And that occurs eminently through divine worship, which is not only aimed at praising God, but also inducing men to do so, as we have indicated above.[78]

---

75   Thomas Aquinas, *In Ps. In psalmos Davidis expositio,* Parma: Pietro Fiaccadori 1863, 25, n.5.
76   Thomas Aquinas, *S.Th.,* I, q.12, a.9 in c.
77   Ibid., I, q. 1, a.4 in c.
78   Ibid., II-II, q. 91, a .1 in c.

Therefore, the most perfect word of man in this life is that which is addressed to God in prayer asking him to manifest his Essence, or, resorting to the beautiful revealed metaphor, that He shows him his Face. This is what St. Thomas explains by commenting on *Psalm* 26:

> This is a particular mark of the one who loves, to seek often after the thing loved. And he indicates what he seeks when he says, *Thy face, O Lord, will I still seek*. This is what Moses was asking for in *Exodus* 33: *Show me thy face*. And the Lord did not immediately show it, but said, I will show thee all good; Luke 10: *Blessed are the eyes that see the things which you see.* And so, David was not without hope, but was still seeking (for it); hence he says elsewhere (possibly *Psalm* 79:4, 8, 20 or *Psalm* 30:17): *Show us thy face* etc.; *Job* 33: *He shall pray to God, and he will be gracious to him: and he shall see his face with joy.*[79]

It is seen here how man can address God with appropriate words, and it is by going precisely to the same ones that God has revealed to him, for he does not find for himself what words to pray with. In the foreword to the commentary on the *Psalms* Aquinas teaches it with clarity and devotion; after indicating that he who prays with the psalms prepares for God to manifest Himself, he adds that the way of praying is by resorting to the words revealed in the Holy Scripture; and then compares the language of the man who prays with that of the child who uses the words that another provides him:

> Therefore Gregory, I Homily, says on Ezekiel, that the voice of psalmody if it is done with the intention of the heart, prepares the way for almighty God through it to the heart, so that he may pour in mysteries or the grace of compunction, by an intent soul or prophecy. The end purpose therefore is for the soul to be joined with God, as the Holy and Most High. The author of this work, however, is signified there in *words of glory*. It should be noted, however, that things are different in the case of Sacred Scripture and in the case of the other sciences. For the other sciences are produced by human reason, but Sacred Scripture is produced through inner urging of divine inspiration, 2 *Peter* 1. *For it is not by human will that prophecy was brought forth, but they spoke inspired by the Holy Spirit.* And so the tongue of man in Sacred Scripture is like the tongue of a child who says words that another provides. *Psalm* 44, *My tongue is like a pen* etc.

---

79   Thomas Aquinas, *In Ps.*, 26, n.8.

2. *Kings* 23. *The Spirit of the Lord has spoken through me, and his speech through my tongue.* And so he says: *in the word of the Lord, or glory*: which are said by revelation. Hence 3. *Kings* 20. *Strike me in the word of the Lord,* that is, in divine revelation.[80]

7   Conclusion

Saint John of the Cross said that man must resort to "figures, comparisons and similarities" to talk about the experience of God. Thus we have seen that St. Thomas Aquinas also teaches that. His theological science, certainly, "can never end by declaring it by words." And so Aquinas himself recognizes it when he sings his praises to God in the hymns of the Office of Corpus Christi. He resorts there, as it could not be otherwise, to the metaphor of bread, which translates to the Body of Christ, as the same Revelation teaches. In his commentary on the Gospel of St. John he explains this metaphor: if the material bread is corporeal food that sustains this life, the spiritual bread is food for the soul, giving it eternal life:

> Jesus said to them: *I am the bread of life,* for as we saw above, the word of wisdom is the proper food of the mind, because the mind is sustained by it: *He fed him with the bread of life and understanding* (*Sir* 15:3). Now the bread of wisdom is called the bread of life to distinguish it from material bread, which is the bread of death, and which serves only to restore what has been lost by a mortal organism; hence material bread is necessary only during this mortal life. But the bread of divine wisdom is life-giving of itself, and no death can affect it. Again, material bread does not give life, but only sustains for a time a life that already exists. But spiritual bread actually gives life: for the soul begins to live because it adheres to the word of God: *For with you is the fountain of life,* as we see in the *Psalm* (35:10).[81]

But this explanation cannot give us a full understanding of the mystery, which remains veiled for the *homo viator*. But Aquinas does not skip resorting to the metaphor of bread, founded on the reality of God's communication of eternal life to the soul through the Body of Christ. And he does it not only to talk

---

80   Ibid., *Prooemium.*
81   Thomas Aquinas, *In Ioann. Super Evangelium S. Ioannis lectura*, Rome: Marietti 1972, c.6, lect.4.

about God, but to talk to God. Thus we find it in the beautiful hymn *Lauda Sion Salvatorem*, of the Mass of *Corpus Christi;* in it, St. Thomas Aquinas praises God with those words that will never be enough to express the mystery, but that resort to the likeness of the bread revealed by God Himself to come to the aid of our poverty: "Praise, O Zion, thy Savior, praise thy Leader and thy Shepherd in hymns and canticles. As much as thou canst, so much darest thou, for He is above all praise, nor art thou able to praise Him enough. Today there is given us a special theme of praise, the Bread both living and life-giving."[82]

In this way, the philosopher not only claims to be in some way a philomyther or lover of metaphors, but also a philotheos or friend of God, as Saint Thomas Aquinas teaches us:

> Since friends have one mind and heart, it does not seem that what one friend reveals to another is placed outside his own heart: *Argue your case with your neighbor* (*Prv* 25:9). Now God reveals his secrets to us by letting us share in his wisdom: *In every generation she [Wisdom] passes into holy souls and makes them friends of God and prophets* (*Wis* 7:27).[83]

Translated by Carlos Rafael Domínguez

Bibliography

Augustine of Hippo, *De Civitate Dei libri XXII*, Paris: J.P. Migne 1900.

Aristotle, *Metaphysics*, ed. by W.D. Ross, Oxford: Clarendon Press 1924.

Aristotle, *Ars Poetica*, ed. by R. Kassel, Oxford: Clarendon Press 1966.

Canals, Francisco, *Sobre la esencia del conocimiento*, Barcelona: PPU 1987.

Canals, Francisco, *Tomás de Aquino, un pensamiento siempre actual y renovador*, Barcelona: Scire 2004.

Cayetano (Thomas de Vio), *Scripta philosophica: De nominum analogía. De conceptu entis*, Rome: Angelicum 1954.

Cúnsulo, Rafael, "Las metáforas ¿son el único camino para conocer a Dios?," *Studium. Filosofía y Teología,* vol. 39, 2017, pp. 43–53.

Ernout, Alfred and Meillet, Antoine, *Dictionnaire Étymologique de la Langue Latine. Histoire des mots*, Paris: Éditions Klincksieck 2001.

---

82   Thomas Aquinas, "Officium Sacerdos," in B.R. Walters, V.J. Corrigan and P.T. Ricketts, *The Feast of Corpus Christi*, Pennsylvania: Pennsylvania State University Press 2007, Missa 1 hymnus 2.

83   Thomas Aquinas, *In Ioann.*, c.15, lect.3.

Gambra, José M, *La analogía en general: síntesis tomista de Santiago M.* Ramírez, Pamplona: EUNSA 2002.

García-López, Jesús, "La analogía en general," *Anuario Filosófico,* vol. 7, 1974, pp. 193–223.

González, Lucero, "La doctrina de Tomás de Aquino sobre la analogía como recurso para el conocimiento natural de Dios. Una meditación filosófica sobre sus límites y alcances," *Revista Perseitas,* vol. 3, no. 2, 2015, pp. 154–74.

González-Arintero, Juan, *La influencia de santo Tomás en la mística de san Juan de la Cruz y santa Teresa,* Salamanca: Convento de San Esteban 1924.

Juan de la Cruz, "Cántico Espiritual," in his *Obras Completas,* Madrid: Editorial de Espiritualidad 1980, pp. 655–897.

Juan de la Cruz, "Dichos de luz y amor," in his *Obras Completas,* Madrid: Editorial de Espiritualidad 1980.

Isabel, Méndez, M. "Consideraciones sobre el mito en Platón y Aristóteles," *Teoría/Crítica,* vol. 6, 1999, pp. 11–6.

Marcelo del Niño Jesús, *El tomismo de San Juan de la Cruz,* Burgos: Tipografía de El Monte Carmelo 1930.

Martínez, Enrique, "Ser, conocimiento y amor," in *Sobre los tipos y grados de conocimiento: Cognoscens in actu est ipsum cognitum in actu,* ed. by C.A. Casanova and I. Serrano del Pozo, Santiago de Chile: RIL–Centro de Estudios Tomistas 2018, pp. 63–91.

McInerny, Ralph, *Studies in Analogy,* The Hague: Martinus Nijhoff 1968.

Ramírez, Santiago, *De analogía,* vols. 1–4, Madrid: CSIC 1972.

Rodríguez, Victorino, "Peculiaridades de la analogía metafórica," *Analogía,* vol. 3, no. 2, 1989, pp. 3–11.

Saranyana, José I., "Tomás de Aquino: significante, significado y palabras fundamentales," *Scripta Theologica,* vol. 11, 1979, pp. 187–95.

Thomas Aquinas, *In Sent. Commentum in quartum librum Sententiarum magistri Petri Lombardi,* Parma: Pietro Fiaccadori 1856–58.

Thomas Aquinas, *In Ps. In psalmos Davidis expositio,* Parma: Pietro Fiaccadori 1863.

Thomas Aquinas, *In Metereol. In libros Aristotelis Meteorologicorum expositio,* Rome: S. C. de Propaganda Fide 1886.

Thomas Aquinas, *Summa Theologiae,* Rome: S. C. de Propaganda Fide 1888–1906.

Thomas Aquinas, *In Met. In duodecim libros Metaphysicorum Aristotelis expositio,* Rome: Marietti 1950.

Thomas Aquinas, *In De Div. Nom. In librum Beati Dionysii De divinis nominibus expositio,* Rome: Marietti 1950.

Thomas Aquinas, *In Rom. Super Epistolam ad Romanos lectura,* Turin and Rome: Marietti 1953.

Thomas Aquinas, *SCG. Liber de veritate catholicae Fidei contra errores infidelium seu Summa contra Gentiles,* Rome: Marietti 1961.

Thomas Aquinas, *De Veritate. Quaestiones disputatae de veritate*, Rome: Editori di San Tommaso 1976.

Thomas Aquinas, *In Ioann. Super Evangelium S. Ioannis lectura*, Rome: Marietti 1972.

Thomas Aquinas, "Officium Sacerdos," in B.R. Walters, V.J. Corrigan and P.T. Ricketts, *The Feast of Corpus Christi*, Pennsylvania: Pennsylvania State University Press 2007.

Vázquez, Daniel, "Metáfora y analogía en Aristóteles: Su distinción y uso en la ciencia y la filosofía," *Tópicos*, vol. 38, 2010, pp. 85–116.

Zagal, Héctor, "Metáfora y analogía en santo Tomás," *Medievalia,* vols. 29–30, 1999, pp. 109–20.

PART 2

The Problems of Interpretation

∴

The Meanings of Doctrine in *De Doctrina Christiana*

Claudio Calabrese

Abstract

This article studies the meanings of the term doctrine in *De doctrina christiana*, as it is necessary to determine the scope of a word that has been integrated into the worldview of Christianity after a long semantic journey. From a methodological point of view, we integrate two perspectives: on the one hand, a review of the secondary literature on Augustine, based on the turning point that the contributions of H.I. Marrou and P. Brown represented. On the other hand, we apply the philological method, since its historical nature lets us understand the nuances of the transition from classical culture to Christianiy. Our contribution to Augustinian studies rests on the following affirmation: the cultural baggage of the grammarian was put in tension by the interpretation of the Scriptures that express, for Christianity, "the truth that God is," with the darkness and ambiguity of human language. The elementary experience of God involved finding an instrument to express a part of that primordial truth and beauty.

Non solum sapienter, sed eloquenter

1   Introduction

In this chapter we focus on the meanings of the term *doctrine* in Augustine's *De doctrina christiana*[1] and its relation with the intellectual tools forged in the context of Greco-Latin culture, but applied now to revelation and persuasion, indissolubly linked to a certain aesthetic effect, of a new kind of audience, the parishioners. This essay debates how classical rhetoric began to be transformed in light of this novelty.

---

1   Augustine, *De doctrina christiana*, ed. and trans. by R.P.H. Green, Oxford: Clarendon Press 1995.

© CLAUDIO CALABRESE, 2021 | DOI:10.1163/9789004448674_006

We reflect on a book that basically maintains a uniform tone, with a coherent work plan and development; the material offered is very diverse, a fact that has in turn produced a very large number of general and specific studies. H.R. Drobner presents an overview of the research up to the year 2000.[2] We complete this with Levering's work.[3] In his study, Drobner presents his understanding of the work: he divides it into three fields: (a) the distinction between *utor* and *fruor* in Book I; (b) the theory of *de signis* in Books I and II, and (c) a study of the Rules of Tyconius, and the use that Augustine makes of them. The relatively little thought given to the formation of Christian rhetoric draws our attention (Book IV). Even though we will pay attention to the controversial question of the two moments of the transcription of *De doctrina christiana*, we suggest that, in this text, the reading of the Scriptures unifies the theme of understanding with that of teaching; we consider, in fact, that this book is a legitimation and an exhortation to the adoption of the classical culture and that, for this, it gave the outlines of a formative curriculum to sustain the foundations of a Christian culture.[4] In this sense, O'Donnell's idea of *De doctrina christiana* has been extremely suggestive: this would be a program that Augustine himself would have liked to follow.[5] When we approach the work of Augustine, we have in mind the observations of Fitzgerald[6] and Vessey[7] on the scope of the renewal of patristic studies in general and Augustine in particular, from the contributions of H.I. Marrou[8] and P. Brown.[9] These two texts,

---

2   See Hubertus Drobner, "Studying Augustine: An Overview of Recent Research," in *Augustine and His Critics: Essays in Honor of Gerald Bonner*, ed. by Robert Dodaro and George Lawless, London: Routledge 2000, pp. 18–34.

3   See Matthew Levering, *The Theology of Augustine. An Introductory Guide to His Most Important Works*, Grand Rapids: Baker Academic 2013, pp. 1–18.

4   Without Augustine, the works of Cassiodorus (6th century) and Isidore of Seville (7th century) are not possible, but they ensured the survival of this ideology. See Gerald A. Press, " 'Doctrina' in Augustine's 'De doctrina christiana,'" *Philosophy & Rhetoric*, vol. 17, no. 2, 1984, p. 100. Also Melissa Markauskas, "Rylands MS Latin 12. A Carolingian Example of Isidore's Reception into the Patristic Canon," in *Isidore of Seville and His Reception in The Early Middle Ages. Transmitting and Transforming Knowledge*, ed. by Andrew Fear and Jamie Wood, Amsterdam: Amsterdam University Press 2016, pp. 177–208.

5   James J. O'Donnell, "Doctrina christiana, De," in *Augustine Through the Ages: An Encyclopedia*, Grand Rapids: Eerdmans 1999, pp. 278–80.

6   Allan D. Fitzgerald, "Tracing the Passage from a Doctrinal to a Historical Approach to the Study of Augustine," *Revue d'études augustiniennes et patristiques*, vol. 50, 2004, pp. 295–310.

7   Mark Vessey, "Introduction," in *Augustine and the Disciplines From Cassiciacum to Confessions*, ed. by Karla Pollmann and Mark Vessey, Oxford: Oxford University Press 2005, pp. 1–21.

8   H.I. Marrou, *Saint Augustin et la fin de la culture Antique*, Paris: Éditions de Boccard 1948.

9   Peter Brown, *Augustine of Hippo: A Biography*, Berkeley and Los Angeles: University of California Press 2000.

very different from each other, have guided the discussion about the place of Augustine in the context of Late Antiquity, that is, his connection with literature and the culture of the time. The first text confronts us with a central question: was Augustine a man who belonged to the cultural decline of the classical world? Is it from here that he nurtured his understanding of Christian novelty? Even though it is clear that Augustine, as all members of the Patristic, belonged to both cultures, the question raised by Marrou opened a new stage in the studies, which we can express as follows: how much of the Classical culture was transformed in the light of the Gospel? Or was it known so early that the reception of the revelation demanded a Christian culture?

The idea of a smooth—and then completely schematic—transition between "syntheses of great worldviews" (like a torch that goes from hand to hand from Plotinus to Thomas Aquinas and Bonaventure) ends with P. Brown, through a more refined study of the socio-cultural context of Late Antiquity.[10] Brown's profound innovation consisted in presenting a biography of Augustine enriched by contextual details and endowed with a fine psychological perception. If the book by H.I. Marrou had been highly controversial, as the *Retractatio* of 1949 shows, this polemic takes on a new perspective with the work by P. Brown, since it gives an innovative direction to Augustinian studies.[11] In both cases, the text *De doctrina christiana* is at the center of the argument. For Marrou,[12] the liberal arts were at the center of the baggage of the intellectual culture of the *paideia* and the *humanitas*, in transit to a medieval Christian culture. Brown's chapter 23,[13] *De doctrina christiana*, begins with a reference to H. Marrou, and we consider that the chapter does not expand too much from the conclusions of the French author regarding the presentation of the scientific-pedagogical program of Augustine. However, its contextual precisions enrich and modify the interpretations of H. Marrou. These questions

---

10   Peter Brown, "Introducing Robert Markus," *Augustinian Studies*, vol. 32, no. 2, 2001, p 183. See also: Mark Vessey, "Foreword," *Augustinian Studies*, vol. 32, no. 2, 2001, pp. 179–80; Robert Markus, "Evolving Disciplinary Contexts for the Study of Augustine, 1950–2000: Some Personal Reflections," *Augustinian Studies*, vol. 32, no. 2, 2001, pp. 189–200.

11   See Vessey, "Introduction," in *Augustine and the Disciplines From Cassiciacum to Confessions*, pp. 1–21.

12   Ibid., pp. 329–540. We used the edition of 1983, which contains the *retractatio* as an addendum (pp. 621–712).

13   Brown, *Augustine of Hippo: A Biography*, pp. 256–66. A few years later, the results were published in two volumes: *De doctrina christiana: A Classic of Western Culture*, ed. by Duane W.H. Arnold and Pamela Bright, Notre Dame: University of Notre Dame Press 1995; and Edward D. English, *Reading and Wisdom: The De doctrina christiana of Augustine in the Middle Ages*, Notre Dame: University of Notre Dame Press 1995.

are still present in the Augustinian studies after almost half a century and has found a new expression in the conference "*De doctrina christiana*: a Classic of Western Culture," which was organized by the University of Notre Dame in 1991. From this perspective, we propose to deal with our topic in the following manner: on the one hand, we stop at the Augustinian consideration of the Scriptures as an expression of the truth that is God and as an aesthetic fact and, on the other hand, we study the continuity and the rupture with the classic rhetorical model, in light of the absolute novelty of the Bible's reading and its status as a revealed word.

2   The Meanings of Doctrina

Thus, we propose to study the transition from classical to Christian culture in a specific aspect so as not to fall into a synthesis devoid of nuances, as P. Brown discourages. We demonstrate in our work that the cultural baggage of the grammarian, trained in the reading and teaching of the classics, was put in tension by the new object of study: the Scriptures that express, in Christian conviction, "the truth that is God," with the darkness and ambiguity of human language. In the solidarity established between the method of knowledge and its object, classical rhetoric could not go unchanged. Therefore, the reading of the believer is tensed towards a certain degree of perfection [*qualis esse debeat*]: the "Christian doctrine" is not something that only remains with the reader, but increases when it is shared with the community [*non solum sibi sed aliis*]; the relationship between "doctrine" and "reading aloud" shows us the ideal of reading and interpreting in an ecclesial way. The relationship that Augustine establishes with the sacred text is not analytic (how did it come to be constituted as such?), but spiritual, or of a hermeneutic attitude that starts from within the text (what does it tell me about the truth that is God?) and that carries an intimately religious impulse.[14] As we read in *Confessions* (11. 2. 3), a contemporary text to the first stage of *De doctrina christiana*, one of the favorite images of Augustine to present the reader's relationship with the Scriptures is that of a dense forest where a deer wanders and eats. The expressive resource as an instrument of understanding acquires a new depth

---

14   The affirmation of M. Cameron, "Augustine and Scripture," in *A Companion to Augustine*, ed. by Mark Vessey, Wiley-Blackwell, Chichester: Malden 2012, that "Augustine looks not so much for *meaning* as for *understanding*, and this difference appears on every page he wrote," (p. 202) corresponds more with contemporary methodological questions than with the exegetical concerns of Augustine.

in Augustine, because a text that expresses the transcendence of God receives the same formal treatment that a profane text does. This conviction did not disguise the central notion of Patristics: the authors of the Bible were inspired by God, who revealed his saving plans as he was dictating. This perspective opened an unrestricted allegorizing understanding; Augustine followed his training as a grammarian: he considers, first of all, the need to clarify the literal sense, to establish later the prophetic aspects.[15]

This application of the grammarian's art to the revealed text produces a twisting of the classical model and will reach its first maturity in the pedagogical models of the Carolingian era. Let us follow the first steps of this profound change. The principle of clarifying the dark passages through the clearest, that Augustine presents in II. 6. 7, comes from a text of Cicero, *De inventione*: Cicero[16] recommended to distinguish between what is written and the will of its author, as he will also do in *Topica*:[17] it is necessary to oppose the text and the intention when the letter of the law and the will of the legislator seem to contradict each other.[18] In *De doctrina christiana*, human words are "signs given by God," (II.2.3) which are properly eloquent in the salvation: rhetoric leads to seek the wisdom of God. As Augustine deepened the understanding of the humanity

---

15 Claudio César Calabrese, "Literatura y teología en el Libro X de 'La ciudad de Dios'," *Classica et Christiana*, vol. 12, 2017, pp. 69–88. See also: Claudio César Calabrese, "Allegory, Myth and Liberal Arts in St. Augustine 'De ordine' I. 8. 24," *Graeco-Latina Brunensia*, vol. 23, 2018, pp. 21–34.

16 Cicero, *De Inventione, De Optimo Genere Oratorum, Topica*, trans. by H. M. Hubbell, London: Heinmann 1949, II, 141: "... *deinde ex utilitatis et honestatis partibus ostendere quam inutile aut quam turpe sit id, quod adversarii cicant fieri oportuisse ut oportere et id quod nos fecerimus aut postulemus, quam utile aut quam honestum sit; deinde leges nobis caras caras esse non propter litteras, quae tenues et obscurae notae sint voluntatis, sed propter earum rerum, quibus de scriptum est, utilitatem et eorum, qui scripserint, sepientiam et diligentiam: postea, quid sit lex, describere, ut ea videatur in sententiis, non in verbis consistere: et iudex is videatur legi optemperare, qui sententiam eius, non qui scripturam sequitur; deinde, quam indignum sit eodem affici supliccio eum, qui propter aliquod scelus et audaciam contra leges fecerit, eye um, qui honesta aut necessaria de causa non ab sentential, sed sibi ab litteris legis recesserit.*"

17 Cicero, *Topica*, XXV, 96: "*Id autem contingit, cum scriptum ambiguum est, ut duae sententiae diferentes accipipossint. Tum opponitur scripto voluntas scriptoris, ut quaeratur verbane plus an sententiae valere debeant.*"

18 Alejandro Guzmán, "Dialéctica y retórica en los *Topica* de Cicerón," *Revista de Estudios Histórico-Jurídicos*, vol. 23, 2010, pp. 161–95. For the theoretical context of the problem see Antoine C. Braet, "Variationen zur Statuslehre von Hermagoras bei Cicero," *Rhetorica: A Journal of the History of Rhetoric*, vol. 7, no. 3, 1989, pp. 246–7; E. Berti, "Le controversia della raccolta di Seneca il Vecchio e la dottrina degli *status*," *Rhetorica: A Journal of the History of Rhetoric*, vol. 32, no. 2, 2014, pp. 125–7; Heinrich F. Plett, *Literary Rhetoric. Concepts – Structures – Analyses*, Leiden: Brill 2010, pp. 33–8.

of Christ and, consequently, the role of the Church in the plan of salvation, he also sharpened his interpretation of the Scriptures, because he departed from the unity of Christ. This allowed him, on the one hand, to advance in the fundamental dogma of the centrality of the Son[19] and, on the other, to order rhetorically the hermeneutics of both Testaments, according to the correlation required by Quintilian.[20] An expressive turn of *Confessions* (7. 21. 27) is revealing the spiritual instances of this continuity: when he contemplated the Scriptures, he found the only face (*una facies*) that contemplated him.

This approach to the concept of doctrine involves distinguishing two very broad fields: one refers to any properly scientific study; another, to the ordering of the knowledge acquired in that study. When Augustine specified the meaning of the term with the adjective *christiana* he implied, in addition to the obvious sense of a knowledge understood in a Christian key, that this search was not only scientific, but also sapiential, that is, the truth founded on the Scriptures and on the tradition. Augustine contrasted this perspective of unity with the pagan teachings, which he considered in terms of multiplicity and confusion.[21]

In this sense, *doctrine* seems to indicate the systematic compendium of Christian teaching or of some particular subject of that compendium; nevertheless, applied concretely to the work that we consider, it does not agree with the content nor with its general sense. The opening of *De doctrina christiana*, in which Augustine reveals the purpose of the work, opens a path to reach the meaning of the term: he proposes to offer "norms" [*praecepta*] for whoever reads and wants to understand the sacred text [*studiosis*] not only to take advantage of those who have exposed their teachings, but also to have a method for transmitting what they have learned: *Haec tradere institui volentibus et valentibus discere.*

When Augustine considers the possible detractors of the *praecepta*, he mentions, in fourth place, those who precisely consider that it is not necessary to

---

19   In this time of dispute with the Manicheans, he needed to demonstrate the deep unity of both Testaments, starting with the prophetic figure of Christ or, in the Augustinian vocabulary, the secret continuity of both: the Old "veiled" (*velatum*) and in the New, the "revealed" (*revelatum*). Augustine, *En. Ps.*, 105, 36. Unless otherwise noted, Latin references to Augustine's works are presented according to the *S. Aurelii Augustini Opera Omnia*—based on Jacques-Paul Migne's *Patrologiae Latinae Elenchus* edition—which can be found in digitalized form in the website www.augustinus.it.

20   Quintilian, *Institutio Oratoria*, ed. by Tobias Reinhardt and Michael Winterbottom, Oxford: Oxford University Press 2006, 7, 10, 16–17.

21   Augustine, *En. Ps.* 31, 2, 18; ep. 233: *Multae enim doctrinae sunt, si tamen doctrinae dicendae sunt, vel superfluae, vel noxiae.*

have "norms," since the understanding of the difficult passages can be reached by means of a divine gift [*divino munere*]; although the divine inspiration is not excluded, the truth is that, just as reading and writing were invented by means of natural reason (*per homines*, according to the Augustinian expression), in *De doctrina christiana* Augustine points out the means that facilitate the understanding of the sacred text and the transmission of what has been learned. He himself presents the opposite examples of Saint Anthony, who learned by heart through attentive listening of the sacred text and who reached his perfect spiritual understanding, and of the Christian slave of barbaric origin, contemporary with the Bishop of Hippo, who learned to read and write perfectly after having asked for it through prayer for three days; it is clear that there is talk about something completely exceptional. For us it is important to insist on this: Augustine does not offer a constituted doctrine of Christian culture, but the hermeneutical foundations for a dialogue *in fieri* between faith and reason.

From the beginning, Augustine clearly shows that the Bible is one of the foundations of Christian culture; for this reason, his effort is aimed at providing comprehension instruments:

> There are certain rules for the interpretation of Scripture [*tractandarum scripturarum*] which I think might with great advantage be taught to earnest students of the word, that they may profit not only from reading the works of others who have laid open the secrets of the sacred writings [*divinarum literarum operta*], but also from themselves opening such secrets to others.[22]

A first approach to the meaning of *doctrina* is intimately linked to the education received in the pagan school, whose knowledge finds a new direction: the understanding of the sacred text. It is not a new instrument, because the *grammaticus* used it in the understanding of classical culture; he has changed, indeed, the textual reality and orientations [*praecepta*] on which the believer exercises his understanding.[23] A first delimitation of the term doctrine is found in the exercise of reading and subsequent comment; here we open two paths: first, what does this reading imply in the context of Late Antiquity? And second, who are these readers and the reasons why Augustine himself warns us over some typologies of them? The final paragraph allows us to understand the direction of the Augustinian argument:

---

22   Augustine, *De doctrina christiana*, Preface 1.
23   This concern is also found in Augustine, *Fid. et symb.*, I, 1.

I, however, give thanks to God that with what little ability I possess I have in these four books striven to depict, not the sort of man I am myself (for my defects are very many), but the sort of man he ought to be who desires to labor in sound, that is, in Christian doctrine, not for his own instruction only, but for that of others also.[24]

In Augustine there is no margin for doubt in the authority of the Scriptures as a revealed word, and, therefore, it is completely foreign to his mentality to judge the truth that the Scriptures express in a critical sense, that is, diverse from the faith; the existential tension between "who I am" and "who should I be" is the experience that leads reading as a path of asceticism to God. For this reason, Book I of *De doctrina christiana* places love at the center of attention, starting with *Mt.* 22: 37–40, since it guides the fruitful (or not) character of reading. The degree of understanding of the Scriptures depends on the degrees of ascent that each reader reaches in this perfection of love. In this concrete sense, every true interpretation is spiritual, because reading and understanding are proportional to the love with which the reader performs these actions; here also lies the need to establish the literal sense, because it is the fundamental step to achieve spiritual reading: not every dark or difficult passage is an allegory or an enigma, therefore it is necessary to clarify thoroughly the meaning of expressions used in an unusual sense or *quaedam verba translata*, according to the Augustinian turn in *De doctrina christiana*.[25] The impulse of love goes from knowing the Scriptures to knowing oneself, because the clarity found in reading becomes light for the reader; this circular correlation is the essence of the Augustinian hermeneutics: if the interpretation transforms an individual, this is also true for humanity.[26]

The figure of the believer who wants to understand puts at stake a central element: if faith requires believing in all the passages of the Bible with the same intensity, this conviction takes root in the experience of the celebration of the Liturgy, since everything concerns Christ: as God [*secundum Deum*], as Head of the Church [*caput Ecclesiae*] and as total Christ [*totus Christus*].[27]

---

24   Augustine, *De doctrina christiana*, 4, 31, 64: *Ego tamen Deo nostro gratias ago, quod in his quattuor libris non qualis ego essem, cui multa desunt, sed qualis esse debeat qui in doctrina sana, id est Christiana, non solum sibi sed aliis etiam laborare studet, quantulacumque potui facultate disserui.*

25   Augustine, *De doctrina christiana*, III, 12, 17.

26   James A. Andrews, *Hermeneutics and the Church in Dialogue with Augustine*, Notre Dame: University of Notre Dame Press 2012, pp. 135–42. Here the author works in depth on the correlation between the notions of *regula fidei* and *regula dilectionis*.

27   Augustine, *Sermons. The Works of Saint Augustine: A translation for the 21st Century*, trans. by Edmund Hill, Brooklyn: New City Press 1990, 341 (1, 1): *Dominus noster Iesus Christus,*

From this horizon, Augustine considers that the most difficult or obscure texts of the Scriptures should be interpreted in the light of others that are more accessible: when a controversy arises, the interpreter must be guided by the biblical doctrinal testimony on disputed questions. This resource widely used by the Bishop of Hippo[28] is typical of the school of the grammarian, according to the model of the *commentarii* of the late-ancient grammarians, Donatus and Servius.[29] The point of connection beyond the historical-conceptual continuity of the grammatical tradition is found in a thin line of understanding: if the Scriptures express in human language the truth that is God, they are true and devoid of all error; however, the task of the interpreters of Scripture is subject to ambiguities, because they must express their own judgment freely.[30]

At this point, we ask ourselves about the purpose of the Augustinian search, that is, how we can consider the emergence of Christian culture or education.[31] In fact, the translation of the work's title depends on the meaning we assign to this purpose. We argue that *doctrina* implies, mainly, the adaptation of the classic rhetorical system to the revealed text; this adaptation is carried out in the following terms: Augustine presents the three levels of style that Cicero studies in *Orator*, but assigning them a different meaning. For Cicero, the styles [*genera*] are closely linked to the dignity of the theme of rhetorical

---

fratres, quantum animadvertere potuimus Paginas sanctas, tribus modis intellegitur et nominatur, quando praedicatur, sive per Legem et Prophetas, sive per Epistolas apostolicas, sive per fidem rerum gestarum, quas in Evangelio cognoscimus. Primus modus est: secundum Deum et divinitatem illam Patri coaequalem atque coaeternam ante assumptionem carnis. Alter modus est: cum assumpta carne iam idem Deus qui homo, et idem homo qui Deus, secundum quamdam suae excellentiae proprietatem, qua non ceteris coaequatur hominibus, sed est mediator et caput Ecclesiae, esse legitur et intellegitur. Tertius modus est: quodam modo totus Christus, in plenitudine Ecclesiae, id est, caput et corpus, secundum plenitudinem perfecti cuiusdam viri, in quo viro singuli membra sumus.

28   We find an eloquent example in Augustine, *De peccatorum meritis et remissione et de baptismo parvulorum*, 1, 2, 2, at the beginning of the Pelagian controversy.

29   L. Holtz, *Donat et la tradition de l'enseignement grammatical. Étude sur l'Ars Donati et sa diffusion (IV-IX siècle) et édition critique*, Paris: CNRS 1981, pp. 25–30. For the development of this subject, with a divergent view of Holtz and his bibliography see: Anna Zago, *Pompei Commentum in Artis Donati partem tertiam. Tomo 1: Introduzione*, ed. by Walter Jost and Wendy Olmsted, Hildesheim: Weidmann 2017, pp. XCIII–CXX.

30   Augustine, *c. Faus.*, 11, 5 and *ep.* 82. 3. At this point, Augustine locates his differences with St. Jerome (*ep.* 28. 40, 3).

31   Augustine maintains, throughout Book 11 (35, 53), that his arguments attempt to ground a "science of the Scriptures;" in the perspective of the Christianity of Late Antiquity, the Bible is the heart of a Christian culture.

exercise and thus distinguishes between high, medium and low;[32] Augustine explicitly rejects this distinction between the levels of style,[33] because for the preacher there are no irrelevant subjects. For this reason, Augustine abandons the dignity of the theme and distinguishes styles based on the intention of the speaker.[34] This turn, fundamental for the gestation of the doctrine understood as culture, is part of the Ciceronian *docere, delectare* and *flectere* triad, and this is defined by the reaction sought in the audience. Although the Ciceronian rhetorical model continues, it is also true that it has undergone a profound transformation, because with the new purpose proposed by Augustine, the classical rhetoric can be applied to the comprehension of all kinds of texts. If the style depends on the audience (Augustine considers the Ciceronian foundations as a preaching key), this idea works on the condition that there is an audience to persuade.[35] The speaker's persuasion about the will of a listener is still standing, but with the emphasis not only on the style, but mainly on the assent; we consider that this is the main reason why Augustine does not call this purpose *flectere* like Cicero, but *movere*. As Augustine warns, between *docere, delectare* and *flectere*, there is not a proper hierarchical relationship, but an interdependent one, since each could not exist separately.[36] This is the general principle that orders the basic sense of *doctrina*.

3   The Encounter with the Scriptures and the Meaning of the Reading

Augustine, as a preacher, needs to find the content of the Scriptures; this text imposes a way of reading that implies a vigorous adaptation of the cultural practices in which he was trained and taught. As a grammarian, he knew that the literal sense constituted the first step of understanding. The path means the attempt to understand beyond the literary sense and its route is a way to dominate the pride of "understanding without difficulty" (the darkness has a moral value, if it leads to reflection):

---

32   See Cicero, *Orator*, 101. B.A. Krostenko, "Text and Context in the Roman Forum: The Case of Cicero's *First Catilinariam*," in *A Companion to Rhetoric and Rhetorical Criticism*, ed. by Walter Jost and Wendy Olmste, Blackwell Publishing: Oxford 2004, pp. 38–57.

33   Augustine, *De doctrina christiana*, IV, 18, 35.

34   Ibid., IV, 19, 38.

35   Mark Vessey, "Augustine among the Writers of the Church," in *A Companion to Augustine*, pp. 246–7.

36   Augustine, *De doctrina christiana*, IV, 22, 51.

And then it happened that even Holy Scripture, which brings remedy for the terrible diseases of the human will, being at first set forth in one language, by means of which it could at the time of the dissemination be through the whole world, was interpreted into various tongues, and spread far and wide, and thus became known to the nations for their salvation. And in reading it, men seek nothing more than to find out the thought and will of those by whom it is written, and through these to find out the will of God, in accordance with which they believe these men to have spoken.[37]

This quote warns us that, for Augustine, reading is a spiritual transformation [*invenire voluntatem Dei*]; if ignorance is equated with illness, it is healed by piety and the hope of knowledge that leads to the Scriptures; in continuity with Neoplatonic philosophy, it is only possible to approach wisdom through a process of purification, that is, the task of clarifying dark passages: pride is broken by work.[38] It is significant, therefore, that we do not find an exhortation to moral life in general, but a claim to reading as asceticism, that is, a dynamic ideal of understanding and purification. Augustine thus specifies the interpenetration of the philosophical reading and the rhetorical resources that arise and return to a praying community (reading as an individual act is not yet fully comprehensible in Late Antiquity). This complex interaction between the grammarian and the lover of philosophy leads the Bishop of Hippo, as we read in the Prologue, to prevent possible refutations of his book, especially against

---

37 Augustine, *De doctrina christiana*, II, 5, 6–7: *Ex quo factum est ut etiam Scriptura divina, qua tantis morbis humanarum voluntatum subvenitur, ab una lingua profecta, qua opportune potuit per orbem terrarum disseminari, per varias interpretum linguas longe lateque diffusa innotesceret Gentibus ad salutem. Quam legentes nihil aliud appetunt quam cogitationes voluntatemque illorum a quibus conscripta est invenire et per illas voluntatem Dei, secundum quam tales homines locutos credimus. Sed multis et multiplicibus obscuritatibus et ambiguitatibus decipiuntur qui temere legunt, aliud pro alio sentientes; quibusdam autem locis quid vel falso suspicentur non inveniunt, ita obscure dicta quaedam densissimam caliginem obducunt. Quod totum provisum esse divinitus non dubito, ad edomandam labore superbiam et intellectum a fastidio renovandum, cui facile investigata plerumque vilescunt.*

38 Christian Tornau, "Augustinus und die neuplatonischen Tugendgrade. Versuch einer Interpretation von Augustins Brief 155 an Macedonius," in *Plato Revived Essays on Ancient Platonism in Honour of Dominic J. O'Meara*, ed. by Filip Karfik and Euree Song, Berlin: Walter de Gruyter 2013, pp. 216–8. This text was important for our work, because it provided clarity on how Augustine received from Neo-Platonism the notion of virtue and the transformations that he then produced through the scriptural notions of love of God and charity ("… für die als Gottesliebe verstandene jenseitige Tugend und schließlich noch einmal für die diesseitige Tugend als Gottes–und als Nächstenliebe," p. 216).

those we can call "pneumatic," since they boast of achieving knowledge without human intervention. His hermeneutical response entails a lasting ethical design: boasting aside, each one must learn from others as much as possible; this goes beyond the empirical data of mutual teaching, because it points to the essentials of charity: readings and common expositions constitute the binding force of a community. For this reason, the use of signs does not only entail an epistemological problem, but a moral act that sustains the community life.

As Augustine has pointed out above, in the human vocation to illuminate the darkness there is a manifest design of God, because dedication and commitment teach a great deal to the human being (*labor*, in Augustinian semantics); this implies that the mystery is available to all who seek it, according to the possibilities of each one. The veil of mystery is an adornment to claim the attention of those who seek: the difficulties are more in the readiness of the reader than in the text itself; here we interpret "disposition" as the degree to which the spiritual signs are confused with the things themselves.[39]

From the Prologue we know that *De doctrina christiana* is addressed to "the students," [*studiosi*][40] and that it could include clerics and educated laics (we want to insist on the distributive sense of the adjective), all those who need a theological hermeneutics. At this point we return to Augustine's objections about the possible challenges at the beginning of his work. *De doctrina Christiana* supports the claim that God speaks to men through men, because

---

39   Augustine, *De doctrina christiana*, III. 5. 9: *Nam in principio cavendum est ne figuratam locutionem ad litteram accipias*. It is important to note that this assertion is part of a brief commentary to 2 *Cor.* 3:6: *Littera occidit, spiritus autem vivificat*.

40   It is illustrative to return to the etymology of *studeo*, intransitive verb (its regime generally goes in dative), with the fundamental meanings of "apply to," "be bound to," and, finally, "investigate;" it has both a technical sense: *studere agriculturae* ("dedicate to agriculture," as used by Caesar in *De bello gallico*, ed. by T. Rice Holmes, New York: Arno Press 1979, 6, 22, 1); as a moral sanction: *studere novis rebus* ("wish novelties," which in the context of Cicero, "Orationes in Catilinam," in *Collegii Reginae Socius, Oxonii e Typographeo Clarendoniano*, ed. by Albert Curtis Clark, Oxford: Scriptorum Classicorum Bibliotheca Oxoniensis 1918, I, 3, implies the will of Catilina to challenge the continuity of the institutional order of the Republic; only at the beginning of the imperial era assumes the meaning of "study," "educate," as for example in Seneca, *Lettres a Lucilius*, trans. by Henri Noblot, Paris: Les Belles Lettres 1964, 94, 20. The adjective *studiosus, -a, -um*, has the fundamental meaning of "having a taste for something" (with genitive or dative forms), then "friend," "admirer," and finally, already in the literature of the time of Augustus, "Applied to the study." See Horace, *Odes et Épodes*, trans. by François Villeneuve, Paris: Les Belles Lettres 2019, 6, 26, 1. The etymology of the Indo-European word is significant: * (s) t- / * (s) -p initial which designates "impression," "concussion," and what results of it. See Alfred Ernout and Alfred Meillet, *Dictionnaire Étymologique de la langue latine. Histoire des mots*, Paris: Librairie Klincksieck 1951, s.v.

He intends to achieve the widest possible dissemination of His word; in turn, Augustine wants to make the rules easier for the understanding of the Bible: "... the most skilful interpreter [*solertissimus indagator*] of the sacred writings, then, will be he who in the first place has read them all and retained them in his knowledge. ..."[41] Augustine advances the objections on the rules of understanding that he proposes.[42] There are three types of objectors in the argument: a) those who manifestly wish to see the moon, but cannot even see the finger, when Augustine points out;[43] b) those who see the finger and where it points, but not the moon;[44] and c) those who only rely on divine inspiration and disregard the rules of interpretation [*nemini esse ista praecepta necessaria*].[45] We recognize those who cannot understand the rules and those who can understand them, but they remain paralyzed at this point (the drama latent in all methodology without awareness of its instrumental nature). As James Andrews warns, the invitation to prayer is also an invitation to deepen the reading (Augustine's recommendation, in short, to the two groups).[46]

Augustine dedicates to this third group, which we have called "pneumatic," a more prolonged reflection, because for him it is more serious to reject the teaching that men give to each other and to depend on enlightenment; the understanding relationship is not merely vertical. For the Bishop of Hippo, this attitude reveals pride and the cure to it is to return to the path of study with humility. While the first two attitudes have to do with the need to strengthen the vertical links of the student, the third is closely linked with the teachers' vocation of learning with humility. An interpretation that does not rest on this axial sense will be unproductive and, therefore, the study will always be necessary. The distrust of education leads to pride: the correlation between learning and teaching is for Augustine the core of this process.

This analysis leads us to consider that the work is not intended only for priests, but for every believer. This affirmation is confirmed when Augustine warns the most serious risk of the "pneumatic" attitude: people could abandon

---

41   Augustine, *De doctrina christiana*, II. 8, 12.

42   Augustine, *De doctrina christiana*, Prol. 2: *Tamquam si lunam vel veterem vel novam sidusve aliquod minime clarum vellent videre, quod ego intento digito demonstrarem ... .*

43   Ibid.: *... illis autem nec ad ipsum digitum meum videndum sufficiens esset acies oculorum ... .*

44   Ibid.: *... arbitrentur se digitum quidem meum videre posse, sidera vero quibus demonstrandis intenditur, videre non posse.*

45   Ibid.: *Qui quoniam nullis huiusmodi observationibus lectis quales nunc tradere institui, facultatem exponendorum sanctorum Librorum se assecutos vel vident vel putant, nemini esse ista praecepta necessaria, sed potius totum quod de illarum litterarum obscuritatibus laudabiliter aperitur, divino munere fieri posse clamitabunt.*

46   Andrews, *Hermeneutics and the Church in Dialogue with Augustine*, p. 122.

the sacramental practice. Therefore, he insists: teaching the Scriptures means teaching to read;[47] the example of the privileged who, being illiterate, understood the Scriptures spiritually is not a measure of the ordinary, it is the exception rather than the rule. Therefore, Augustine insists that the direction of his argument [*res*] goes against those who believe that the Scriptures can be learned without human guidance.[48]

The reading deepens its meaning understood as a gift: the Incarnation has arranged a completely new state of Humanity and it means, in the scriptural understanding, that there are not only individual readers, because the common love of Christ also entails a common reading of his word. The neglect of the human (love of neighbor) or divine aspect (inspiration) implies ignoring the providential order. The interpretation of the canonical texts has an inherent *telos*, because God is part of the economy of salvation; this idea of reading reflects God's desire to engender his love in humanity. This understanding is peremptory, because the private or public interpretation is oriented to discern the will of God.[49] This means that the constitution of the canon is a reality prior to reading; however, Augustine's concern is practical and not theoretical: he does not discuss the formation of the canon, but he recommends the readings of greater ecclesial benefit.[50]

Augustine resorted to the classic schemes of oral persuasion to interpret texts; all the currents and experiences known to him were merged at the time of conversion, when he adapted to the whole point of view of the Scripture. He was not an exegete like St. Jerome (or Origen of Alexandria in the Greek language), but essentially a preacher; from his readings, he proposed an interpretative scheme, and, in this way, he contributed to the conception of reading as exegesis. The dynamism that characterizes the thought of Augustine is also present in the relationship with the Scriptures, because he adjusted this link

---

47   Augustine, *De doctrina christiana, Prol.* 9: ... *qui autem ipsas litteras tradit, hoc agit ut alii quoque legere noverint ... .*

48   Ibid.: ... *qui ... sine duce homine gaudent nosse ...* He immediately gives the argument that we consider fundamental against the attitude of those we have called "pneumatics:" those who only consider dependence on God continue, nevertheless, to write and teach (*Prol.,* 8: *Sed cum legit et nullo sibi hominum exponente intellegit, cur ipse aliis affectat exponere ac non potius eos remittit Deo, ut ipsi quoque non per hominem sed illo intus docente intellegant?*).

49   Ibid., III, 1, 1: *Homo timens Deum, voluntatem eius in Scripturis sanctis diligenter inquirit.*

50   Michel A. Fahey, "Augustine's Ecclesiology Revisited," in *Augustine from Rhetor to Theologian,* ed. by Joanne McWilliam, Ontario: Wilfrid Laurier University Press 1992, pp. 179–80 Here he presents the relationship between canon formation and the importance of apostolic foundation churches.

throughout his life. Undoubtedly, this experience is organized by *De doctrina christiana*; as Cameron points out, it is a mistake to circumscribe this work to the understanding of the Bible;[51] the previous point is clearly present: its importance lies fundamentally in the establishment of principles to move from literal enlightenment to spiritual understanding; the reform of these rules on the fly, in properly exegetical works such as *De Trinitate* or *De Genesi ad litteram*, does not obstruct the idea that *De doctrina christiana* is the nucleus of the link with the Bible.[52] Let us see the statement in the text. Augustine had always manifested his lack of knowledge of the scriptures, at least since 391, the date of his ordination to the priesthood. In Books I-III of *De doctrina christiana*, he reflects on this topic in a more general presentation: what moves the exegete? What do you look for in the Scriptures (love of God and neighbor)? What steps should the process of interpretation have and what instruments are required for the task? Of this complex process, we are particularly concerned about the moment in which Augustine reflects on the debt to classical culture. In II. 17. 27, Augustine refutes the fable of the nine muses from Varro's *Antiquitates*:[53] a king of an unknown city asked three craftsmen to make three statues of the Muses and they agreed that the author of the best work would receive the payment; as the artists presented very similar works in art, the king bought nine for a temple dedicated to Apollo; later Hesiod imposed the names with which we know the Muses. After this criticism, part of a series of arguments against superstition, Augustine presents the general principle for the acceptance or rejection of Classical Culture: regardless of the truth or not of Varro's explanation, "still we ought not to give up music because of the superstition of the heathen, if we can derive anything from it that is of use for the understanding of the Holy Scripture."[54] Will we abandon reading, because it was a gift from Mercury? Will we forsake justice or the law, because the Gentiles worshiped them in temples?[55] Then he holds this principle with a Pauline quote: the truth, where it is found, belongs to God:

---

51   Michel Cameron, "Augustine and Scripture," *A Companion to Augustine*, p. 201.

52   Ibid.

53   Burkhart Cardanus, *Antiquitates Rerum Divinarum*, 2 vols., Wiesbaden: Franz Steiner 1976, pp. 225ff. Jörg Rüpke, "Rationalité et Société Romaine," in *Dans le laboratoire de l'historien des religions*, ed. by Francesca Prescendi and Youri Volkhine, Geneva: Labor et Fides 2011, pp. 404–5.

54   Augustine, *De doctrina christiana*, II. 17. 28: ... *nos tamen non propter superstitionem profanorum debemus musicam fugere, si quid inde utile ad intellegendas sanctas Scripturas rapere potuerimus ...* .

55   Ibid.: *Neque enim et litteras discere non debuimus quia earum repertorem dicunt esse Mercurium, aut quia iustitiae virtutique templa dedicarunt, et quae corde gestanda sunt in lapidibus adorare maluerunt, propterea nobis iustitia virtusque fugienda est.*

Nay, but let every good and true Christian understand that wherever truth may be found, it belongs to his Master; and while he recognizes and acknowledges the truth, even in their religious literature, let him reject the figments of superstition, and let him grieve over and avoid men who, "when they knew God, glorified him not as God, neither were thankful; but became vain in their imaginations, and their foolish heart was darkened. Professing themselves to be wise, they became fools, and changed the glory of the incorruptible God into an image made like to corruptible man, and to birds, and four-footed beasts, and creeping things (*Rom.* 1, 21–23)."[56]

From the St. Ambrose's principle [*omne verum a quocumque dicatur a Spiritu Sancto est*],[57] Augustine found the measure to incorporate the classical model to the understanding of revelation.[58] Christianity forged a culture, that is, a world of symbols mediated by language (we give the term its maximum extension), because this religious experience is situated, from the beginning, in the field of faith (to be Christian is to have faith in the Person of Christ). Therefore, no aspect of life is outside the consideration of faith: not only worship, but everything is elevated to grace and redemption. This means, at the same time, that supernatural life does not replace the natural order of human existence, but presupposes it and perfects it. As Juan Antonio Widow[59] points out, the theological virtues are proper to the supernatural order, and there are no corresponding ones in the natural order; nevertheless, they perfect the higher

---

56   Ibid.: *Immo vero quisquis bonus verusque Christianus est, Domini sui esse intellegat, ubi-cumque invenerit veritatem, quam conferens et agnoscens etiam in Litteris sacris supersti-tiosa figmenta repudiet, 'doleatque homines atque caveat qui cognoscentes Deum non ut Deum glorificaverunt aut gratias egerunt, sed evanuerunt in cogitationibus suis et obscura-tum est insipiens cor eorum; dicentes enim se esse sapientes stulti facti sunt et immutaverunt gloriam incorruptibilis Dei in similitudinem imaginis corruptibilis hominis et volucrum et quadrupedum et serpentium.'* (Rom. 1:21–23).

57   Ambrosiaster, *Glossa I Cor XII, 3,* PL 17, 245. About this author, see: Pierre Courcelle, *Recherches sur saint Ambroise: 'Vies' anciennes, culture, iconographie,* Paris: Etudes Augustiniennes 1973; Pierre Courcelle, "Ambroise de Milan 'professeur de philosophie'," *Revue de l'histoire des religions,* vol. 181, no. 2, 1972, pp. 147–55.

58   See Jean Claude Fredouille, *Tertulien et la conversion de la culture antique,* Paris: Études Augustiniennes 1972. We are debtors of the author's analysis model; the study on the importance and nature of Tertullian's culture is adapted to the way in which his faith unfolds, understanding it in terms of "a continuous conversion." This process is more evi-dent applied to Augustine (there are no records of hostility as in Tertullian).

59   Juan A. Widow, "La cultura clásica y el Cristianismo," *INTUS-LEGERE,* vol. 3, no. 2, 2009, pp. 151–2.

faculties of man, the understanding by faith and the will for hope and, above all, for charity. Christianity expresses a central conviction: virtue perfects the world of man. Every perfective development of the human being is incorporated into the Christian life; therefore, virtue takes root in a nature constituted by a spiritual soul and a material body. Faith is the cognitive habit, participation of the knowledge with which God knows himself (the object is God himself). Revelation requires a network of symbols and analogies established by language (and its limitations), that is, by a culture that expresses tension towards God.

In this sense, Augustine takes up in Book IV of *De doctrina christiana*, after a long life of study and predication, the theme of the expression and communication of the Scriptures.[60] In this book, he laboriously presents continuity between Christian practice and rhetoric, since this art constituted the synthesis of culture in Late Antiquity: the whole of the liberal arts culminated in rhetoric, the highest educational achievement. From the time of his passage through Manichaeism, Augustine taught rhetoric in the public chair of Milan;[61] he will not abandon this practice, because as a priest and bishop he taught, he preached, and he had an intense epistolary exchange for the purpose of spiritual and doctrinal direction. These experiences feed the reflections of Book IV; at this point, the preacher comes to meet his classical education; it is remarkable the conscience of Augustine about the need to work this relationship as deeply as possible.

Augustine's arguments are almost entirely in the field of classical rhetoric; he considers rhetoric as a criterion from which Christian practice is weighed. As we noted above, rhetoric could not simply be ignored or rejected, because it was the fertile ground for revelation to take root; this means that Christianity was inextricably linked to the horizon of classical culture; however, Augustine's attempt to reach a synthesis with his own cultural context has permanently encountered detractors.[62] His allegorical exegesis is frequently criticized for being artificial and arbitrary[63]; the question for Augustine could

---

60   For the possible explanations about the almost thirty years of distance between the writing of the Books I to III and IV, see Charles Kannengiesser, "The Interrupted *De doctrina christiana*," in *De doctrina christiana: A Classic of Western Culture*, ed. by Duane W.H. Arnold and Pamela Bright, Notre Dame: University of Notre Dame Press 1995, pp. 4–14.

61   Augustine, *Conf.*, IV. 2.2.

62   See Christoph Schäublin, "*De doctrina christiana*: A Classic of Western Culture?," in *De doctrina christiana: A Classic of Western Culture*, pp. 46–67.

63   This idea is presented with special force in Robert Markus, "World and Text in Ancient Christianity I: Augustine," in his *Sings and Meaning. World and Text in Ancient Christianity*, Liverpool: Liverpool University Press 1996, p. 18: "What is critically important to note is that Augustine insists that the biblical author's text does not have a meaning, but that

be the following: can the means of expression be placed on the literal meaning of a specific passage? In practice, his response was normally positive, and he came very close to the rhetorical conception of sophistry, criticized openly by Augustine. In Book IV of *De doctrina christiana*, he painstakingly defined the use that Christians give to eloquence: its purpose, its practices and its rules, both as continuity and as a break with the classical tradition. Sometimes there is a clear continuity, because the purpose is the same (this also includes the same practices for different purposes); there is also an opposition to fundamental principles. Our author moves from one side to another, between acceptance, rejection and modification of classical eloquence. An immediate point of agreement with the classical tradition is that the speaker must not only be an "expert in talking," but fundamentally a good man[64]; that is to say that, beyond technical considerations, moral qualities are fundamental for Quintilian: *bonus* implies integrity and a solid cultural formation for a positive influence in political life. Quintilian's method to educate the perfect speaker has a strong presence in Augustine, because in *Institutio oratoria* we read that the breadth of knowledge must determine the formation.[65] The primacy of the

what that text refers to, the things or events it tells of, can also have their meaning." The meaning of the narrative as a divine action results to the author foreign to the explanation. To understand his position, we must return to the beginning of his chapter, in which he notes that his way of approach is "incorrigibly" pre-modern (p.1), that is, fundamentally alien to the world of Late Antiquity.

64   Quintilian, *Inst. orat.*, XII, 1, 1: ... *vir bonus dicendi peritus* ... It is undoubtedly a conclusion of Plato. See "Gorgias," trans. by W. Dudley, in *The Collected Dialogues of Plato*, ed. by E. Hamilton and H. Cairns, Princeton: Princeton University Press 1961, 460 c. And, for this reason, it poses a deeper definition than the Ciceronian approach in *De inventione* I, 5, "eloquence by art." Robert Wardy, *The Birth of Rhetoric: Gorgias, Plato and their Successors*, London: Routledge 1996: "The *De oratore* never achieves a final resolution; Cicero endlessly vacillates between ill-defined positions on whether eloquence requires knowledge by playing endlessly with the scope and substance of 'knowledge.' " (p. 103).

65   Quintilian, *Institutio oratoria*, X, 1, 5. Christian Tornau, "Augustinus und das 'hidden curriculum': Bemerkungen zum Verhältnis des Kirchenvaters zum Bildungswesen seiner Zeit," *Hermes*, vol. 130, no. 3, 2002, p. 318: "Augustinus hatte, zunachst als Schuler, spater als Dozent, nahezu sein ganzes Leben in der Schule verbracht, bevor er sich nach seinem Bekehrungserlebnis im Alter von 31 Jahren endgultig von ihr ab- und einem christlich-asketischen Leben zuwandtete. Infolgedessen ist seine Auseinandersetzung mit dem spatantiken Bildungswesen zugleich die unter streng christlichem Maßstab erfolgende kritische Aufarbeitung eines wesentlichen Teils der eigenen Biographie. So unbestreitbar es ist, daß das Christentum Teil und pragendes Element der spatantiken Kultur ist, darf das Verhaltnis des Christen zur ihn umgebenden Kultur, zur 'Welt', doch niemals selbstverständlich oder unreflektiert sein." Although the idea of "hidden curriculum" can be considered an excessive extrapolation of the author, we are interested in the arguments to demonstrate that the whole of the culture of Late Antiquity walked towards the dialogue

moral ideal in the education of a rhetorician was undoubtedly a profound innovation of Quintilian and his decisive difference with Cicero.[66] How is the realization of this ideal, especially in relation to the ability to argue independently over the truth? Quintilian offers a new conception of the rhetoric, since he established an original relationship with other knowledge: more science to reach a true argumentative foundation.[67] In Book IV, Augustine presents the classical perspective on Christian novelty; he does it in these terms: there is no place to delight without ideas, because if something is said with elegance, it is also true for the audience.[68] Augustine considers that it is necessary to teach rhetoric, since wisdom without eloquence is not used by the Church or by the State; here the influence of the *De inventione* of Cicero[69] as well as the extension of this idea to the Church is evident. He considers that the primacy of wisdom over all art was recognized by classical theorists—as we previously saw in Quintilian—although they did not know the wisdom "that descends from the Father of Lights."[70] For this reason, eloquence and wisdom are proportional to the depth with which he took advantage of the reading of Scripture.[71]

The systematization of Quintilian[72] made rhetoric a pedagogical instance, through the balance between content density and formal resources; Augustine

---

with Christianity, and its consequence: Christianity as a culture is constructed through dialogue with the ancient "world;" this dialogue is never evident or thoughtless.

66   Maria Silvana Celentano, "Oratorical Exercises from the Rhetoric to Alexander to the *Institutio oratoria*: Continuity and Change," *Rhetorica: A Journal of the History of Rhetoric*, vol. 29, no. 3, 2011, pp. 357–65.

67   Arthur E. Walzer, "Quintilian's *Vir Bonus* and the Stoic Wise Man," *Rhetoric Society Quarterly*, vol. 33, no. 4, 2003, p. 33: "Quintilian starts with ordinary effective rhetorical tactics (...) as 'speaking well' for him means 'speaking effectively' as much as it does speaking ethically."

68   Augustine, *De doctrina christiana*, IV, 5, 7: *Qui (id est "orator") vero affluit insipienti eloquentia, tanto magis cavendus est quanto magis ab eo in his quae audire inutile est, delectatur auditor et eum quoniam diserte dicere audit, etiam vere dicere existimat.*

69   Cicero, *De inventione*, 1.1.

70   Ibid. *Si hoc ergo illi, qui praecepta eloquentiae tradiderunt, in eisdem libris in quibus id egerunt, veritate instigante coacti sunt confiteri, veram, hoc est supernam quae a Patre luminum descendit sapientiam nescientes, quanto magis nos non aliud sentire debemus, qui huius sapientiae filii et ministri sumus?*

71   Ibid. *Sapienter autem dicit homo tanto magis vel minus, quanto in Scripturis sanctis magis minusve profecit, non dico in eis multum legendis memoriaeque mandandis, sed bene intellegendis et diligenter earum sensibus indagandis.*

72   Alan G. Gross, "The Rhetorical Tradition," in *The Viability of the Rhetorical Tradition*, ed. by Richard Graff, Arthur E. Walzer and Janet M. Atwill, Albany: State University of New York Press 2005, p. 32. Kathy Eden, *Hermeneutics and the Rhetorical Tradition. Chapters in the Ancient Legacy and Its Humanist Reception*, New Haven: Yale University Press 2005, pp. 20–40.

urged the teaching of rhetoric not only for the intrinsic needs of Christian culture, but also for the polemical and apologetic nature of his preaching; for this
reason, he insists on the ethical, metaphysical and religious contents of dialectical processes. Logically it could not be a simple addition but a new rhetorical
design, because, on the one hand, he linked the logical-philosophical root of
the rhetorical discipline with a hermeneutic of the sacred text,[73] and, on the
other hand, he continued the pragmatic sense of rhetoric, now understood as
a pedagogical purpose, since it was addressed to an audience.[74] *De Doctrina
Christiana* is the point of reference of all theoretical reflection, where there
is consideration of the thematic background of the discourses [*modus inveniendi*] and the way of communicating [*modus proferendi*].

The concept has changed profoundly: we find the assumptions of traditional
rhetoric, but completely transformed by their encounter with the Scriptures.
The thematic distribution of the *De doctrina christiana* shows Augustine's
concern in the formulation of the nascent Christian rhetoric, since in the first
three he investigates the *modus inveniendi* and only in the last the *modus proferendi*; this is a significant indication of the eminently thematic perspective
and that he does not worry about founding a new *Ars Rhetorica*. In this way, the
logic of understanding the revealed word is expressed in a normative framework, where the thematic treatment prevails; in this sense we affirm that it
was the model of medieval theoretical elaboration. We have considered how
the historical aspects of the subject are presented, but the panorama would be
incomplete if we do not think about the tensions within Augustine himself,
between his intellectual formation and his identity as bishop of Hippo. These
tensions are expressed in the constant search for usefulness in the interpretation of the Scriptures and in the conditions for eloquence: we thus establish
the nucleus of the arguments of Book IV, since Augustine always seems to be
stalked by the possibility of irrelevance in the task of exegesis or preaching.
We understand, in fact, that for this reason the Bishop of Hippo insists on the
understanding of the Scriptures in accordance with the norms of classical eloquence; thus, he expresses the conviction that these authors, divinely inspired,
are the wisest and the most eloquent.[75] There is the possibility, however, that

73   Christine Mohrmann, "Saint Augustine and the 'Eloquentia,'" in her *Études sur le latin des
      chrétiens I*, Rome: Edizioni di storia e letteratura 1961, pp. 356–8.

74   Augustine develops this topic in detail in *De catechizandis rudibus*, a work completed
      around the year 400. About this see Andrews, *Hermeneutics and the Church in Dialogue
      with Augustine*, p. 21.

75   Augustine, *De doctrina christiana*, IV, 6, 9: *Nam ubi eos intellego, non solum nihil eis sapientius, verum etiam nihil eloquentius mihi videri potest.*

they are not understood: to a lesser understanding of the audience (Augustine speaks in the first person) it will seem that they lack the capacity to be understood, but the truth expressed is always the same; in these circumstances natural conditions and assiduous dedication are manifested.[76]

The interpretation of Saint Paul (*Rom* 5, 3, 5) shows us how Augustine understood the interrelation between wisdom and eloquence. The Latin text that he has on hand is the following: "*Gloriamur in tribulationibus, scientes quia tribulatio patientiam operatur, patientia autem probationem, probatio vero spem, spes autem non confundit; quia caritas Dei diffusa est in cordibus nostris per Spiritum Sanctum qui datus est nobis.*"[77] Augustine first clarifies that the Apostle did not follow the rules of eloquence to construct his exhortation; with a forced turn for our sensibility, *imperite peritus*, he considers the primacy of wisdom, and he presents the rhetorical figures of the Pauline fragment: what in Greek is called *klimax* and in Latin "gradation" (sentences or words that create a crescendo of sense), Augustine mentions a second "ornament" or *decus*, which the Greeks called *kommata* and the Latin *ambitus sive circuitus*, ordered in the syntactic period.[78] Augustine concludes: "Well, just as we do not say that the Apostle followed the rhetorical precepts, we do not deny that eloquence followed wisdom."[79] This quote is a true synthesis of the relationship between classical tradition and its use by Christianity to understand and explain the Scriptures: the eloquence of the Scriptures is not artificial or deliberate, but the natural expression of true words.

Augustine's concern to show that eloquence depends on wisdom is also evident in passages where he discusses how eloquence is acquired.[80] At the beginning of Book IV, he states that he will give us the rules of eloquence

---

76   Ibid.: ... *in qua proficere noster intellectus, non solum inventione, verum etiam exercitatione deberet.*

77   The Apostle's text is quoted in IV, 7, 11: "We glory in tribulations also: knowing that tribulation worketh patience; and patience, experience; and experience, hope: and hope makes not ashamed; because the love of God is shed abroad in our hearts by the Holy Ghost which is given unto us."

78   Augustine's doubts about the meaning and scope of Greek terminology are also found in Cicero, the translator. For "periods," the Latins have different terms and Cicero himself uses different words: *ambitus, circuitus, comprehensio, continuatio* or *circumscription*, or he simply transliterates the Greek term. See: James D. Williams, *An Introduction to Classical Rhetoric. Essential Readings*, Chichester: Wiley-Blackwell 2009, particularly: "Cicero and the Latinization of Greek Rhetoric," pp. 273–315, and "The End of The Classical Period: Libanius and Augustine," pp. 416–526.

79   Augustine, *De doctrina christiana*, IV, 7, 11.

80   Winrich Löhr, "Christianity as Philosophy: Problems and Perspectives of an Ancient Intellectual Project," *Vigiliae Christianae*, vol. 64, no. 2, 2010, pp. 164–5.

that he learned in school and then taught; they are useful, but he considers
that it is not the place to explain them (they are of secondary importance).
For Augustine it is more important to read and listen in order to acquire eloquence (one must privilege at the same time what is said and how it is said);
for him, eloquence is not a question of rules, because whoever possesses
eloquence, he applies them, not so that his words are eloquent.[81] There is a
direct relationship with the way a child learns to speak: listening and prac-
ticing; he does not need, in fact, grammar, if he lives among men (intuition is
absolutely decisive).[82] When someone teaches, the simple learning of rules is
not a properly educational act, because the truth is a gift and not something
simply achieved with effort. From the apostolic root, the fragment of Saint
Paul shows that Christian preaching and rhetoric are intended to convince
from the truth; in this way, Augustine takes distance from the so-called Second
Sophistic, centered on verbal virtuosity, destined to influence the listeners,
but disregarding the true content of what is communicated. The emphasis
on the rhetorical dimension is the central observation of Augustine towards
the end of Book IV (30, 63): who is willing to speak publicly must pray, "for
God to put in his mouth propitious words (or literally 'good preaching')."[83] He
proposes, in short, that life is the most eloquent witness of the truth and that
words are his reflection and, implicitly, its opposite: if life is a lie, words lack
force.[84] This claim takes us to a central point: the Patristic maintained that the
Scripture expresses the truth that is God, unlike the works of the classical culture that occasionally and obscurely could do it. *The truth that is God* is what
the exegete seeks and what the preacher teaches. In this way, the distinction
between *res* and *signa* (beginning of Book I) acquires a new depth: the plural
res is the Trinitarian faith as it is expressed in the *signa* of Scripture.[85] The

---

81   Augustine, *De doctrina christiana*, IV, 3, 4.

82   Ibid., 4.3.5.

83   Ibid., 4. 30. 63: ... (*orator*) *oret ut Deus sermonem bonum det in os eius* ...

84   Ibid., 4. 30. 62: ... *qui, cum dicat bene, vivit male* ... About this, see Theo Kobusch "Christliche
      Philosophie. Das Christentum als Vollendung der antiken Philosophie," in *Beitrage zur
      Altertumskunde*, Munchen and Leipzig 2002, p. 239, has pointed out: "In diesem Sinne soll
      die These vertreten werden, daß das Christentum selbst auch eine Form der Philosophie
      darstellt, weil es sich als die Vollendung der gesamten griechischen Philosophie,
      besonders auch der platonischen verstanden hat." We consider interesting to rescue this
      thesis (against the dominant opinion in the academic circles) about Christianity as a real-
      ization of Greek philosophy and especially the Platonic one (especially if we consider the
      case of Augustine).

85   See Kaija Anneli Luhtala, *Grammar and Philosophy in Late Antiquity. A Study of Priscian's
      Sources*, Amsterdam and Philadelphia: John Benjamin's Publishing Company 2005,
      pp. 141–2.

reading of the interpreter has the same purpose as the Scripture: the love of God and neighbor in God or, in Augustine's terms, "love of the truth;"[86] the ways that he reflects on the signs to express the truth that is God are presented and discussed in Books II and III, and the resources for their expression is the subject of Book IV.[87]

If we accept that the Scripture (what the Holy Spirit has dictated) is a literary work, this also implies that Augustine accepts the "fall" of language, darkness and ambiguities, difficulties inherent in human reality (therefore the Text requires exegesis); the aesthetic delight of literature requires the joint space of imagination, intuition, sensitivity and rationality. The Scripture is an inspired word of God, but it assumes the difficulties and obscurities of the human language.[88] Therefore, the Scripture became a work in accordance with the sensitivity of cultured people; more importantly, the Word and its exegesis was the instrument by which God guides and inspires the will of believers, educated or ignorant, to the only necessary: the love of God and the love of neighbor. Much of patristic exegesis interpreted the Scriptures, not in the manner of modern scholars, but as pastors of the congregation; this leads us to the encounter of a first "Christian aesthetic," shaped by the desire to teach and transform the listener with the truths of faith. The end of the Law and the Scriptures is the love of a Being that is necessary to enjoy: Enjoying, in this sense, refers to the goodness of God: "But what God does about us

---

86   Augustine, *De doctrina christiana*, III. 24. 34.

87   Anne-Isabelle Bouton-Touboulic, "Deux interprétations du scepticisme: Marius Victorinus et Augustin," *Les Études philosophiques*, vol. 2, 2012, pp. 227–8: "On note que la bipartition cicéronienne logique morale devient sous la plume de Victorinus une distinction divin-humain qui recoupe la physique et l'éthique. Surtout, il insiste sur le fait que Cicéron a employé le terme studium, pour désigner l'étude de ces domaines qui s'offre à l'orateur. Celle-ci s'oppose au savoir parfait, dont relève aussi la *perfecta philosophia* qui possède tous les éléments de celle-ci, mais qu'aucun orateur ne peut prétendre atteindre pleinement; c'est pourquoi en ce cas leur simple *studium* est préconisé. Nous avons donc affaire à deux appropriations différentes de la même définition, l'une rapportée à son sujet, l'autre à son objet; chez Augustin, Licentius défend une définition zététique de la sagesse humaine, tandis que Victorinus réserve à l'orateur une 'étude' (*studium*) éloignée de la perfection philosophique." Although the present article is especially dedicated to Marius Victorinus, the arguments show the efforts of Augustine to overcome the skepticism of Cicero, his source.

88   Susannah Ticciati, *A New Apophaticism: Augustine and the Redemption of Signs*, Leiden, Brill 2013, p.137: "The distinction between *frui* and *uti* (I. 3) is thus superimposed on the *res-signum* distinction, and will pervade the whole of *DDC*; it is the means whereby Augustine links what he has to say about language with what he has to say about beings who 'mean' and about the fundamentally desirous nature of those beings."

refers to his own goodness. We exist because God is good, and because we exist, we are good."[89]

Augustine had a theological attitude towards language and literary art and he thus took distance from classical theory; what we have called "Christian aesthetics" is then the language of the Christian faith, as we find it in the Scriptures and in the words of the preacher: the formation of a culture where the core of the Christian faith operates. This is the love that unifies the Christian community, especially because it allows communication between men to take place. The consciousness of language due to the "fall" sustains the thought of *De doctrina christiana*: according to Augustine, the preacher must work to articulate his understanding of the faith, and he must search until he finds words suitable for the level of his listeners. This is the speech of love towards the listener's heart. The Scriptures made an intensive use of figurative speech, and it is for this reason that Augustine pays so much attention to the theory of meaning in his educational works. It is common in Christian exegesis to think that God stopped speaking directly with man, after the communication between man and God was broken in the fall. However, God continued to speak to human beings obliquely, through signs, thus adapting his Word to an imperfect understanding.

4   Conclusion

We have presented the modifications of the term *doctrina* in the light of a deeper transformation: the emergence of the foundations of an emergence of a cultural Christian culture paradigm. The noun *doctrina*, in effect, deployed new semantic fields, from the encounter with reading in the Christian sense; if the Scriptures express the truth that is God, but with the ambiguity of human language, reading implies a transformation of the person. At the same time, we pointed out that it was not only an individual activity, but also a task of the community and had a liturgical meaning. At this point two paths open: a) the rise of the reader from literalness to allegorical understanding (*modus inveniendi* is the Augustinian expression for this process); b) as readers naturally we do not have the same degree of preparation or experience, it is necessary to share with the community what he found (we remember that this community

---

89   Augustine, *De doctrina christiana*, 1. 32. 35: *Sed neque sic utitur ut nos; nam nos res quibus utimur ad id referimus ut Dei bonitate perfruamur; Deus vero ad suam bonitatem usum nostrum refert. Quia enim bonus est, sumus; et in quantum sumus, boni sumus.*

is founded on listening to the word of God). This second moment (*modus profiriendi*) required a pedagogical mediation: what to explain and with what instruments were he inextricably linked in the transcendent axis of this teaching, sustained by an absolute act of faith: the person of Christ.

The classical tradition had extensive experience in the art of persuasion; from the Sophists onwards, resources were systematized early by Greek-language theorists and were directed to convince or move an audience, regardless of the truth of the arguments. In Rome, the figure of the orator will be the culmination of the *humanitas*, according to two different models, Cicero and Quintilian: the former dedicated more to the technical path of art and the latter also concerned about moral education [*vir bonus dicendi peritus*]. Augustine, as we saw, was a *grammaticus* formed in the commentary of texts, by the models of Donatus and Servius, and also in oratory, by the measure of Cicero and Quintilian. With these tools, Augustine offered the *praecepta* to understand and teach the Scriptures; we have used the term "tension" in our work to explain the changes produced by the solidarity between the old method and a new object: the truth enters as a metaphysical and theological absolute and its individual and community discernment, in an eschatological key.

We have considered the historical-doctrinal aspects of the subject, but the panorama would be incomplete if we did not think about the tensions, within Augustine himself, between his intellectual formation and his identity as bishop of Hippo. These tensions express the constant search for usefulness in the reading of the Scriptures and in the conditions to express that experience in an eloquent way: let us thus establish the nucleus of the arguments that organize Book IV, since Augustine is always haunted by the possibility of irrelevance in the task of exegesis or preaching. Therefore, we consider that he also expresses the conviction that biblical authors, divinely inspired, are the wisest and the most eloquent; thus, there is the possibility of not understanding: if there is a lack of capacity to understand in the audience, the speaker may seem incompetent.

We saw that the theological interpretation of language and literature implied a distancing from classical theory; "Christian aesthetics" is the expressive medium of the Christian faith: the formation of a culture where the core of the Christian faith operates. The awareness of the state of language as a result of the fall sustains the thought of the *De doctrina christiana*: the Scriptures made intensive use of figurative speech, and this required special tools for interpretation; for that reason Augustine pays so much attention to the theory of meaning in his educational works: the absolutely elementary experience of God implies primordial truth and beauty.

Translated by Carlos Rafael Domínguez

Bibliography

Andrews, James A., *Hermeneutics and the Church in Dialogue with Augustine*, Notre Dame: University of Notre Dame Press 2012.

Arnold, Duane W.H. and Bright, Pamela, *De doctrina christiana: A Classic of Western Culture*, Notre Dame: University of Notre Dame Press 1995.

Augustine of Hippo, *De doctrina christiana*, ed. and trans. by R.P.H. Green, Oxford: Clarendon Press 1995.

Augustine of Hippo, "De catechizandis rudibus," in *Ancient Christian Writers*, vols. 1–63, ed. and trans. by Joseph P. Christopher, New York: Newman 1946, vol. 2.

Augustine of Hippo, *L'istruzione cristiana*, Milan: Arnoldo Mondadori 2000.

[Augustine of Hippo], *Sermons. The Works of Saint Augustine: A Translation for the 21st Century*, trans. by Edmund Hill, Brooklyn: New City Press 1990.

Berti, E., "Le controversia della raccolta di Seneca il Vecchio e la dottrina degli *status*," *Rhetorica: A Journal of the History of Rhetoric*, vol. 32, no. 2, 2014, pp. 94–147.

Bouton-Touboulic, Anne-Isabelle, "Deux interprétations du scepticisme: Marius Victorinus et Augustin," *Les Études philosophiques*, vol. 2, 2012, pp. 217–32.

Braet, A. C., "Variationen zur Statuslehre von Hermagoras bei Cicero," in *Rhetorica: A Journal of the History of Rhetoric*, vol. 7, no. 3, 1989, pp. 239–59.

Brown, Peter, *Augustine of Hippo: A Biography*, Berkeley and Los Angeles 2000.

Brown, Peter, "Introducing Robert Markus," *Augustinian Studies*, vol. 32, no. 2, 2001, pp. 181–7.

Caesar, *De bello gallico*, ed. by T. Rice Holmes, New York: Arno Press 1979.

Calabrese, Claudio César, "Allegory, Myth and Liberal Arts in St. Augustine 'De ordine' I. 8. 24," *Graeco-Latina Brunensia,* vol. 23, 2018, pp. 21–34.

Calabrese, Claudio César, "Literatura y teología en el Libro X de 'La ciudad de Dios," *Classica et Christiana*, vol. 12, 2017, pp. 69–88.

Cameron, Michel, "Augustine and Scripture," in *A Companion to Augustine*, ed. by Mark Vessey, Chichester: Wiley-Blackwell 2012, pp. 200–14.

Cardanus, Burkhart, *Antiquitates Rerum Divinarum*, vols. 1–2, Wiesbaden: Franz Steiner 1976.

Celentano, Maria Silvana, "Oratorical Exercises from the Rhetoric to Alexander to the *Institutio oratoria*: Continuity and Change," *Rhetorica: A Journal of the History of Rhetoric*, vol. 29, no. 3, 2011, pp. 357–65.

Cicero. *De Inventione, De Optimo Genere Oratorum, Topica*, trans. by H. M. Hubbell, London: Heinmann 1949.

Cicero, "Orationes in Catilinam," in *Collegii Reginae Socius, Oxonii e Typographeo Clarendoniano*, ed. by Albert Curtis Clark, Oxford: Scriptorum Classicorum Bibliotheca Oxoniensis 1918.

Courcelle, Pierre, *Recherches sur saint Ambroise: 'Vies' anciennes, culture, iconographie*, Paris: Etudes Augustiniennes 1973.

Courcelle, Pierre, "Ambroise de Milan 'professeur de philosophie,' " *Revue de l'histoire des religions*, vol. 181, no. 2, 1972, pp. 147–55.

Drobner, Hubertus, "Studying Augustine: An Overview of Recent Research," in *Augustine and His Critics: Essays in Honor of Gerald Bonner*, ed. by Robert Dodaro and George Lawless, London: Routledge 2000, pp. 18–34.

Eden, Kathy, *Hermeneutics and the Rhetorical Tradition: Chapters in the Ancient Legacy and Its Humanist Reception*, New Haven: Yale University Press 2005.

Ernout, Alfred and Meillet, Alfred, *Dictionnaire Étymologique de la langue latine. Histoire des mots*, Paris: Librairie Klincksieck 1951.

Fahey, Michel A., "Augustine's Ecclesiology Revisited," *Augustine from Rhetor to Theologian*, ed. by Joanne McWilliam, Ontario: Wilfrid Laurier University Press 1992, pp. 173–82.

Fitzgerald, Allan D., "Tracing the Passage from a Doctrinal to an Historical Approach to the Study of Augustine," *Revue d'études augustiniennes et patristiques*, vol. 50, 2004, pp. 295–310.

Fredouille, Jean Claude, *Tertullien et la conversion de la culture antique*, Paris: Études Augustiniennes 1972.

Gross, Alan G., "The Rhetorical Tradition," in *The Viability of the Rhetorical Tradition*, ed. by Richard Graff, Arthur E. Walzer and Janet M. Atwill, Albany: State University of New York Press 2005, pp. 31–46.

Guzmán Brito, A., "Dialéctica y retórica en los *Topica* de Cicerón," *Revista de Estudios Histórico-Jurídicos*, vol. 23, 2010, pp. 161–95.

Holtz, L., *Donat et la tradition de l'enseignement grammatical. Étude sur l'Ars Donati et sa diffusion (IV-IX siècle) et édition critique*, Paris: CNRS 1981.

Horace, *Odes et Épodes*, trans. by François Villeneuve, Paris: Les Belles Lettres 2019.

Kannengiesser, Charles, "The Interrupted *De doctrina christiana*," in *De doctrina christiana: A Classic of Western Culture*, ed. by Duane W.H. Arnold and Pamela Bright, Notre Dame: University of Notre Dame Press 1995.

Krostenko, B.A., "Text and Context in the Roman Forum: The Case of Cicero's First *Catilinariam*," in *A Companion to Rhetoric and Rhetorical Criticism*, ed. by Walter Jost and Wendy Olmsted, Oxford: Blackwell Publishing 2004, pp. 38–57.

Levering, Matthew, *The Theology of Augustine: An Introductory Guide to His Most Important Works*, Grand Rapids: Baker Academic 2013, pp. 1–18.

Löhr, Winrich, "Christianity as Philosophy: Problems and Perspectives of an Ancient Intellectual Project," *Vigiliae Christianae*, vol. 64, no. 2, 2010, pp. 160–88.

Luhtala, Kaija Anneli, *Grammar and Philosophy in Late Antiquity: A Study of Priscian's Sources*, Amsterdam and Philadelphia: John Benjamin's Publishing Company 2005.

Markauskas, Melissa, "Rylands MS Latin 12. A Carolingian Example of Isidore's Reception into the Patristic Canon," in *Isidore of Seville and His Reception in the Early Middle Ages: Transmitting and Transforming Knowledge*, ed. by Andrew Fear and Jamie Wood, Amsterdam: Amsterdam University Press 2016, pp. 177–208.

Markus, Robert, "Evolving Disciplinary Contexts for the Study of Augustine, 1950–2000: Some Personal Reflections," *Augustinian Studies*, vol. 32, no. 2, 2001, pp. 189–200.

Markus, Robert, "World and Text in Ancient Christianity I: Augustine," in his *Signs and Meaning: World and Text in Ancient Christianity*, Liverpool: Liverpool University Press 1996, pp. 1–45.

Matthew, Levering, *The Theology of Augustine: An Introductory Guide to His Most Important Works*, Grand Rapids: Baker Academic 2013.

Mohrmann, Christine, "Saint Augustine and the 'Eloquentia,' " in her *Études sur le latin des chrétiens I*, Rome: Edizioni di storia e letteratura 1961, pp. 351–70.

Plett, Heinrich F., *Literary Rhetoric: Concepts – Structures – Analyses*, Leiden: Brill 2010.

Pollmann, Karla and Vessey, Mark, *Augustine and the Disciplines from Cassiciacum to Confessions* Oxford: Oxford University Press 2005.

Press, Gerald A., " '*Doctrina*' in Augustine's '*De doctrina christiana*,' " *Philosophy & Rhetoric*, vol. 17, no. 2, 1984, pp. 98–120.

Quintilian, *Institutio Oratoria*, ed. by Tobias Reinhardt and Michael Winterbottom, Oxford: Oxford University Press 2006.

Rüpke, Jörg, "Rationalité et Société Romaine," in *Dans le laboratoire de l'historien des religions*, ed. by Francesca Prescendi and Youri Volokhine, Geneva: Labor et Fides 2011, pp. 385–405.

Schäublin, Christoph, "*De doctrina christiana*: A Classic of Western Culture?," in *De doctrina christiana: A Classic of Western Culture*, ed. by Duane W.H. Arnold and Pamela Bright, Notre Dame: University of Notre Dame Press 1995, pp. 46–67.

Seneca, *Lettres a Lucilius*, trans. by Henri Noblot, Paris: Les Belles Lettres 1964.

Ticciati, Susannah, *A New Apophaticism: Augustine and the Redemption of Signs*, Leiden: Brill 2013.

Tornau, Christian, "Augustinus und die neuplatonischen Tugendgrade. Versuch einer Interpretation von Augustins Brief 155 an Macedonius," in *Plato Revived Essays on Ancient Platonism in Honor of Dominic J. O'Meara*, ed. by Filip Karfik and Euree Song, Berlin: Walter de Gruyter 2013, pp. 215–40.

Tornau, Christian, "Augustinus und das 'hidden curriculum': Bemerkungen zum Verhältnis des Kirchenvaters zum Bildungswesen seiner Zeit," *Hermes*, vol. 130, no. 3, 2002, pp. 316–37.

Vessey, Mark, "Augustine Among the Writers of the Church," in his *A Companion to Augustine*, ed. by Mark Vessey, Chichester: Wiley-Blackwell 2012, pp. 240–54.

Vessey, Mark, "Foreword," *Augustinian Studies*, vol. 32, no. 2, 2001, pp. 179–80.

Walzer, Arthur E., "Quintilian's *Vir Bonus* and the Stoic Wise Man," *Rhetoric Society Quarterly*, vol. 33, no. 4, 2003, pp. 25–41.

Wardy, Robert, *The Birth of Rhetoric: Gorgias, Plato and their Successors*, London: Routledge 1996.

Widow, Juan A., "La cultura clásica y el Cristianismo," *INTUS-LEGERE*, vol. 3, no. 2, 2009, pp. 145–58.

Williams, James D (ed.)., *An Introduction to Classical Rhetoric: Essential Readings*, Chichester: Wiley-Blackwell 2009.

Zago, Anna, *Pompei Commentum in Artis Donati partem tertiam. Tomo. 1: Introduzione*, Hildesheim: Olms-Weidmann 2017.

The Myth of Self-Knowledge in Genesis 1–2

The Fascination of the Encounter

Gustavo Esparza

Abstract

My purpose in this paper is to analyze the encounter between Adam and Eve as it is described in Genesis 1–2. Here I consider the myth as a valid source of self-knowledge, inasmuch as through its narration it is possible to experience the moment of fascination in which "man" realizes that "woman" is "bones of his bones and flesh of his flesh." I will emphazise that this expression is developed through a phenomenological process which implies, in turn, a pedagogical path to form in man the capacity to understand the woman as the culminating point of creation, and that, being "like" me means being different from me.

1   Introduction

The purpose of this investigation is to deepen the concept of encounter and the conditions that, according to the biblical account of *Genesis*, were necessary for Adam to find Eve. I will argue that the narrative structure presents a mythical logic and pedagogy since one of its aims is to present the phenomenological process through which the encounter between man and woman occurs as a moment of self-knowledge. I have in mind the existing discussion about the "epistemic privilege of the first-person," which argues that it is only possible to justify the knowledge of personal experiences insofar as I am myself the one who experiences them, and, therefore, I notice the evidence of its reality and epistemic validity. However, according to these approaches, affirming the existence of an outside world leads to a problem of objective justification since I must demonstrate that someone who is not me exists and is capable of experiencing psychic states similar to those I experience; although in some cases the acceptance of an external world allows the state of mental states to be validated, this contrast refers ultimately to the ratification of personal states themselves.[1]

---

1 About this topic see Cynthia MacDonald, "Externalism and First-Person Authority," *Synthese*, vol. 104, no. 1, 1995, pp. 99–101; pp. 117–8. Amie L. Thomasson, "Self-Awareness and

© GUSTAVO ESPARZA, 2021 | DOI:10.1163/9789004448674_007

Even though these approaches can be fruitful at a certain level of argumentation, referring to the problem of how "I am aware that I am aware," the applicability of such postulates depends on (a) the psychological experience with which we demonstrate that a content of consciousness is such, and (b) the validity of the arguments or evidence which the external world (the others) present to justify the view that the psychic states themselves are (in)correct. Within this framework, I claim that the scope of what self-knowledge means is limited by the hypothesis that my knowledge of myself is only knowing what "I" feel, experience or think.

My proposal is to redirect the reflection of self-knowledge in a different way. I will consider that the interpretation of phenomena does not necessarily imply the physical experience of events to arouse understanding. I will argue that the mythical text offers sufficient expressive resources to ensure that the reading experience of the story and its subsequent interpretation operates as a personal life experience.[2] In this sense, the methodology will be philosophical; specifically it will be a hermeneutical phenomenology,[3] and so I will not consider theological and historical-religious points of view,[4] since the central interest is to deepen the concept of encounter as a moment of self-knowledge.

Self-Knowledge," *Psyche*, vol. 12, no. 2, 2006, pp. 11–12; Lynne Rudder B., "Social Externalism and First-Person Authority," *Erkenntnis*, vol, 67, 2007, pp. 299–300; Mathew Parrot, "Expressing First-Person Authority," *Philosophical Studies*, vol. 172, 2015, pp. 2215–7.

2 I take into account two essays by Paul Ricoeur in his *Du texte à l'action. Essais d'herméneutique II*, Paris: Ed. Du Seuil 1986, in order to support this statement: "De l'interprétation" (pp. 11–35) and "Hermeneutique philosophique et hermenéutique biblique" (pp. 119–133).

3 I consider the essay by Sebastian Luft, "A Hermeneutic Phenomenology of Subjective and Objective Spirit: Husserl, Natorp and Cassirer," in *The Yearbook for Phenomenology and Phenomenological Philosophy*, vol. 4, 2011, p. 213. He demonstrates there that such methodology constitutes two traditions that were considered antagonistic: Marburg's neo-Kantianism and Husserl's phenomenology. The main thesis is that comprehension of a transcendental realm could be achieved by intuition and conceptual constitution, something that has been in dispute since Natorpian philosophy and Husserlian philosophy were considered antagonistic: "In general, the methodological opposition between phenomenology and Kantianism can be seen as a paradigmatic debate over this question of adequately studying what one could call 'the transcendental realm,' and it is precisely a dispute over *intuition* versus *construction* as the basis for analysis with regard to the transcendental realm … in order to analyze this transcendental realm, both methodological principles are needed."

4 Paul Ricoeur (*Du texte à l'action*) claims that "la 'confession de foi' qui s'exprime dans le documents bibliques est inséparable des *formes* de discours," p.120. Therefore, to affirm that I will not develop this perspective would seem as a contradiction. Nevertheless, what I claim is that I will not make a theological study on Genesis, but a phenomenological interpretation in which the main characters realize and express a joy for "being" humans, something that the biblical text considers as a *conditio sine qua non* to achieve self-knowledge.

The structure of the paper is as follows: in the second section, I will present the biblical account of Genesis trying to highlight the main *aporia* derived from this mythical account. The third section will define the conditions of the encounter as a pedagogical dialectic that proposes that the interrelation of the first human being with the different natural beings (or his identification as non-human-being) is a necessary step to recognize Eve as different from the rest of creatures of the world. The fourth section will study fascination as the warning of the encounter as a phenomenon; it stands out that the recognition of the otherness that accompanies my own being is not a logical conclusion, but an emotional experience. The fifth section assesses the overall results to show that the encounter between Adam and Eve is possible because of the fascination of overcoming loneliness; the structure of the logical and pedagogical phenomenological process of this event is emphasized. Finally, the conclusions will propose that the mythical narrative—its logical rationality—is constituted within the framework of a pedagogy that fosters the emotional character of the event so that this text is an archaic resource that motivates the encounter of the human being with the world and with the other.

2   The Creation of the Human Being: From Solitude to Encounter

In the biblical account of Genesis, after the creation of the world, the creation of the human being is narrated. The process described in the first chapter is as follows: in the beginning God created the light to divide day and night; these tasks are completed on the first day. On the second day, God creates the firmament and separates it from the waters. On the third day, the waters are separated from the dry land and then the creation of live plants occurs. On the fourth day, the great lights are created; the sun is assigned to the day and the moon and the stars to the night. On the fifth day, animal life is created, and it appears in the water and in the sky. Every form of life is blessed and receives the mandate to be fruitful. On the sixth day, God first creates the beasts of the earth and then creates the human being in "his own image." The text reads, "in the image of God he [was] created; male and female he created them."[5]

This is the creation story described in chapter 1. In the second chapter, the creation of the world and of the human being is narrated thus:

---

5   Genesis 1:26–27.

Then he breathed into his nostrils a breath of life, and thus man became a living being ... The Lord God took the man and settled him in the Garden of Eden to cultivate and take care of it ... And the Lord God said, "It is not good that the man should be alone; I will make him a helpmate for him." And out of the ground the Lord God formed every beast of the field, and every fowl of the air; and brought them unto Adam to see what he would call them: and whatsoever Adam called every living creature, that was the name thereof. And Adam gave names to all cattle, and to the fowl of the air, and to every beast of the field; but for Adam there was not found a helpmate for him. And the Lord God caused a deep sleep to fall upon Adam, and he slept; and he took one of his ribs, and closed up the flesh instead thereof. And the rib, which the Lord God had taken from man, made he a woman, and brought her unto the man. And Adam said, "This is now bone of my bones, and flesh of my flesh: she shall be called Woman, because she was taken out of Man."[6]

With both narratives, a phenomenological process is established, the culmination of which is the encounter of man (*'is*) and woman (*'issha*). Adam, although he is a creature that lives in a "good" world created by God, is incapable of making a connection with any other being. Before the task of naming each living creature, a process of successive approximation is established in which the human being names the world; the whole world is a cosmos of consciousness for "life" as something created and, therefore, as a cause for wonder. The consciousness of being, according to Ernst Cassirer,[7] is the first cause of wonder: "which objects first awakened wonder in man and thus set him upon the road of philosophic reflection? Were these objects 'physical' or 'spiritual'? Was it the order of nature or man's own creations which here took precedence?"[8]

With the distinction between the quality of the phenomenon as physical and spiritual objects, Cassirer is aware that the myth offers a peculiar way of conceiving the world or, in terms of the author, a specific "point of view"[9] that constitutes the way of knowing the world. With regard to this, it is important to remember what Carl Hamburg points out: "no meaning can be assigned to any

---

6 Genesis 2:7, 2:15–23.

7 The three volumes of Cassirer's *The Philosophy of Symbolic Forms, Volume I: Language; Volume II: Mythical Thought; Volume III: Phenomenology of Knowledge,* trans. by Ralph Manheim, New Haven and London: Yale University Press 1955, are henceforth quoted as *PSF* I–III.

8 Ernst Cassirer, *The Logic of Humanities,* trans. by Clarence Smith Howe, New Haven: Yale University Press 1961, p. 41.

9 *PSF,* III, p. IX.

object except in reference to the pervasive symbolic-relation types of space, time, cause and number which 'constitute' objectivity in all domains, with the modifications characteristic of the [symbolic forms (myth, language, science)]."[10] If we apply this to Adam's lack of amazement when naming the creatures, then it is possible to foreshadow an anthropological inability to reach an emotional bond between the human being and the rest of the creatures in the world. Since the meaning, according to Cassirer, originates in the context of a "symbolic pregnancy," where the difference between the subject and the object is recognized and accepted as a duality of identity in which the agent is seen as a being different from the other, then we will have to consider that the process of naming the animals cannot be presented as a moment of symbolic pregnancy.[11]

Adam's loneliness, underlined in the biblical account,[12] exposes a first intention of this myth; although the narrative insists that before the creation of the human being there was a cosmic and living world (the plant and animal world), the narration underscores the following: "*It is not good* that the man should be alone."[13] This sentence is a problem of interpretation: how can goodness be lacking in divine creation? For Augustine this loneliness does not expose an imperfection in the world, but a narrative resource through which the ontological superiority of the human being over the *animalia* is underlined; according to him, by the rational nature of the human being: "(he) is better than the animals in virtue of reason, since only reason which judges concerning them is able to distinguish and know them by name."[14] However,

---

10   Carl Hamburg, "Cassirer's Conception of Philosophy," in *The Philosophy of Ernst Cassirer*, ed. by P.A. Schilpp, Evanston: The Library of Living Philosophers 1949, p. 84.

11   Cassirer defines "symbolic pregnance" as follows: "By symbolic pregnance we mean the way in which a perception as a sensory experience contains at the same time a certain nonintuitive meaning which it immediately and concretely represents. Here we are not dealing with bare perceptive data, on which some sort of apperceptive acts are later grafted, through which they are interpreted, judged, transformed. Rather it is the perception itself which by virtue of its own immanent organization, takes on a kind of spiritual articulation—which, being ordered in itself, also belongs to a determinate order of meaning. In its full actuality, its living totality, it is at the same time a life 'in' meaning. It is not only subsequently received into this sphere but is, one might say, born into it." *PSF*, III, p. 202.

12   In the biblical text, there are two passages that mention this same event: "And the Lord God said, 'It is not good that the man should be alone; I will make him a helpmate'." The second states: "And Adam gave names to all cattle, and to the fowl of the air and to every beast of the field; but for Adam there was not found a helpmate for him." Genesis 2:18, 20.

13   Genesis 2:18. Emphasis added.

14   Augustine, *On Genesis. Two Books Against the Manichees and On the Literal Interpretation of Genesis: An Unfinished Book*, trans. by Roland J. Teske S.J., Washington, D.C.: The

in the interpretation of John Paul II, this original loneliness is characterized by the impossibility of finding another creature that, physically and spiritually, was an image of God:

> [The] first meaning of man's original solitude is defined on the basis of a specific test or examination which man undergoes before God (and in a certain way also before himself). By means of this test, man becomes aware of his own superiority, that is, that he cannot be considered on the same level as any other species of living beings on the earth.[15]

In this text, the human being is in a world of physical objects and living creatures, but there is no other spiritual being like him with whom to identify himself. According to this, then, what would be the basic conditions that allow Adam to find Eve and, at the same time, allow him to recognize her as a human being? What is the meaning of the expression: "This is now bone of my bones, and a flesh of my flesh: she shall be called Woman, because she was taken out of Man"?[16] I will argue that the uniqueness of the moment of this encounter is constituted by the fulfillment of three conditions explained in the first chapters of Genesis, which are pedagogically organized to highlight the fascination of the meeting: A. Adam requires the "I don't find" to understand himself as a being (singular). In this first stage, "not being" functions as a necessary resource to constitute the recognition of being (universal). B. Adam reaches an identification and differentiation in a negative way. At this second stage, the first human is aware that there is no one like "me" on three levels: (i) organic (I can't identify another "body" as "mine"); (ii) psychological (I don't "perceive" another "animal" like me); (iii) ontological (there is no other being like "I am"). C. When Adam finds Eve, he formulates that she is "bones of my bones and flesh of my flesh."[17] With this linguistic expression one can see an astonishment at finding someone like "me." Adam and Eve appear as a complementary duality. The identity achieved by each of them is based on the individual difference of the characters.

Catholic University of America Press 2001 (*The Fathers of the Church*, vol. 84), Book 2, Chap. 11, § 16, p. 112.

15 John Paul II, "The Meaning of Man's Original Solitude," § 6. General Audience, October 10th, 1979, available in <http://www.vatican.va/content/john-paul-ii/en/audiences/1979/documents/hf_jp-ii_aud_19791010.html>.

16 Genesis 2:23.

17 Genesis 2:24.

3   Not Being as No Encounter: The Singularity of Self-Knowledge

I will begin with the questions that will lead the investigation in this section: what is the logic of the encounter of Adam and Eve? How can both characters recognize themselves as human if there was no animal like them? It is
clear that the narrative structure of the first chapters of Genesis develops a
negative dialectic: the human being is alone, and there is no one like him to
help him in his task of naming animals; among the animals, there is no one to
accompany him. God, as the absolute creator, rules: "it is not good that the man
should be alone."[18] In this regard, it is important to highlight two ideas. First,
human loneliness is expressed in the anatomical and morphological difference
between the human animal and the rest of the animals; whatever happens, all
the animals are willing to obey, but none expressed a corporality like that of
humans. Second, conscious loneliness does not appear in the morphological
opposition between humans and animals, but in the process of naming each
living creature.

      The first access to an ontological self-consciousness is possible in the bodily
distinction that occurs during the naming task. To analyze the idea, I will consider the philosophy of the body developed by Cassirer,[19] which follows the
Theoretical Biology of Jakob von Uexküll.[20] Cassirer claims that:

> reality is not a unique and homogenous thing; it is immensely diversi-
> fied, having as many different schemes and patterns as there are different
> organisms. Every organism is, so to speak, a monadic being. In the world
> of a fly, says Uexküll, we find only "fly things"; in the world of a sea urchin
> we find only "sea urchin things."[21]

According to these ideas, it is possible to maintain that in a world of human
beings we will only find "things of human beings." With this simple idea,
Cassirer develops his new definition of the human being as "animal symbolicum."[22] Relying on anatomical differentiation, what Cassirer offers is a review
of the possible functional circles of each animal's anatomy. The ability to
adapt to a way of life reveals a complex network of organic and psychological

18   Genesis 2:18.
19   Ernst Cassirer, *An Essay on Man: An Introduction to a Philosophy of Culture*, New York:
          Doubleday Anchor 1945, pp. 40–4.
20   Jakob Uexküll, *Theoretical Biology*, New York: Harcourt, Brace & Company 1926.
21   Cassirer, *An Essay on Man*, p. 41.
22   Ibid., p. 44.

relationships through which the central characteristic of the world of life of the species in question is appreciated. However, in the case of the human being, his anatomical and psychological vitality is not enough to express its essence since throughout the history of mankind a new relational capacity has been expressed, a way of symbolic adaptation with the environment.[23]

In this regard, Uexküll studies the function of the anatomical structure—mainly the task developed by different neuron systems of each species—in the process of adaptation to the environment. According to the biologist, the difference between reactive systems is not due to the physical conditions in which the organism lives or to the anatomical conditions of the individual, but to an interrelation of both. In this context, the (a) inner world of an animal is bodily linked to the (b) outer world to which the animal reacts by creating the (c) world of action corresponding to the animal. About this interaction, Uexküll states: "The entire function-circle formed from inner world and surrounding-world (the latter divisible into world of action and world-as-sensed) encompassing a whole which is built in conformity with a plan, for each part belongs to the others, and nothing is left over to chance."[24]

Cassirer, following this idea in volume three of his *magnum opus* and adding a detailed analysis of apraxia and aphasia disease, claims that it is possible to establish a pattern to assess the distance between the organic world (as mere existence) and human culture (as the world of the human being):

> The aphasiac or apractic seems to have been thrust one step backward along this path which mankind had to open up by a slow, steady endeavor. Everything that is purely mediated has in some way become unintelligible to him; everything that is not tangible, not directly present, evades both his thinking and his will. Even though he can still apprehend and in general correctly handle what is "real," concretely present, and momentarily necessary, he lacks the spiritual view into the distance, the vision of what is not before his eyes, of the merely possible. ... In this sense the pathology of speech and action gives us a standard by which to measure the distance separating the organic world and the world of human culture, the sphere of life and the sphere of the objective spirit.[25]

The importance of this previous text allows us to understand the value of the body in the constitution of a world of meaning. The impossibility to operate

23   Ibid., pp. 42–3.
24   Uexküll, *Theoretical Biology*, p. 127.
25   *PSF*, III, p. 277.

according to the biological resources that define the human being because of the atrophy suffered, reveals, for Cassirer, the value of the anatomical structure as an indispensable means in the exercise and experience of culture.[26]

According to this, while for Uexküll there is no vital imperfection and for Cassirer the anatomical evidence is a resource to understand the functional circle of the animal world, it can be affirmed that the parade of the animal species in front of the human shows a process of identification of the worlds of each living being.[27] The overall result of this task is the understanding of the differences between the animal world and the human world. On this, John Paul II says the following: "Thus formed, man belongs to the visible world; he is a body among bodies. Taking up again and, in a way, reconstructing the meaning of original solitude, we apply it to man in his totality. His body, through which he participates in the visible created world, makes him at the same time conscious of being 'alone.' "[28]

Within the narrative context, the human body ceases to be an organic form of the world with vitality; now, as a result of this continuous confrontation between species, a state of loneliness is experienced as a result of the naming of the animals. The paradox of this process is that although man is seen as a peculiar animal of the world that operates and acts according to various biological laws,[29] he will notice a fundamental difference that leads him to recognize his uniqueness. John Paul II notes that the

> text also enables us to link man's original solitude with consciousness of the body. Through it, man is distinguished from all the *animalia* and is separated from them, and also through it he is a person. It can be affirmed with certainty that man, thus formed, has at the same time consciousness and awareness of the meaning of his own body, on the basis of the experience of original solitude.[30]

---

26   I have presented these ideas in the following essay: Gustavo Esparza, "Ernst Cassirer: una fundamentación biológica de la definición del ser humano como 'animal simbólico,'" *Open Insight*, vol, 10, no. 18, 2019, pp. 136–9.

27   Genesis 2:20: "the man gave names to all the cattle, all the birds of the air, and all the wild animals; but none proved to be the suitable partner for the man."

28   John Paul II, "Man's Awareness of Being a Person," § 5. General Audience, October 24th, 1979, available in <http://w2.vatican.va/content/john-paul-ii/en/audiences/1979/documents/hf_jp-ii_aud_19791024.html>.

29   To biblical account, there are certain biological laws that do not apply to human beings, such as pain, death, and so on. These limitations come as punishments for original disobedience. See Genesis 3.

30   John Paul II, "Man's Awareness of Being a Person," § 6.

In this way, it is appreciated that the original loneliness is the recognition of the differences between the creatures; Adam deduces that his human body does not exhaust the totality of his essence in pure animal existence, but that his anatomical structure is hardly the starting point for the experience of a complex network of vital relationships that at that moment he feels unable to experience, despite feeling qualified for it. This tension that arises from the recognition of a superior capacity and the warning of the non-existence of a human world translates into the main dialectical opposition that leads to the consciousness of loneliness.

The second resource of ontological self-awareness that is possible during the naming process[31] is the assignment of a linguistic code with which Adam establishes a hierarchy of vital forms. The name does not constitute an essential alteration of the species in general, but a way of knowing the species in particular.[32]

In this way, the cognitive activity of the human being obtains a resource to name the world of creation, but without company. Cassirer explains that linguistic codes have their origin in the appearance of a "god" (or "demon") that through the presentation of all living species promotes an overwhelming emotional experience in humans. It can be affirmed that the main function of the mythical activity, in all its modalities (ritual, linguistic, artistic, pictorial, etc.), is the stabilization of this presence through these intermediate codes through which it is possible to connect with the deity. Every mythical act maintains as a general mission the intermediation of human nature with those forces and mysteries that are manifest in nature: "[The myth, as symbol], is a spontaneous law of generation; an original way and tendency of expression which is more than a mere record of something initially given in fixed categories of real existence."[33]

As Cassirer explains, following Usener's theory, there are three stages or nominal classifications that we can trace in the history of religious thought: "momentary deities" (Augenblicksgötter), "special gods" (Sondergötter) and "personal gods" (persönliche Götter?).[34] The first kind, the "momentary deities," are

---

31   Genesis 2:20.

32   Genesis 2:19–20.

33   Ernst Cassirer, *Language and Myth*, New York: Dover Publications 1946, p. 8. See also *PSF*, I, pp. 117–120; *PSF*, II, pp. 22–23, 98–99, 200–206; *PSF*, III, pp. 90–91, 108–111.

34   Cassirer studies this evolution on *Myth and Language* (pp. 17–23), following the theory developed by Herman Usener, *Götternamen. Versuch einer Lehre von der Religiösen Begriffsbildung*, Bonn: Friedrich Cohen 1896. Based on the German philologist, the neo-Kantian considered the naming process in Roman (pp. 73–79) and Greek cultures (pp. 122–144, pp. 279–314, pp. 330–365).

characterized by the uniqueness of the moment and whose appearances are not related to each other: "These beings do not personify any force of nature, nor do they represent some special aspect of human life. ..."[35] That moment of appearance is fleeting and appears as a sudden revelation of a superior being at which moment it is unfathomable. Therefore, in these moments the emotion that awakens in the human being and that prevents him from communicating with the instantaneous deity is hidden in the singularity of the moment. Here the particular event is privileged; there is no call to a continuous relationship; there is only mystery and wonder.[36]

In the second stage of this linguistic framework, the "special gods" appear; they are characterized by personifying nature. Here the human being tries to stabilize the presence of the divine through the continuity of temporal events by abstracting natural events; if the deity is delighted by creation, then creation is the proper way to communicate with the god:

> As intellectual and cultural development progresses, our relation toward the outer world changes proportionately from a passive to an active attitude. Man ceases to be a mere shuttlecock at the mercy of outward impressions and influences; he exercises his own will to direct the course of events according to his needs and wishes. ... [The special gods] have as yet no general function and significance; they do not permeate existence in its whole depth and scope, but are limited to a mere section of it, a narrowly circumscribed department. But within their respective spheres have attained to permanence and definite character, and there with to a certain generality.[37]

In this conceptual stage, the purpose is to build an intellectual resource through which man can reach the presence of the absolute. Although it seems that it is the god who is present through a diaphanous sequence of instants, it is the community-constituted ritual activity that makes visible

---

35   Cassirer. *Myth and Language*, p. 17.
36   Usener defines the conceptuation of this experience in these terms: "Wenn die augen-blickliche Empfindung dem Dinge vor uns, das uns die unmittelbare nähe einer Gottheit zu Bewusstsein bringt, dem Zustand in dem wir uns befinden, der Kraftwirkung die uns überrascht, den Werth und das Vermögen einer Gottheit zumisst, dann ist der Augenblicksgott empfunden und geschafen. In voller Unmittelbarkeit wird die einzelne Erscheinung vergöttlicht, ohne dass ein auch noch so begrentzer Gattungsbegriff irgend-wie hereinspielte: das eine Ding, das du vor dir siehst, das selbst und nichts weiter ist der Gott." Usener, *Götternamen*, p. 280.
37   Cassirer, *Myth and Language*, p. 19.

the presence of the divine; the naming of these deities occurs as the result of an interweaving between the disconcerting and the everyday, between what is barely glimpsed and what, at the same time, becomes familiar in certain contexts.[38]

At the final stage, the "personal gods" are revealed as the result of a philological approach.[39] While at the previous phases the names of the divinities are coupled with community activity and from it they acquire their distinctive sign, in the case of this last stage there is a detachment of the naturally conceived and that conceived by means of the name:

> The many divine names which originally denoted a corresponding number of sharply distinguished special gods now fuse in one personality, which has thus emerged; they become the several appellations of this Being, expressing various aspects of his nature, power and range.[40]

As can be seen, here the emotional stabilization caused by the presence of the divine is possible by virtue of the proper name: the possibility of referring through a specific sign allows the human being to invoke the name of the deity. There is no longer the transience of the moment, nor the metaphor of nature that links the human being with a specific superior being, but a linguistic code that makes it possible to relate "word" and "presence."

Cassirer recognizes that these results achieved by Usener, beyond their philological value, represent the methodological configuration that implies the recognition of otherness by means of a name. Although the entire treatise of the German philologist focuses on the understanding of the process of appointing divine beings, this allows Cassirer to assume those results to apply them to the process of the appearance of an archaic meaning within the mythical world; just as the world of words historically allowed the naming of the absolute through the transit of transience, moving beyond the metaphor and

---

38   Usener begins his study naming these gods as "transparent gods" (*durchsichtige Götter*), but then he uses the term "special gods" (*Sondergötter*) to clarify the communitarian origin in which the process of naming these deities appears. Usener, *Götternamen*, pp. 75–6.

39   The appearance of these "personal gods" is one of the main results achieved by Usener. Although the appearance of these beings can be verified in the Homeric poems, the great intellectual synthesis literally expressed by Homer about them stands out. Although the personifications of deities are lost in the cultural nebula, it is worth the philological tracking by Usener to show the configuration of these personal deities. Usener, *Götternamen*, p. 330.

40   Cassirer, *Myth and Language*, p. 21.

finding its culmination in personification, for Cassirer it is clear that this process can be traced in the world of mythical awareness.[41]

Now, if what this long and necessary process described by Usener and Cassirer is a necessary path for the linguistic codification of a reality in its primal state, how should we consider that Adam had named Eve without a similar analogous process? It must be remembered that, according to the biblical account, the process through which the new creature is called by its name does not present a gradual progress, but due to a spontaneous act is identified as "Eve." With the formula: "This one, at last, is bone of my bones and flesh of my flesh; this one shall be called 'woman,' for out of 'her man' this one has been taken,"[42] there is the charm of meeting another being like the being that I am. Adam knows Eve from the first moment and for that reason he names her "bone of my bones and flesh of my flesh." The experience of emotion, instead of being an overwhelming moment that is silently transmuted, becomes a jubilant expression with which the man personally identifies with the woman.

The story is clear in showing that before the experience of loneliness that the human had experienced and his lack of emotion, the jubilant irruption that arises in the encounter between man and woman appears. The charm of witnessing another human animal and its subsequent identification as "flesh of my flesh" reflects the awareness of an absolute moment that, according to the naming process described by Usener and Cassirer, should be expressed as a silence or a translucent moment barely noticeable. In front of man, there is someone who is "image of God"[43] and for that reason he recognizes himself as a being that is equal to him, as a being that analogically depends on his creator.

---

41   This is the idea that Cassirer develops after the synthesis he presents of Usener's work: "The value of such observations for the general history of religions lies in the fact that here a dynamic concept of deity has taken the place of the static ones with which both are wont to operate; that the god or daemon is not merely described according to his nature and significance, but that the law of his origin is taken into consideration. If empirical science ... finds itself faced with problems of this sort, surely no one can deny philosophy the right to essay them, and bring its own principles and interests to bear on their solution." Cassirer, *Myth and Language*, p. 23.

42   Genesis 2:23.

43   Genesis 1:27. "So God created man in his *own* image, in the image of God created he him; male and female created he them." About this, John Paul ii explains two important ideas: (i) "Man and woman constitute two different ways of the human 'being a body' in the unity of that image." John Paul ii, "Creation as a Fundamental and Original Gift," § 7. General Audience, January 2nd, 1980, available in <http://www.vatican.va/content/john-paul-ii/en/audiences/1980/documents/hf_jp-ii_aud_19800102.html> The second text is the following: (ii) "The Creator is he who 'calls to existence from nothingness,' and who establishes the world in existence and man in the world because he 'is love' ... It also signifies, according to the first narrative, *beresit bara*, giving. It is a fundamental and

If we establish that the amazement and fascination with meeting another being depends on being an "image of God" it would seem that, consequently, this emotional exaltation should extend to the entire creation, since the biblical account emphasizes that God is the creator of everything that exists and, in that sense, it would be understandable that the human being would find God in all beings as his creator: "God looked at everything he had made, and found it very good."[44] This is, at least, Erich Fromm's thesis, according to which the experience of "God" is constituted by the interrelation between a daily event and the constitution of its conceptual image, through the overlapping of an event called as a consequence of a divine force, the human being develops and incorporates the experience of the superior and, as a reflex psychic act, the fascination of superiority. According to the same author, only the progressive warning that divinity is constituted in human nature itself and not in its alienation, leads to the astonishment of one's life force and as a species; all interest in transcendence depends on the understanding of the intimate as infinite. In human nature itself lies its ultimate goal and basic principle of action.[45]

In contrast, Alejandro Llano has noted that the fascination that comes from the recognition and naming of a divine reality does not lie in the assumption

---

'radical' giving, that is, a giving in which the gift comes into being precisely from nothingness." John Paul II, "Creation as a Fundamental and Original Gift," § 11. Unlike other authors who consider that the term "image of God" represents being-alike-God (see Erich Fromm, *You Shall be as Gods. A Radical Interpretation of Old Testament and its Tradition*, New York: Fawcet Premier 1966, pp. 125–40), John Paul II considers that the "image" is related to the capability to donate everything because of love. In this text, then, we can assume that the expression said by Adam constitutes the moment he delivers everything he has done (and been) to her and vice versa. The joy represents the very moment in which both find each other, but, mainly, the instant in which both recognize themselves as creatures in the image of God, what specifically implies that they were created to donate themselves: Adam *be*longs to Eve; Eve *be*longs to Adam.

44   Genesis 1:31.

45   Erich Fromm writes: "There is a simultaneous permanence and change in any living being; hence, there is permanence and change in any concept reflecting the experience of a living man. However, that concepts have their own lives, and that they grow, can be understood only if the concepts are not separated from the experience to which they give expression. If a concept becomes alienated—that is, separated from the experience to which it refers—it loses its reality and it is transformed into an artifact of man's mind. The fiction is thereby created that anyone who uses the *concept* is referring to the substratum of *experience* underlying it. Once this happens—and this process of the alienation of concepts is the rule rather than the exception—the idea expressing and experience has been transformed into an ideology that usurps the place of the underlying reality within the living human being." Fromm, *You Shall be as Gods*, p. 17. Emphasis in the original.

that the human being is infinity in all its splendor, but that our ability to notice the breath of the superior is a reaction to the analogue and dependent structure of our nature; as human beings we depend and return to divinity to find meaning in our common activities in that environment. In this sense, the astonishment to which it refers the human being is not an emotion motivated exclusively by the discovery of the singular human being, but by the recognition of the divine image to which it brings us back.

According to this, it can be understood that the experience and naming between Adam and Eve revolves around the warning of the "image of God" to which each one refers to the other. Only in the individuality of Eve, as a creature that is an image of divinity, does the man find the fascination of having found another being that is an analogical image and dependent on its creator. Therefore, naming the new creature as "flesh of my flesh and bones of my bones"[46] reveals that in the mystery of existence there is a new unique and personal creature. This act of "finding" appears next to the "name" as a unit that delights the intimacy of the conscience of the other and the understanding of this being as another with which the man identifies himself; here there is no dialectical process of discovery: naming is finding.

Walter Benjamin has expressed with wonderful precision the importance of naming nature. Through the process of naming things, nature is translated into a spiritual world that is unique to the human being, not by virtue of the essence of material objects, but of the properties of language. With this designation in which all creatures receive a name, the world is unified around the given designation:

> All nature, insofar as it communicates itself, communicates itself in language, and so finally in man. Hence, he is the lord of nature and can give names to things. Only through the linguistic being of things can he get beyond himself and attain knowledge of them in the name. God's creation is completed when things receive their names from man, from whom in name language alone speaks. Man can call name the language of language (if the genitive refers to the relationship not of a means but of a medium), and in this sense certainly, because he speaks in names, man is the speaker of language, and for this very reason its only speaker.[47]

---

46   Genesis 2:23.

47   Walter Benjamin, "On the Language as Such and the Language of Man," in *Selected Writings, vol. 1 (1913–1926)*, ed. by Marcus Bullock and Michael Jennings, Cambridge: Harvard University Press 1997, p. 65.

The spirituality achieved, then, implies a process attributable to the human being; in the process of denomination a spiritual characteristic is granted. The same author explains that while nature, through its existence, permanently expresses the essential reality, they cannot communicate this peculiarity because the world is a sign that needs to be decoded. But among all creation the unique creature capable of undertaking this task needs a logos with which to interpret this spiritual reality imbued with the natural world. The passage from the expressed to the communicated constitutes a reconfiguration of existence as a physical sign towards a coded name. In this way, the process that drives the designation of names translates existing signs into communicable meanings.[48]

Due to this process of denomination, a problem arises: if the animals were created as a first attempt of company because it was not good for man to be alone, what good is extracted from this task? What is the meaning of this loneliness within the purposes of the text? The end of the appointment of creation reveals the absence of adequate help for Adam; the recognition process translates into a fragmented self-identification: there is no other being like the human animal.[49] Although the creation, according to the narrative, "is good," at this point it is established that the consciousness acquired by the character indicates that something "is not."

On the apparent lack of goodness, Augustine reminds us that one of the objectives of *Genesis* is the expression of a message that can be understood by the human intellect, which implies a pedagogical process that guarantees the appropriation of revealed truth. Thus, the formula "The Lord God said: 'It is not good for the man to be alone. I will make a suitable partner for him,'"[50] does not expose a stage of consciousness achieved by the creator. According to Augustine, in the deity reflection it is not necessary to conclude that the world "is" good, but with this expression, "it was done," the judgment, action and absolute creation of the world are unified. Therefore, the text proposes

---

48   Benjamin writes about it: "Language therefore communicates the particular linguistic being of things, but their mental being only insofar as this is directly included in their linguistic being, insofar as it is capable of being communicated." Benjamin, "On the Language," p. 63.

49   In the biblical text we read: "And the Lord God said, It is not good that the man should be alone; I will make him a helpmate for him. And out of the ground the Lord God formed every beast of the field, and every fowl of the air; and brought them unto Adam to see what he would call them: and whatsoever Adam called every living creature, that was the name thereof. And Adam gave names to all cattle, and to the fowl of the air, and to every beast of the field; but for Adam there was not found a helpmate for him." Genesis 2:18–20.

50   Genesis 2:18.

a dialectic in which reason assimilates the step from not being (nothing) to being (creation): "For what is said more fittingly of God insofar as it can be humanly said ... These ineffable things had to be said in this way by a man to men so that they might profit."[51]

In this way, the creation myth and its linguistic articulation constitute a mediation resource to support the idea that the human being is not a resource of the material world and, therefore, the world is not essentially spiritual; human nature ends in an organic reality that specifies it in the world, but transcends it since it was created according to the "image of God."[52] In this regard, John Paul II, underscores the negative sense to confirm the self-consciousness achieved by Adam:

> All this part of the text is unquestionably a preparation for the account of the creation of woman.[53] However, it possesses a deep meaning even apart from this creation. Right from the first moment of his existence, created man finds himself before God as if in search of his own entity. It could be said he is in search of the definition of himself. A contemporary person would say he is in search of his own "identity." The fact that man "is alone" in the midst of the visible world and, in particular, among living beings, has a negative significance in this search, since it expresses what he "is not."[54]

In this way, theology has expressed that the purpose of the biblical account is not in the expression "is not good," but in the consciousness of loneliness, in the need of man to donate to woman and vice versa. The intimate relationship achieved by the man/woman in their duality allows the confirmation of the uniqueness of what each person is. Only with the willingness to offer another human being is it possible to ratify Adam and Eve as human beings who need the donation to understand themselves as animals of the world.

With the expression "It is not good for the man to be alone,"[55] a negative pedagogy is highlighted in which it is necessary the recognition of otherness as everything that "I am not" to realize what "I am." However, the subject's knowledge that is expressed as "ipseity" is a knowledge of the world; this identity is constituted as a hierarchical difference that does not deny the

---

51   Augustine, "On Genesis," cap. 5, § 22, p. 159.
52   Genesis 1:27.
53   He refers to Genesis 2:15–22.
54   John Paul II, "The Meaning of Man's Original Solitude," §8.
55   Genesis 2:18.

natural world, but emphasizes that the human being, as a rational animal, is aware of its vital environment. In order for this objective to be narratively expressed, *Genesis* describes a progressive presentation of the bodies in front of the human body to constitute the original loneliness. The pedagogical purpose of the narrative is to inform the reader that in the natural and animal world there is no other being with whom it is possible to achieve identity; it is only the encounter between man and woman that constitutes the motive of self-knowledge.

Carlos Llano explains that the non-being, although it does not exist and, therefore, is nothing, implies a cognitive path as a necessary means to achieve what "is." The opposition to existence and its denial confirm the peculiarity and way of being that the existing is recognized as itself in this dialectical action. Llano claims that: "The enigma of the origin of the idea of non-being is found in the content of what understanding understands when it is first understood as the present reality."[56] In this way, the problem can be placed on the same plane as the "non being" pursues as a shadow the "being" that expresses itself hopelessly in a singular way; "existing being" is recognized as opposed to "non-existing being." The same author, as part of the general solution of the problem he faces, emphasizes that the consciousness of being offers the possibility of distinguishing the nature of the object: "to what or to whom does this first knowledge of being refer?"[57]

If we apply these results to the process described in *Genesis* about naming the world, it can be said that Adam concludes that he is not like the creatures of the world. The identity sought by the human being cannot be derived from the question "*what* is in the world?" The only option for self-knowledge is to move towards "*who* is in the world?" In this sense, Adam becomes aware that the natural world does not accompany the human being and, therefore, through this relationship it is not possible to sustain the encounter between the natural world and the human animal.

As can be seen, the objective up to this point of the biblical account has been the description of the insufficiency of living creatures to accompany the human being. In any case, through this process the need for a new creature that, at this point, does not exist, is ratified. In the next section we will discuss the task that must be solved to achieve the encounter.

---

56   Carlos Llano, *Etiología de la idea de la nada*, Mexico City: Fondo de Cultura Económica 2004, p. 19.

57   Ibid. These ideas can be deepened in the study that Cassirer offers about "Perception of things and perception of expression." Cassirer, *The Logic of Humanities*, pp. 86–116.

4   Being as an Encounter: From Dream to Self-Knowledge

Now I will try to answer the following question: what kind of creature could
reflect an emotion different from that achieved in any of the living creatures already known? I will argue that in *Genesis* lies a creative process that
is revealed through a hermeneutical analysis consisting of these aspects: (1)
the human sleeps; (2) to wake up; (3) to find Eve; and (4) to express about
her: "This one, at last, is bone of my bones and flesh of my flesh; this one shall
be called 'woman', for out of 'her man' this one has been taken."[58]
    I will begin by studying (1): Adam's dream.[59] While the man (*'adam*) "sleeps,"
but without "dreaming,"[60] God creates the woman from his ribs. This process,
for John Paul II, begins "with the desire of finding a being like himself."[61] If
until now the creation of the myth of man ['*adam*] has not found identity in
another being, then the existence of a new being in the world develops. This
fact, for John Paul II, reflects an action that is not explicitly expressed, but represents the breaking of loneliness due to the absence of another being like me:

> Perhaps, therefore, the analogy of sleep indicates here not so much a
> passing from consciousness to subconsciousness, as a specific return to
> non-being (sleep contains an element of annihilation of man's conscious
> existence). That is, it indicates a return to the moment preceding the cre-
> ation, that through God's creative initiative, solitary "man" may emerge
> from it again in his double unity as male and female.[62]

With the image of awakening, the story goes from the expression of "man"
['*adam*] as a generic reality of the human creature to the personal distinction
between "man" ['*is*] and "woman" ['*issah*] as the manifestation of the new

---

58   Genesis 2:23.
59   "So the Lord God cast a deep sleep on the man, and while he was asleep, he took out one
      of his ribs and closed up its place with flesh." Genesis 2:21.
60   John Paul II distinguishes between the act of dreaming, drowsiness and sleep, as the psy-
      chological activity that is derived from this action. Although the comment is anachronis-
      tic, it was important for the author to differentiate between the participatory possibilities
      that the man ['*is*] had during the creation of the woman ['*issah*]; when remarking the
      absence of an unconscious state, the attributions of any form of desire or indirect partic-
      ipation are nullified since the man was in torpor.
61   John Paul II, "The Original Unity of Man and Woman," § 9. General Audience, November
      7th, 1979, available in <http://www.vatican.va/content/john-paul-ii/en/audiences/1979/
      documents/hf_jp-ii_aud_19791107.html>.
62   Ibid., § 8.

human being. What this passage emphasizes is that, after the dream, humanity expresses itself in the differentiated unity of the virile and the feminine. Therefore, the stupor to which the first man submits remains as part of the same prayer and divine promise that accompanied the task of naming animals: "it is not good that the man should be alone; I will make him a helper fit for him."[63]

If until then the parade of animal and plant beings "none proved to be the suitable partner for the man,"[64] there is no reason to infer that the promise of finding company through the appointment of the world had failed, since the experience of loneliness was considered a necessary stage to see who would be the end and culmination of this project.

With respect to (2), the "awakening" of man ['is], it is important to remember that "The Lord God then built up into a woman the rib that he had taken from the man."[65] This passage expresses the unity of three activities that, although they differ from each other, are consistent with the general intent of the myth: (a) the search for another being like me, (b) the creation of another being like me, and (c) the recognition of another being like me. John Paul II acknowledges that, since the biblical language is exposed as a mythical narrative, it is possible to underline the ductility of the term "dream" as an essential note in the development of an intentional hope.[66] At this point it cannot be separated that Adam sleeps in the midst of his search for a being similar to him, and yet the only creative participation of man is reduced to the donation of his rib. This allows us to underline an idea about the desire to overcome the experience of loneliness: the woman is a creation of God and not of Adam, which confirms that man and woman are in creation.

Now, if the woman was conscious before the man, is it possible to give her a passive recognition by knowing the man? That is, is the promise of the entire process described here, as well as the promise of a help similar to hers only attributable to man? Although it cannot be argued that there was a similar process between man and woman, it can be asserted that Eve is looking for another being with whom she can identify. The plausibility of this interpretation would only emphasize the personal similarity of Adam and Eve in the tasks that both fulfill in the world. In any case:

---

63   Genesis 2:18.
64   Genesis 2:20.
65   Genesis 2:22.
66   See John Paul II, "The Original Unity of Man and Woman," § 5–8.

The Bible narrative seems to go beyond the dimension of man's subconscious. If we admit, moreover, a significant difference of vocabulary, we can conclude that the man (*'adam*) falls into that "sleep" in order to wake up "male" and "female." In *Genesis* 2, 23, we come across the distinction *'is-'issah* for the first time. Perhaps, therefore, the analogy of sleep indicates here not so much a passing from consciousness to subconsciousness, as a specific return to non-being (sleep contains an element of annihilation of man's conscious existence). That is, it indicates a return to the moment preceding the creation, that through God's creative initiative, solitary "man" may emerge from it again in his double unity as male and female.[67]

The "encounter" between Adam and Eve, characterized by a moment of joy and recognition, is achieved in this way: "The man said: 'This one, at last, is bone of my bones and flesh of my flesh; this one shall be called 'woman,' for out of 'her man' this one has been taken'."[68] If this expression is analyzed in the light of those achieved so far, it is appreciated that, although Adam discovers that "he is not a woman" and that Eve "is not a man," this understanding focuses on the identity character that is offered through human otherness. Before the warning of the feminine singularity, Eve will recognize in the man the particular being next to which she can ratify her singularity. Adam will notice in her the climax of creation. In both cases, the warning of the other as a singular and unique being is constituted as an anthropological meeting configured pedagogically and whose purpose is the simultaneous naming of the other.

The interest of the narrative context is to crystallize that loneliness is a *sine qua non* formative condition for another body to be understood as human. Adam is not a man by virtue of woman, but thanks to her he is known as such and vice versa. With the expression "This one, at last, is bone of my bones and flesh of my flesh," the passage exposes an essential homogeneity typical of the human race, but highlights the anthropomorphic differences of both. Adam and Eve are human beings and among them they express an adequate way of existing that, without exhausting itself in difference, in its duality highlights the harmony of the unity that humanity reveals. Therefore, instead of reflecting what each one is not, in the expression "this one, at last, is" it is exalted in the context of an intimate emotion.[69]

---

67   John Paul II, "The original Unity of Man and Woman", § 8.

68   Genesis 2:23.

69   This result is similar to the one presented by John Paul II: "Man finds himself alone before God mainly to express, through a first self-definition, his own self-knowledge, as the original and fundamental manifestation of mankind. Self-knowledge develops at the same

With the expression we are flesh of the same flesh and bones that find intimacy in the bones of the other, an emotional narrowing is established by the
affective impact of finding and finally linking with another that, without being
"I," is "like" me. In this passage, woman is the culmination of man's dream;
man is also revealed as the end of the creation of women; both are surprised
to have found themselves in the duality that each represents for the other.
Adam expresses to Eve that I am "yours,"[70] and she expresses that I am "yours."
Individuality and difference remain, difference and opposition are accen-
tuated, and emotion reduces them to a binding difference. The harmony of
opposites narrows thanks to the encounter.

5   The Myth of Self-Knowledge: Fascination as an Encounter

Emotional activity in itself is not a means of encounter, but the operation
through which the agent notices a worldwide phenomenon. However, the
emotional apprehension of the phenomena, instead of offering a differential
resource for the subject's approach to the particular object, presents the phenomenon as a homogeneous multiplicity of events that do not reach a particular differentiation. For Cassirer, the act of knowing begins when there is a
differentiation between the singular and the universal. In this way, knowledge
is constituted as a representation on three levels: expressive, representative

---

rate as knowledge of the world, of all the visible creatures, of all the living beings to which
man has given a name to affirm his own dissimilarity with regard to them. In this way,
consciousness reveals man as the one who possesses a cognitive faculty as regards the
visible world. With the knowledge that, in a certain way, brings him out of his own being,
man at the same time reveals himself to himself in all the peculiarity of his being. He
is not only essentially and subjectively alone. Solitude also signifies man's subjectivity,
which is constituted through self-knowledge. Man is alone because he is 'different' from
the visible world, from the world of living beings. Analyzing the text of Genesis we are, in
a way, witnesses of how man 'distinguishes himself' before God-Yahweh from the whole
world of living beings (*animalia*) with his first act of self-consciousness, and of how he
reveals himself to himself. At the same time, he asserts himself as a 'person' in the visible
world. Sketched so incisively in *Genesis* 2.19–20, that process is a search for a definition of
himself." John Paul II, "Meaning of Man's Original Solitude," § 10.

70   In English it is not possible to appreciate the richness of the Spanish terms "*tuyo*" (mas-
culine possessive pronoun) and "*tuya*" (feminine possessive pronoun). These possessive pronouns are composed of two personal pronouns which are "You-I" (tu-yo/tu-ya).
In some way, we could deduce from the Spanish word that someone has donated him/
herself to other person, but he or she continues being the very same (soy tu-yo/tu-ya);
this donation formula (tuyo/tuya) reveals an intimate difference between those who give
themselves.

and significant. In each of these epistemological stages, although it is diversified into a variable plurality of forms of knowledge, the common operational unit is symbolic.[71]

Now, the epistemic representation does not appear originally; it starts as an organic apprehension of a stimulus and continues evolving until it becomes a concept.[72] Herbert Read[73] and Fernando Zamora[74] have deepened this point by explaining that the primary epistemological act is the warning of a sensitive image; the senses appropriate their corresponding object not by virtue of the subject's consciousness, but by an organic reaction of the bodily form. From this, the impossibility of the human being to notice company, in part, is due to the anatomical differences between man and animals; the human being, although it is an animal, differs from the rest of the *animalia* and in spite of it, in its encounter with the rest of living beings it does not reach an emotion when knowing them. This expressive bond is reached only in the encounter with Eve. The uniqueness of the moment is noted not by the existence of the woman, but by the ability of the human to configure a stabilized image of himself and Eve.

That said, we must ask ourselves: What are the conditions that allow Adam's encounter with Eve? The text, in particular, raises a moment of emotional shock when the man says: "This one, at last, is bone of my bones and flesh of my flesh."[75] With this formula, the protagonist makes clear the existence of the only being in the world that has been created in his image and likeness; the woman is also an "image of God"[76] that allows Adam to achieve a personal identity. Adam is an animal creature of the world that only finds in woman the possible means of self-understanding. It is important to keep in mind that a similar operation occurs in Eve: in her, there is also a moment of joy when she meets Adam, since he is the only creature in the world that allows personal recognition.

---

71   In strict sense this is the long path developed by Cassirer on *PSF*, III. The *expression* process is considered in the Part I (pp. 43–104), the *representational* phase is studied on Part II (105–278), and the *signification* is Part III concern (pp. 279–480). As we can see this is a phenomenological study of knowledge as the subtitle of the volume suggests.

72   This is a complex process, as Cassirer has shown. See *PSF*, III, pp. 105–327.

73   Herbert Read, *Icon and Idea. The Function of Art in the Development of Human Consciousness*, New York: Schocken Books 1965, pp. 17–34.

74   Fernando Zamora, *Filosofía de la imagen*, Mexico City: Universidad Nacional Autónoma de México, pp. 105–232.

75   Genesis 2:23.

76   Genesis 1:26.

The importance of the linguistic formula constructed by Adam is characterized by expressing a singular basis with which he manages to access a universal reality attributable to each "human being;" in other words, with the expression of man, the general form that will make sense of all subsequent particular events is established. Eve has found in him the intermediary for the donation of all her womanly self; thanks to the woman, the man assumes the responsibility to donate everything he has named in the creation; both become responsible for the natural and animal world to yield it to the other. Through the biblical narrative the reader witnesses how the unity of the world merges into the emotion of an encounter that attests to the origin and sense of full surrender to the other.

It is important to keep in mind that since the text emphasizes a duality in the names of the protagonists, there is an essential difference between the first man ['adam] and the later protagonists presented as man ['is] and woman ['Issah], because the "original loneliness" that prevented human beings from emotionally linking with creation is dissolved by the meeting of both. Thanks to the fact that the woman appears before the man, the self-knowledge of one's own animal being as a human species becomes possible: the man ['is] is like her and the woman ['issah] is like him. The creation story confirms that, regardless of the purpose of the human being, the unity that makes the encounter possible is only feasible on the body frontier of the opposite being that is another human being different from the self that defines me, but that, at the same time, in its difference, it allows me to confirm myself in the affirmation I am "yours" or, as it is suggested in Spanish, "I am you-me" (soy tu-yo).

In this way, the pedagogical work of the narrative that had endeavored to configure everything that man is not, now, in the creation of the human being as man and woman, reveals a link through which the original loneliness ends. Thanks to Eve the dream ends; only in Eve is it possible to suppress loneliness and recognize the original creation plan. Through the presentation of the man to the woman, the universal edges are articulated in which the personal being is ratified giving meaning to that pristine expression that seals the unity of the human being: this is now flesh of my flesh and bone of my bones, because in the image and likeness of God we have been created.

6   Mythical Pedagogy: Narrative as a Formative Function

If so far the effort has been directed to specify what were the contextual conditions in which Adam and Eve met, what remains to be considered are the formative characteristics of this text. With the previous presentation we solved the anthropological problem that we established at the beginning, but there is still the question of how it is possible to attribute this mythical explanation to any "I." In this section, I will try to solve this problem by trying to answer the following questions: What is the general function of the myth? Can it be attributed a "formative" intentionality?

The function of myth is the articulation of the word about reality. Both Ernst Cassirer[77] and Lluís Duch[78] affirm that the human being, before the linguistic conformation of the experiences, suffers the world. In this particular case, however, the function operates as an attenuation of the expressive possibilities of linguistic affirmation. It is enough, for this, to think that while God dictated "Then God said, 'Let there be light,' and there was light,"[79] in the case of humans, he could only call what had already been created: "And Adam gave names to all the cattle, and the birds of the air and each beast of the field."[80] This previous idea allows us to affirm that, in the divine word, once it is pronounced it becomes existence, but in the case of the human word, the being needs to be narrated; in the word of God there is no narration, but presence; in the (primitive) word of man there is a myth that represents being.

The essence of the world and what is understood by it is achieved archaically thanks to myth. Through the narrative, the agent does not strive to create a reality, but to stabilize the experience of astonishment of encountering the being of reality. From the narrative an interpretive framework of the phenomenon is developed. Through the encounter with the other that presents itself, the possibility of astonishment is opened as a first operation or as a reflection of a mythical stage. This transition from the warning of a phenomenon to the mythical configuration implies an interpretive resource that is accessed through the language offered by the experience of the phenomenon; only through the representation of the word made reality, can the human being narrate.

The myth, therefore, does not depart from reality, since it becomes its *conditio sine qua non*. However, access to that purpose must be deployed through a human representation. Through narration, the human being is placed in an integral framework of divine activity. Usener,[81] in that sense, had already delimited mythology as the methodological content through which access to the history of the gods is possible. The cultural effort that represented

---

77   Cassirer, *Language and Myth*, pp. 83–99.
78   Lluís Duch, *Mito, interpretación y cultura*, Barcelona: Herder 2002, pp. 65–131.
79   Genesis 1:3.
80   Genesis 2:20.
81   See Usener, *Götternamen*, pp. V–VII.

transcending the emotional outburst caused by the gods of the moment to reach the personal gods is part of a long struggle of the human being to stabilize emotions and articulate an appropriate linguistic sign with which to represent reality.

If we recognize in the human faculties—particularly in imagination and fantasy—the power to build resources that in fact do not exist in the world, it is understandable that the myth exalts the "possible" as a frontier of meaning. In this way, that idea of myth as something that denies or lies implies, in an analogous way, the conception of "being" as "nothing."[82] Myth is constituted as an epistemological legality, as a resource for the constitution of the world of cultural experience.

All the meaning and function of this particular symbol is linked to the concatenation of the vitalities that unite the community; therefore, while mythical thought becomes aware of the world, an interpretive network of vital existence is stirred; the entire universal empire that lacks a homogeneous structure, through mythical function becomes accessible, becomes a resource where the orientation of the individual in the cosmos becomes possible. However, we must understand this guiding characteristic, in the broadest sense of the term, is not only directive signaling, but also conformation, community, training.

Through the activity of the subject that accompanies an ideal structure, it is revealed and promoted to all members of the community. The individual is not an isolated entity that subsists in its own reality, but it rather understands itself as a singular being that maintains a coordination relationship with the community environment with which it develops. The community, in this sense, constitutes the social framework that allows access to the designation of everyday experience as an anthropological experience. Only in the heart of the community is the human being seen as such.

Within pedagogical thinking, it is J.A. Comenius who better understood the formative function of myth in general and the history of Genesis in particular. On the basis that this story expresses both the ideal to which we must return (Genesis 1–2) and the cause of our human condition (*Gen* 3–4), the author's theological effort materializes in the development of a system to return human nature to its original state. For the author, given the tragic loss of the presence of God, educational work must strive to offer a counterweight to the conventional tendencies of daily life that arose from the expulsion from paradise. For the Czech educator, then, in the myth there is more than a fantasy narrative, it

---

82   *PSF*, II, pp. 73–82.

reveals and expresses the general structure that a pedagogical formation must assume.[83]

The myth, for Comenius, is not exhausted in its narrative instance, but in this only a first revealing function is fulfilled. Throughout the discursive expression, the possibility of interpreting the reconstructive phases through which it will be possible to propel human nature towards its original state is opened: (a) diagnosis, (b) ideal, (c), human ages, (d) educational contexts, (e) activities, (f) material resources and (g) return, constitute, more or less, the didactic project developed by the author. If in the understanding of the human being as a being created as "imago Dei" (*diagnosis*) the archaic essence of man is revealed, then there is no other purpose than the return to the origin (*ideal*). This path can only be achieved through the understanding of the human being as a living being that evolves evolutionarily (*human ages*) and that, in each of these stages, there is an educational agent (*educational context*) that, backed by an adequate bibliography, acts and resources (*activities and material resources*), allow man to return to his original state described in Genesis.

For Lluís Duch, this pedagogical process should not be recognized as an *ad extra* resource but as a constituent of the narrative activity. Every expressive warning finds in the narrative the grammatical framework to combine and organize individual experiences in a coherent whole; for this author, then, there can be no myth without logos or pedagogical praxis. Starting from the fact that the crisis of the human being is grammatical, the means to return to the narrative possibilities (mythical and logical) require the cultural coordination through which to train each individual from the idea of the whole.

Therefore, myth as narration will not only be presented as a spoken discourse, but as an active expression, as an action that drives the reorganization of human nature.

7   Conclusion

In this work we analyzed the conditions that, according to Genesis, were necessary for the 'encounter' between Adam and Eve to be possible. It was suggested that this myth, while detailing the process of creation of man ['*adam*],

---

83   Juan A. Comenio, *Pampedia*, trans. by Federico Gómez, Madrid: UNED 1992, pp. 37–104. These ideas had been developed in a previous essay: Gustavo Esparza, "Pedagogía del mito en J.A. Comenio. De la educación a la formación de la naturaleza humana," in *Mito, conocimiento y acción. Continuidad y cambio en los procesos culturales*, ed. by Claudio Calabrese, Gustavo Esparza and Ethel Junco, New York: Peter Lang 2019, pp. 147–82.

expresses an original (primitive) context in which the human being distinguishes its being as a man ['is] and as a woman ['issah]. Through this analysis, simultaneously, two characteristics of the text were identified: a pedagogy of myth and a logic of myth.

On the pedagogy of myth, it was suggested that the narrative structure of Genesis was characterized by a negative dialectic. To highlight human nature, the text exposes the differences that man maintains with the creatures of the natural world and the animals. Due to a nomenclature process, the human being recognizes creation as a physical and vital reality that, although it is constituted as the context in which the human being lives, operates as a cultural mediation resource for the recognition of personal being.

It was observed that, in the task of naming living beings Adam perceives himself as alone in the world. This experience forms a narrative process that emphasizes what the human being is not; this stage allows humans to underline the experience of meeting women. But the emphasis of the biblical story is on the pedagogical process through which it is possible to configure the conditions that make self-knowledge possible: the awareness of loneliness and the subsequent encounter with women operate as contrasting experiences. This dialectic allows the individual to configure the fascination of the encounter between Adam and Eve.

With respect to the logic of myth, it was said that the Genesis account contains the basic principles through which it is proposed to delineate the nature of the encounter of the human being. By opposing man to the plant and animal world, a differentiation is established between beings. In the process of hierarchy of modes of existence, an identity is achieved that opposes the body structure as its own and distinct from the rest of the beings in the world. The objective of this myth is to accentuate the essential differences between the parts that constitute the world. The importance of exposing these contexts through emotions and emotional shocks configures vital spaces as functional operational circles of the species; man, as a man, does not exalt himself jubilantly before the creatures of the world; in naming the animal world a border is delineated that does not satisfy the personal interest of living in the world. The inability to unite species, body, form and world, results in a becoming aware of this singular loneliness.

However, in the face of the experience of meeting the "new creature," Adam experiences a joyful fascination: she is the opposite of the rest of the beings in the world and is also the only creative being with which he reaches an emotional bond. The same process occurs with Eve, in the face of the inability to relate to the world, the only creature capable of increasing her joy is Adam; thanks to him, creation is no longer offered as the opposite of personal being, but is the vital environment in which each one as a male and female can be donated. The unity that both achieve does not degrade their differences; it is because of this opposition that both approach each other, and due to this radical difference, they can form a single flesh in whose daily manifestation the singularities of men and women will be noticed.

All the mythical sense of the text studied indicates that, from the fascination of the encounter between two beings, the first condition of unity arises to link men and women. The second condition indicates that, from the recognition of otherness as a unique and singular reality comes the awareness of other beings as alien to my own reality, but in the recognition of their essence, vegetable, animal or human, mutual donation is forged. In the fascination of the encounter with the other, it is the only viable way to achieve self-knowledge.

Translated by Carlos Rafael Domínguez

Bibliography

Augustine of Hippo, "*On Genesis*: Two Books on Genesis Against the Manichees and On the Literal Interpretation of Genesis. An unfinished Book," trans. by R.J. Teske, Washington, D.C.: Catholic University of America 2001 (*The Fathers of the Church*, vol. 84).

Benjamin, Walter, "On the Language as Such and the Language of Man," in *Selected Writings, vol. 1 (1913–1926)*, ed. by Marcus Bullock and Michael Jennings, Cambridge: Harvard University Press 1997.

Cassirer, Ernst, *An Essay on Man: An Introduction to a Philosophy of Culture*, New York: Doubleday Anchor 1945.

Cassirer, Ernst, *The Philosophy of Symbolic Forms. Volume I. Language*, trans. by Ralph Manheim, New Haven and London: Yale University Press 1955.

Cassirer, Ernst, *The Philosophy of Symbolic Forms. Volume II. Mythical Thought*, trans. by Ralph Manheim, New Haven and London: Yale University Press 1955.

Cassirer, Ernst, *The Philosophy of Symbolic Forms. Volume III. Phenomenology of Knowledge*, trans. by Ralph Manheim, New Haven and London: Yale University Press 1955.

Cassirer, Ernst, *Language and Myth*, trans. by Susanne K. Langer, New York: Dover Publications 1946.

Cassirer, Ernst, *The Logic of Humanities*, trans. by Clarence Smith Howe, New Haven: Yale University Press 1961.

Comenio, Juan A., *Pampedia*, trans. by Federico Gómez, Madrid: UNED 1992.

Duch, Luis, *Mito, interpretación y cultura*, trans. by Francesca Babí and Domingo Cía, Barcelona: Herder 2003.

Esparza, Gustavo, "Ernst Cassirer: una fundamentación biológica de la definición del ser humano como 'animal simbólico,' " *Open Insight*, vol, 10, no. 18, 2019, pp. 125–144.

Esparza, Gustavo, "Pedagogía del mito en J. A. Comenio. De la educación a la formación de la naturaleza humana," in *Mito, conocimiento y acción. Continuidad y cambio en los procesos culturales*, ed. by Claudio Calabrese, Gustavo Esparza and Ethel Junco, New York: Peter Lang 2019, pp. 147–82.

Fromm, Erich, *You Shall Be as Gods: A Radical Interpretation of Old Testament and its Tradition*, New York: Fawcet Premier 1966.

Hamburg, Carl, "Cassirer's Conception of Philosophy," in *The Philosophy of Ernst Cassirer*, ed. by P.A. Schilpp, Evanston: The Library of Living Philosophers 1949, pp. 73–120.

John Paul II, "Man's Awareness of Being a Person." Accessed August 13, 2018. http://w2.vatican.va/content/john-paul-ii/en/audiences/1979.index.html#audiences.

John Paul II, "The Meaning of Man's Original Solitude." Accessed August 13, 2018. <http://w2.vatican.va/content/john-paul-ii/en/audiences/1979.index.html#audiences>.

John Paul II, "The Original Unity of Man and Woman." Accessed August 13, 2018. <http://w2.vatican.va/content/john-paul-ii/en/audiences/1979.index.html#audiences>.

John Paul II, "Creation as a Fundamental and Original Gift." Accessed August 13, 2018. http://www.vatican.va/content/john-paul-ii/en/audiences/1980.index.3.html.

Llano, Carlos, *Etiología de la idea de la nada*, Mexico: Fondo de Cultura Económica 2004.

Luft, Sebastian, "A Hermeneutic Phenomenology of Subjective and Objective Spirit: Husserl, Natorp and Cassirer," *The Yearbook for Phenomenology and Phenomenological Philosophy*, vol. 4, 2011, pp. 209–48.

Lynne, Rudder B., "Social Externalism and First-Person Authority," *Erkenntnis*, vol, 67, 2007, pp. 287–300.

MacDonald, Cynthia, "Externalism and First-Person Authority," *Synthese*, vol. 104, 1995, pp. 99–122.

Parrot, Mathew, "Expressing First-Person Authority," *Philosophical Studies*, vol. 172, 2015, pp. 2215–37.

Read, Herbert, *Icon and idea: The Function of Art in the Development of Human Consciousness*, New York: Schocken Books 1965.

Ricoeur, Paul, *Du texte à l'action. Essais d'herméneutique II*, Paris: Ed. Du Seuil 1986.

Thomasson, Amie L., "Self-Awareness and Self-Knowledge," *Psyche*, vol. 12, no. 2, 2006, pp. 1–12.

Uexküll, Jakob, *Theoretical Biology*, New York: Harcourt, Brace & Company 1926.

Usener, Herman, *Götternamen. Versuch einer Lehre von der religiösen Begriffsbildung*, Bonn: Friedrich Cohen 1896.

Zamora, Fernando, *Filosofía de la imagen. Lenguaje, imagen y representación*, Mexico City: UNAM 2013.

The Notion of Subjectivity as Reflected in Early Notions of the Afterlife

Jon Stewart

Abstract

This article argues that we can track specific stages in the development of subjectivity by tracing the different accounts of the afterlife. As the sense of subjectivity and individuality becomes more pronounced, this is reflected in ever more refined views of the underworld or heaven, as the case may be. An attempt is made to establish the basic framework of this claim with just a few examples, which can be used as the point of departure for a more detailed study. The article examines the Mesopotamian, Hebrew, Greek, Roman and Medieval Christian views of the afterlife, which, when taken together, clearly show an undeniable trajectory.

Hegel was the first to suggest that the idea of human subjectivity was something that emerged historically, taking millennia to develop the ideas about it that are intuitive to us today.[1] His theory is that as humans emerged from nature, they first had no clear sense of themselves, and this was an idea that only started to arise in ancient Greek society.

Inspired by this theory, Bruno Snell, in his *The Discovery of the Mind*, and Charles Taylor, in his *Sources of the Self*, try to follow up on Hegel's intuition in different ways. As a classical philologist, Snell attempts to argue for Hegel's general thesis about the rise and development of subjectivity based primarily on linguistic evidence. He thus traces in minute detail the changes in the usage of different Greek words from Homer onward. By contrast, Taylor's *Sources of the Self* traces the development of inwardness with the eye of a philosopher.

---

1   This paper was originally given as a lecture at the workshop: "Individual and Collective Subjectivity: Historical and Contemporary Issues," that took place at the Institute of Philosophy and Sociology of the Polish Academy of Sciences, Warsaw, June 26, 2019. This work was produced at the Institute of Philosophy, Slovak Academy of Sciences. It was supported by the Agency VEGA under the project Synergy and Conflict as Sources of Cultural Identity, No. 2/0025/20.

    Bruno Snell, *The Discovery of the Mind: The Greek Origins of European Thought*, trans. by T.G. Rosenmeyer, Cambridge, MA: Harvard University Press 1953. Charles Taylor, *Sources of the Self: The Making of Modern Identity*, Cambridge, MA: Harvard University Press 1989.

© JON STEWART, 2021 | DOI:10.1163/9789004448674_008

However, his work is in a sense overly focused on philosophy in that it takes almost exclusively philosophical texts as its sources. While Taylor mentions Homer very briefly, his actual analysis begins with Plato. Thus, he overlooks the vast number of works in ancient literature, history and drama that could also be fruitfully used to support his thesis. Moreover, Taylor's work is focused primarily on the modern period, as is implied in the subtitle of the work, *The Making of Modern Identity*. While he purports to give a historical account of the development of the concepts of inwardness and the self, there are major gaps in the narrative. For however rich it might be, the first part of his account, which runs from Plato to Augustine to Descartes, leaves much unexplored.

Following in this research tradition, I wish to claim that the development of inwardness and subjectivity is an important feature of Western culture. These are ideas and conceptions which, although largely absent among the ancients, are widely celebrated today in our modern world. But these concepts are complex and in a sense too intuitive and too close for us to see them with a critical distance. We take them to be obvious, and this blinds us to their historical genesis.

Since this is such a broad topic, some principle of selection must be employed in order to make it manageable. In this paper I wish to focus specifically on early views of the afterlife. It is, I think, uncontroversial to claim that the view of humans after death in all cultures is closely related to their views of the self in general. My thesis is that we can track specific stages in the development of subjectivity by tracing the different accounts of the afterlife. As the sense of subjectivity and individuality becomes more pronounced, this is reflected in ever more refined views of the underworld or heaven, as the case may be. I believe that the basic framework of this claim can be established with just a few examples, which can be used as the point of departure for a more detailed study. I will thus examine the Mesopotamian, Hebrew, Greek, Roman and Medieval Christian views of the afterlife, which, when taken together, clearly show an undeniable trajectory. Suffice it to say that these individual treatments must remain perfunctory since the goal is to provide not an in-depth analysis of each individual case (for which specialized works are much better suited) but rather a synoptic overview which facilitates an understanding of the movement I wish to sketch. Finally, it should be noted that there is a substantial scholarly literature on the subject of images of the afterlife in antiquity.[2] These range from literary to anthropological studies. None of them

---

2 See, for example, Herbert Weir Smyth, "Conceptions of Immortality from Homer to Plato," in *Harvard Essays on Classical Subjects*, ed. by Herbert Weir Smyth, Boston and New York: Houghton Mifflin 1912, pp. 239–83. Christiane Sourvinou-Inwood, *'Reading' Greek*

takes the approach employed here, and none of them is particularly interested in the question of subjectivity or individuality.

1   The Mesopotamian and Hebrew View of the Afterlife

The Sumerian underworld is known as Kur, Irkalla, Kukku, Arali, or Kigal. Glimpses of it appear in a number of surviving texts, for example, "Ishtar's Descent to the Netherworld," "Nergal and Ereshkigal," and most famously *The Epic of Gilgamesh*.[3] In *Gilgamesh* the gods decide that the hero Enkidu must die.[4] As he lies ill, Enkidu has a dream in which he sees the underworld. His account provides a colorful picture of the Mesopotamian pendant to Hades. Although there is an afterlife, it is a miserable one. Like the Greek underworld, the place where the dead go is a concrete physical location in the real world. It is a gloomy and dreary place that is ruled by Ereshkigal, the Queen of the underworld and her record-keeper Belit-Sheri. Enkidu describes it as a place where "people sit in darkness."[5] The dead have their bodies transformed into bird-like creatures with wings and feathers. They eat and drink only black dust. Enkidu sees once great kings and princes now languishing in this place of despair. Stripped of their previous positions, they appear in this land of the dead like servants or slaves. The key feature of the underworld is thus that it has a levelling effect on all human beings. This expresses the basic truth that everyone dies. Death makes no exception for nobility, wealth, power or fame. The good and the evil all in the end must perish in death.

This picture is similar to the one presented in some of the books of the Old Testament under the name Sheol or the Pit.[6] While this place is never described

---

Death to the End of the Classical Period, Oxford: Clarendon Press 1995. Alan E. Bernstein, *The Formation of Hell: Death and Retribution in the Ancient and Early Christian Worlds*, London: University College London Press 1993. Isabel Moreira and Margaret Toscano (eds.), *Hell and Its Afterlife: Historical and Contemporary Perspectives*, Farnham and Burlington: Ashgate 2010.

3   *The Epic of Gilgamesh*, trans. by N.K. Sanders, Harmondsworth: Penguin 1960. See Jean Bottéro, "The Mythology of Death," in his *Mesopotamia: Writing, Reasoning, and the Gods*, trans. by Zainab Bahrani and Marc Van De Mieroop, Chicago and London: University of Chicago Press 1992, pp. 268–86. Samuel Noah Kramer, *History Begins at Sumer*, Philadelphia: University of Pennsylvania Press 1956, pp. 154–67.

4   *The Epic of Gilgamesh*, p. 89.

5   Ibid., p. 92.

6   See Philip Johnson, *Shades of Sheol: Death and Afterlife in the Old Testament*, Downers Grove: InterVarsity Press 2002. Martin Ravndal Hauge, *Between Sheol and Temple: Motif Structure and Function in the I-Psalms*, Sheffield: Sheffield Academic Press 1995 (*Journal for the Study of the Old Testament*, no. 178).

in much detail, it is consistently mentioned as a dark and dreary place. Also in common with the Mesopotamian view there is no judgment and no sense of rewards or punishments. This is something that is frequently referred to in the Book of Job and Ecclesiastes, both of which lament that in the end it all amounts to the same thing. In other words, in death no differentiation in made between rich and poor, noble and common, wise and foolish, righteous and sinful. In both Job and Ecclesiastes there is clearly a tone of dissatisfaction with this arrangement.

2   The Greek Underworld in Homer

The Greek underworld, Hades, is represented perhaps most famously in Book XI of Homer's *Odyssey*,[7] when Odysseus is commanded to go there in order to consult with the prophet Tiresias and get instructions about how to return home. The motif of a hero visiting the underworld while still alive is a well-known one in Greek mythology and is often referred to with the term *katabasis* (κατάβασις) or "descent."[8] This motif is also found in Mesopotamian literature. The mythological figures Herakles, Theseus and Orpheus all visit Hades in different circumstances. While these heroes manage to return from the land of the dead, the trip is perilous, and there is a sense that there is something unnatural about these visits.

According to ancient Greek geography, the Ocean was conceived as a great river that encircled the known world. Thus, it is constantly referred to as a "stream."[9] The underworld is located at the limit of the river, in a place that the sun does not reach, again a specific geographical location. After having arrived there, Odysseus, following the detailed instructions of Circe, performs a series of sacrifices in order to appease the gods of the underworld. He pours the blood of the sacrificial animals into a bowl, and the dead souls then come to him desiring to drink from it. This is the key for them to recognize Odysseus

---

7   *The Odyssey of Homer*, trans. by Richmond Lattimore, New York: Harper Collins 1965. See Christiane Sourvinou-Inwood, "To Die and Enter the House of Hades: Homer, Before and After," in *Mirrors of Mortality: Studies in the Social History of Death*, ed. by Joachim Whaley, New York: St. Martin's Press 1981, pp. 15–39. Walter Burkert, *Greek Religion*, trans. by John Raffan, Cambridge: Harvard University Press 1985, pp. 190–215.

8   See Radcliffe G. Edmonds III, *Myths of the Underworld Journey: Plato, Aristophanes, and the 'Orphic' Gold Tablets*, Cambridge, Cambridge University Press 2004. Bruce Louden, "Catabasis, Consultation, and the Vision," in his *Homer's Odyssey and the Near East*, Cambridge and New York: Cambridge University Press 2011, pp. 197–221.

9   E.g., *The Odyssey of Homer*, Book XI, line 21, p. 168.

and speak with him. But since Odysseus' goal is to consult with the prophet Tiresias, he, again following Circe's directives, draws his sword and, in the first instance, prevents the other souls from drinking. It should be noted that, in contrast to other variants on the motif of underworld visits, Odysseus does not descend into Hades as such, but rather the dead souls come up to him, attracted by the blood of the sacrificial animals, and after their discussions with him, they return.

The underworld episode in the *Odyssey* provides valuable insight into Greek religious practice and views of the afterlife. As Odysseus learns, the dead souls are no longer physical beings. When he tries to embrace the soul of his beloved mother, Antikleia, he cannot hold on to her: "Three times / I started toward her, and my heart was urgent to hold her, / and three times she fluttered out of my hands like a shadow / or a dream."[10] When he fails to understand this, she explains to him that this is "what happens, when they die, to all mortals. / The sinews no longer hold the flesh and the bones together, / and once the spirit has left the white bones, all the rest / of the body is made subject to the fire's strong fury, / but the soul flitters out like a dream and flies away."[11] The human soul is thus immaterial and separable from the body. After the body is cremated, the soul endures in an incorporeal form. The souls are thus referred to as *skiai* (σκιαί), that is, "shades" or "shadows." This conception can be seen as the forerunner of many different dualistic views that conceive of the mind and the body as distinct substances as, for example, in Plato.

There is, however, something odd or inconsistent in the conception of the dead souls as portrayed here since, despite the fact that they are immaterial, Odysseus is able to frighten them off with his sword, which one would expect would simply pass through them. But even if it didn't, the souls are dead anyway, and it is hard to understand why they would fear being injured or even killed a second time given their present condition. Equally odd is the fact that the spirits desire to drink the sacrificial blood that Odysseus has prepared. Drinking and eating, of course, hardly make sense if one does not have a body. But this notion is common in other ancient cultures such as that of the Egyptians, who buried their dead with food and drink. These contradictions point to a conception of immortality that is still closely tied to the natural human realm. The dead souls are very much like the living and are concerned exclusively with affairs of the living. There is no conception here of a higher sphere where the souls live an elevated, more sublime existence.

---

10   Ibid., Book XI, lines 205–8, p. 173. See also lines 390–5, p. 178.
11   Ibid., Book XI, lines 218–22, pp. 173f.

The Greek conception has not yet fully emancipated itself from the natural sphere.

The picture of Hades bears certain similarities to the Mesopotamian underworld and the Hebrew Sheol. Despite the fact that the individual is conceived as surviving death, the new existence in Hades is by no means a desirable one. While most of the souls are apparently not experiencing any direct form of punishment, they are nonetheless clearly miserable and languishing. Odysseus meets his fallen comrade from Troy, the mighty warrior Achilles, and tries to console him. Achilles, however, rejects this consolation and speaks the famous lines, "I would rather follow the plow as thrall to another / man, one with no land allotted him and not much to live on, / than be a king over all the perished dead."[12] This is a profound statement coming from a man known as the exemplification of the warrior ethic, where personal honor is the supreme principle. Life in the underworld is so odious to him that it would be better to be a slave and still be alive. To a great warrior like Achilles, the thought of being a slave was absolutely the lowest, most humiliating and disgraceful thing imaginable. But yet even this is better than life in Hades. The reason that Achilles and the other souls are so miserable is presumably that they are deprived of any meaningful activity that characterizes the life of the living. They can no longer win glory by conquering their enemies or undertaking adventures. Given that their sense of self-identity is defined by this, they seem to languish in inactivity, deprived of the meaning that only the mortal condition can provide.

Odysseus then sees a series of mythological figures: of special interest are Tityos, Tantalus, and Sisyphus, who are all portrayed as suffering terrible punishments for grave crimes that they committed.[13] Tityos has his liver constantly gnawed by two vultures, while Tantalus suffers from eternal hunger and thirst, although he is painfully close to both food and water. Once again, this picture would seem to be inconsistent with the idea that these figures are shades without bodies of flesh and blood. Finally, Sisyphus is condemned continually to push a large rock up a hill only to see it fall back down again. While the other souls in Hades are clearly miserable, they are not explicitly punished for any wrongdoings; only these souls suffer specific punishments. This can be regarded as the origin of the conception of Hell as described, for example, in Dante. The idea of Hell is, of course conceived as a place where the souls are subject to varying kinds of punishments in accordance with the gravity of their sins. But it will be noted that, on this Greek conception, this represents

---

12   Ibid., Book XI, lines 488–91, p. 180.
13   See Christiane Sourvinou-Inwood, "Crime and Punishment: Tityos, Tantalos and Sisyphos in *Odyssey* 11," *Bulletin of the Institute of Classical Studies*, no. 33, 1986, pp. 37–58.

only a small number of the souls in Hades. On the Greek view, the underworld is conceived not primarily as a place of punishment but simply as a place of general despair and misery.

The trip to the underworld is also about the search for knowledge. This motif is also found in *The Epic of Gilgamesh*. Both Gilgamesh and Odysseus are renowned heroes on a quest. This means that they must undertake great journeys in order to achieve their ends. While Gilgamesh does not travel to the underworld as such, like Odysseus, he nonetheless gains knowledge about the secrets of human mortality. Odysseus wants, above all, to return home, but in order to do so, he needs the knowledge that only Tiresias can provide. But once in the underworld, he does not miss the opportunity to acquire new knowledge about the nature of life and death as well as concrete information about the fate of friends and family. Not all of this knowledge is immediately useful to him for the task at hand, yet he lingers there for a long time to learn as much as he can. Thus, not all knowledge must have a clear-cut utilitarian end. Like Gilgamesh, Odysseus goes to the ends of the earth, to the underworld and returns with knowledge. Siduri serves as Gilgamesh's divine guide to the underworld, just as Circe tells Odysseus how to find and safely enter Hades. The Greek story seems in a sense more optimistic than the Mesopotamian one in that Odysseus uses the knowledge he has gained in order to return home. By contrast, Gilgamesh, despite all that he has learned, has still not managed to overcome death. Nonetheless, the two stories bear much in common, for example, the focus on the inevitability of death, the pessimistic view of the underworld, the negative relations with the gods, the value of friendship and comradery, the importance of self-restraint, and the dependence on divine good will.

The idea of an underworld journey has the function of serving as a kind of revelatory vision. It allows the hero to see and understand certain things that are usually not accessible to people. The protagonist sees things in the land of the dead that are beyond the realm of mundane human experience, and this information constitutes an important basis for a general world-view that is relevant for cosmology, anthropology, etc. Gilgamesh was described as someone "who saw mysteries and knew secret things."[14] The underworld thus serves as a source of knowledge about the profound questions of human existence. Given this, it is no wonder that this motif was seized by later authors, such as Virgil and Dante, who used it as an explanatory tool for different things in their own cultural context.

---

14   *The Epic of Gilgamesh*, p. 61.

3   The Greek Underworld in Plato

At the end of the *Gorgias* Socrates presents a mythological account of the nature of life after death that draws on what is found in Homer, whom he refers to directly.[15] This passage has puzzled scholars for different reasons. First, it is not entirely clear how it fits with the foregoing arguments in the work or what purpose it is meant to serve philosophically. Second, Socrates presents the mythological tale straightforwardly and affirms its truth without any hint of his characteristic critical analysis.[16] This seems to contradict his general methodology, which takes nothing for granted and puts everything to the test of reason. Finally, it is a matter of debate how this account fits with Socrates' other treatments of life after death in Plato's other works, most notably the *Phaedo*, the *Symposium*, and the *Laws*. There are thus many open questions surrounding this passage.

However, what is interesting for our purposes is the view of human beings that is implied in the picture of the underworld that Socrates presents. The account that he gives is generally in agreement with what we find in Homer, but Socrates emphasizes and elaborates on a specific aspect that is undeveloped in the *Odyssey*, namely, the question of rewards and punishments. In contrast to the account given in Homer, in the myth that Socrates recounts, all of the souls are judged for their behavior in life. Socrates says,

> Now, there was in the time of Kronos a law concerning mankind which has remained in force among the gods from that time to this. The law ordains that, when his time has come to die, a man who has lived a righteous and holy life shall depart to the Isles of the Blessed and there live in complete happiness, free from evils, but that the man whose life has been wicked and godless shall be imprisoned in the place of retribution and judgment, which is called Tartarus.[17]

Instead of all the souls going to a single place, here there are thus two possible destinations. With this we can see an early version of the idea of heaven and hell in the Christian tradition.

---

15   Plato, *Gorgias*, trans. by Walter Hamilton and Chris Emlyn-Jones, London: Penguin 2004, p. 133, 525d-e, p. 134, 526c-d.

16   Ibid., p. 131, 523a: "Give ear then, as they say, to a very fine story, which will, I suppose, seem just a legendary tale to you but is a fact to me; what I am going to tell you I tell you as the truth."

17   Plato, *Gorgias*, p. 131, 523a-b.

Socrates recounts that in the early days the judgment took place while the people were still alive, specifically on the day when they were destined to die; moreover, their judges were also living. But this arrangement was problematic since evil people could unfairly influence their judgments by giving the misleading appearance that they were moral and righteous. Socrates explains, "Many whose souls are wicked are dressed in the trappings of physical beauty and high birth and riches, and when their trial takes place they are supported by a crowd of witnesses who come to testify to the righteousness of their lives."[18] As a result, people with evil characters managed to get a favorable judgment and be sent to the Isles of the Blessed, and those with good characters to Tartarus.

When Pluto and those in charge of the underworld complained about this, Zeus could not allow the injustice to stand. He then made three changes. First, he ordained that people should be judged naked, so that they could not hide anything or influence the judges by their expensive clothes. Second, he made it such that people did not know the day of their death so that they could not make special arrangements for their trials. Third, he decided that the judges themselves should be dead and should likewise be naked in order to ensure that they were incorruptible. Zeus then appointed three of his sons to be judges after their deaths: Minos, Rhadamanthus and Aeacus. In the *Odyssey*, it is mentioned that Odysseus sees Minos in the underworld, but there is no elaboration given of the nature or procedure of his judgments.[19] Rhadamanthus is also mentioned by way of allusion, although not in the underworld scene.[20] He is portrayed simply as dwelling in and perhaps ruling over the Elysian Field (which presumably corresponds to the Isles of the Blessed), but there is no mention of his role as judge. The element of judgment thus remains undeveloped.

The myth recounted by Socrates develops and extends the notion of divine justice that only existed in embryonic form in Homer. Here Pluto is upset about the injustices that arise concerning the judgments, and Zeus himself takes action to correct this. This view demonstrates an awareness or expectation that the gods act justly and are concerned with correct judgments. Moreover, the idea of judging people naked so that they can hide nothing also approaches our intuitive sense of what justice should be. This is a more satisfying picture of the afterlife than the one presented in Homer.

---

18   Ibid., p. 131, 523c.
19   *The Odyssey of Homer*, Book XI, lines 568–72, p. 182.
20   Ibid., Book IV, lines 564–5, p. 79.

Socrates explains that the soul is separated from the body at death. The body maintains its physical features as in life, and the soul, although immaterial, also visibly displays the moral character of the deceased: "once it is stripped of the body all its qualities may be seen, not only its natural endowments but the modifications brought about by the various habits which its owner has formed."[21] Thus, the judges can see the moral character of the individual transparently by looking at his disembodied soul. This also seems to correspond to an intuitive sense of divine justice. The divine judges have the ability to see the precise nature of each individual in a way that would never be possible for living judges evaluating living people. Thus a divide is created between fallible human justice and divine justice. While human beings do the best that they can by creating laws and legal institutions in order to determine justice, they are still fallible, and miscarriages of justice do sadly take place. This is a fact of human existence, regardless of how good the given laws or judges are. But divine justice is not constrained in the same way. It can attain perfection in judgment since the judges are able to see the exact moral characters of individuals. They have complete knowledge, and their judgments are not clouded by deceptions and lying testimony. This idea strengthens the sense that there is something absolutely right and wrong, despite the fact that in the human sphere there is never any complete agreement about such things. With the idea of divine judgment, there is nowhere to hide. Everyone will get exactly what he or she deserves based on their moral character.

Moreover, the value of the individual increases, since now the moral character of every single human being is what is decisive. Each person is evaluated for his or her own merits. In death they can no longer be helped by their wealth or social standing. Their families or friends cannot come to their assistance. Now the dead souls stand completely alone and naked, that is, transparent before their judges. The individual moral character is thus more important than one's traditional roles in society or the family. Individual choice and responsibility now become tantamount, while custom and tradition are reduced to a secondary role. The idea of being judged naked and, indeed, as a disembodied soul also marks a shift from the outward to the inward. What is important is not the clothes that one wears or even the body that one possesses. One's outward roles in the family or society are likewise irrelevant. Instead, what is supremely valuable is the inward soul, which is invisible while one is alive.

An interesting deviation from the later Christian conception involves the notion of reincarnation, which, although not stated explicitly, is implied in

---

21   Plato, *Gorgias*, p. 132, 524d.

the myth that Socrates recounts.[22] He explains the twofold goal of the punishments. There are hardened, unrepentant sinners who can never be redeemed. Their terrible punishments serve as examples to others. However, for the other sinners—presumably the vast majority of souls—the punishments serve the function of improving them. Their moral failings are curable. This picture implies that the souls will return to life with improved moral characters. Thus the whole process of judgement, punishment and moral redemption is designed to prepare people for their next life. It might be claimed that there is something intuitive about this model since in this way the punishments are made to serve a constructive purpose. When we punish children, the idea is that they will learn from this and be better adults for it. Likewise, when we punish criminals, the hope is that they will thereby be rehabilitated and eventually be able to resume a productive role in society. But if there is no future perspective, there is no constructive point to punishment. This seems to be a problem if the souls in the myth were simply to remain dead and suffer in the underworld forever. There is no point in trying to improve their characters since they will never become moral agents again. This problem is solved with the idea of reincarnation.

Moreover, if people are made to suffer eternal punishment, a disproportion seems to arise. For an individual finite sin, or even a number of them, one is made to suffer infinitely in eternity. Although we might derive a sense of vengeful satisfaction from seeing sinners suffer for their misdeeds, the principle of the punishment fitting the crime is violated. Why should we be made to suffer forever for a single misdeed or moment of weakness? The idea of reincarnation also solves this problem since it implies that the punishments are finite and that afterwards one will be given another chance. Only in the case of the incurable sinners is the punishment eternal.

Given all this, the point of the myth that Socrates recounts seems to be to motivate people to act justly. Socrates states straightforwardly, "I put faith in this story, and make it my aim to present my soul to its judge in the soundest possible state."[23] This reinforces the conclusion of the dialogue that one should strive for justice: "All other theories put forth in our long conversation have been refuted and this conclusion alone stands firm: that one should avoid doing wrong with more care than being wronged, and that the supreme object of a man's efforts, in public and in private life, must be the reality rather than

---

22   Socrates develops a theory of reincarnation in the *Republic*. See *The Republic of Plato*, trans. by Allan Bloom, New York: Basic Books 1968, Book X, pp. 292–303, 614a–621d.

23   Plato, *Gorgias*, pp. 134f., 526d.

the appearance of goodness."[24] The question remains about the value of the myth for Socrates' purposes. If he believes that his argument has already thoroughly demonstrated the importance of acting justly, why does he need to mention a myth as well? In any case, we can see in the myth a further development in the conception of individuality and inwardness from what was seen previously in Homer.

4   The Roman Underworld

Corresponding to Book XI of the *Odyssey*, Book VI of the *Aeneid* depicts the hero's descent to the underworld.[25] While it is clear that Virgil is using the text from Homer as his model, there are some significant differences in the depictions, and these provide rich material for comparison and contrast. Once again it is possible to discern a clear elaboration of the concept of life after death and divine justice.

In Virgil's account of the underworld, the souls are differentiated much more specifically by their individual circumstances. First, Aeneas sees crowds of souls trying to cross the river Styx in the boat of Charon, who only allows the buried to come aboard. The unburied are not permitted to make the crossing but are forced to endure first a hundred years of wandering on the shores. Then there are the souls of children who died before they reached adulthood; then those who were executed unjustly on false charges. These souls are given a new trial in the afterlife and thus a chance to prove their innocence. This is described as follows: "Minos, the president of the court, shakes the lots in the urn, summoning the silent dead to act as jurymen, and holds inquiry into the lives of the accused and the charges against them."[26] This recognizes that there is something special and unique about the moral life of each individual. Moreover, the souls of dead children are recognized as full human beings. The account that Virgil gives here resembles in some ways that which Socrates recounts at the end of the *Gorgias*, where Minos and the other judges are mentioned.[27]

Aeneas and his guide the Sibyl come to a fork in the road, with Elysium on the one side and Tartarus on the other. With this division of the underworld into a heaven and a hell, Virgil follows the myth recounted by Socrates in

---

24   Ibid., p. 135, 527b.
25   Virgil, *The Aeneid*, trans. by David West, London: Penguin 1990.
26   Ibid., Book 6, lines 433–6, p. 127.
27   See Plato, *Gorgias*, pp. 131–6, 523a-527e.

contrast to that found in the *Odyssey*. Aeneas is not allowed to enter Tartarus since he is pure and virtuous, but the Sibyl describes the place in great detail.[28] She outlines all of the different crimes that people have committed and the terrible punishments that they are suffering. Here the degree of detail involved goes well beyond Socrates' myth. We can clearly see in the Sibyl's descriptions the inspiration for Dante's elaborate portrayals in the *Inferno*, where he creates a detailed system of gradated punishments for the different crimes and sins.

In Tartarus, the Sibyl explains, Rhadamanthus is the ruler, and he upholds the laws and exacts the punishments on the sinners (another point of commonality with Socrates' account). Moreover, he gets them to confess the crimes that went undetected during their lives.[29] This is an idea that was presumably created in order to resolve the problem of divine justice. We might think of the question of justice as having two aspects. If there is divine justice, then no one who is innocent would ever be punished, and no one who is guilty of some crime would ever get away with it with impunity. With regard to the first part, Aeneas first sees the judge Minos who corrects the injustices that have happened to the innocent who were wrongly punished. Now Rhadamanthus rectifies the second half of the concept of injustice by punishing those who got away with crimes undetected. It will be recalled that this was a key element in Job's complaint. He could not understand why, given God's infinite power and justice, bad people seem to get away with their ill-deeds and live happy and prosperous lives. The answer to this that Job was given is, in effect, that it is a mystery and one needs to believe that God is just, despite all appearances to the contrary. In Virgil's underworld, this problem is resolved. While some evil people might have gotten away with their crimes in life, they will be caught by Rhadamanthus, made to confess, and punished accordingly. On this account, there is no escaping responsibility for one's ill-deeds. There is perfect divine justice, and it is clear to see. It is no longer a mystery that needs to be taken on faith. The wicked are made to suffer for their crimes, and, as in Dante, one feels a sense of satisfaction in seeing that justice is done, especially when one reads about their heinous crimes. While there are injustices in the world, these will all be corrected in the afterlife. This can be seen as a great psychological help to victims who suffer injustices in this world since it assures them that if they simply be patient and bravely endure the wrong done to them for a while, then after death they will in fact be vindicated and rewarded, while the ones who did them harm will be punished.

---

28   Virgil, *The Aeneid*, Book 6, lines 563–637, pp. 130–2.
29   Ibid., Book 6, lines 568–70, p. 131.

Another new element here is that of the confession of the guilty party. In Socrates' account, the judges could see the moral characters of the individuals transparently since the latter were naked, and this seemed to be a guarantee for the correctness of their judgment. However, there always remains something slightly unsatisfying about such cases when unrepentant swindlers and manipulators stick to their claims of innocence even in the face of overwhelming and conclusive evidence to the contrary. Now here in Virgil this problem is also resolved since not only are such souls rightly judged by others but importantly they are also made to confess their own guilt. This seems to be a more certain vindication of the justice of their condemnation. The ultimate recognition of their own misdeeds is morally satisfying to see.

In Homer, it is not obvious what the dead souls in Hades are actually doing. They seem to have no real activity but are simply hanging around or wandering about. Similarly, in both the Mesopotamian and the Jewish underworld, the souls also seem to be simply sitting there languishing in darkness and despair. By contrast, here in Virgil's underworld, all of the souls have specifically appointed activities. The souls who committed some evil deed are made to suffer, whereas the souls who led virtuous lives, such as Aeneas' father Anchises, are enjoying themselves, engaging in exercise, music, dancing and other enjoyable activities. Once again, the picture of the afterlife presented by Virgil seems much more satisfying to our basic moral intuitions.

This happy picture does not bear critical scrutiny with regard to the underlying philosophical anthropology. For example, it is not clear how physical exercise makes any sense for disembodied souls. Moreover, Aeneas is said to see the dead souls of his fellow Trojan warriors, who take "the same joy in their chariots and their armor as when alive."[30] The idea seems to be that the warriors can still practice their military skills in the afterlife since this is a source of pleasure, even though they have no need to engage in warfare and thus no need of such skills. But it would seem impossible for an immaterial shade, who cannot even be grasped, to wear armor. Perhaps most absurd in this picture is the image of them feeding and caring for their horses in Elysium. It is clear that Virgil wants to portray this condition as a positive form of a continued earthly existence with all of the pleasures and joys that one experienced during life. Since tending to horses is a pleasant pastime for some, this requires that horses also be present in the afterlife.

It is noted that here Aeneas sees the souls of his fellow Trojans, "the ancient line of Teucer, the fairest of all families, great-hearted heroes born in a better

---

30   Ibid., Book 6, lines 655–6, p. 133.

time."[31] Given Virgil's goal of glorifying the heroes of Troy as the forerunners of the Romans, it stands to reason that they would be depicted as noble and dignified, enjoying a happy existence in Elysium. This should be contrasted with the picture of the Greek heroes from Troy who are described earlier. They are in neither Elysium nor Tartarus, and their location is described simply as "the place set apart for brave warriors."[32] Although some of these Greeks are interested to see Aeneas and to talk to him, others are portrayed in a decidedly cowardly fashion:

> But when the Greek leaders and the soldiers of Agamemnon in their pha-lanxes saw the hero and his armor gleaming through the shadows, a wild panic seized them. Some turned and ran as they had run once before to get back to their ships, while others lifted up their voices and raised a tiny cry, which started as a shout from mouth wide open, but no shout came.[33]

Here the goal is clearly to emphasize the greatness of Aeneas as a warrior, who can instill such fear in the Greeks merely by his appearance. In contrast, to the Trojans in Elysium, they appear as weak and undignified. The obvious absurdity in this picture is that it is difficult to understand why they would fear that Aeneas would do them harm if they are already dead anyway.

In Elysium Aeneas is united with the ghost of his father, Anchises, who died during the journey from Troy. He now in a sense takes over as guide from the Sibyl and tells of the rationale and organization of this part of the underworld. He presents a doctrine of reincarnation. People are born, live their lives, and then die and come to the underworld. There the souls drink from the water of the river Lethe, which causes them to forget their past lives.[34] Then they are prepared to return to mundane existence again, where they are given a new body and can live a new life. Scholars have identified elements of Platonism and Stoicism in the cosmology that Anchises presents, but it is uncertain to what degree Virgil's vision of these things was widely shared in the Rome of his day. In any case, there is a clear mind-body dualism at work. The spark of life is fire, which comes from heaven.[35] The body is simply physical matter, which decays and is perishable, while the soul endures. With an echo of Plato's

---

31   Ibid., Book 6, lines 649–50, p. 133.
32   Ibid., Book 6, lines 479–80, p. 128.
33   Ibid., Book 6, lines 488–94, p. 128.
34   Ibid., Book 6, lines 713–6, p. 135.
35   Ibid., Book 6, lines 730–1, p. 135.

Phaedo,[36] the body is even portrayed as a "prison" to the soul and the cause of both grief and joy.[37]

Anchises seems to indicate that even the souls in Elysium were in some ways sinful and needed to pay for their missteps in different ways, before they could be allowed to enjoy the afterlife. He explains that the souls "are put to punishment, to pay the penalty for all their ancient sins. Some are stretched and hung out empty to dry in the winds. Some have the stain of evil washed out of them under a vast tide of water or scorched out by fire."[38] These sins are thus taken seriously, but they are apparently of a different category than the far more serious crimes committed by the inveterate and hardened sinners, who are punished in Tartarus.

Anchises emphasizes the key point: "Each of us suffers his own fate in the after-life."[39] Once again we have seen that there was a levelling effect in the Mesopotamian and the Jewish afterlife. Even in the Homeric underworld the dead souls seemed all to be treated equally, despite the differences in their moral characters. Now, however, people are evaluated individually. The moral life of each person is of interest to the gods, and people are judged and held responsible for their own decisions and actions. This represents a new conception of individuality and an increased awareness and appreciation for the realm of inwardness and subjectivity of each person. This in turn generates a demand for individualized justice.

5   Dante's Christian View

For the *Inferno*, Dante is clearly inspired by the accounts of the underworld in Homer in the *Odyssey* and especially Virgil in the *Aeneid*.[40] However, being ignorant of Greek, he was considerably less familiar with the former. Just as these ancient epic poets portrayed the underworld and used it in different ways as a part of their own narrative, so also Dante exploits this motif and even makes it central to his own work. Indeed, Dante alludes to Aeneas' visit to the underworld directly, before undertaking his own journey.[41]

---

36   Plato, *Phaedo*, in *The Last Days of Socrates*, trans. by Christopher Rowe, London: Penguin 2010, p. 114, 62b.

37   Virgil, *The Aeneid*, Book 6, lines 735–6, p. 135.

38   Ibid., Book 6, lines 739–43, p. 135.

39   Ibid., Book 6, lines 743–4, p. 135.

40   *Dante's Inferno*, trans. by Mark Musa, Bloomington and Indianapolis: Indiana University Press 1995.

41   Ibid., Canto II, lines 13–5, p. 27.

The purpose of the underworld scenes in both Homer and Virgil is one of knowledge. In the *Odyssey*, Odysseus is told by Circe that before he can continue his journey home, he must visit the underworld and ask for help from the prophet Tiresias.[42] The prophet tells him what he needs to do to complete his voyage successfully and even explains how he will die.[43] This episode plays an important role in the narrative since it anticipates the adventures that Odysseus will have in the second half of the work and gives him invaluable guidance about what he must do in order to arrive back home safely.

In the *Aeneid*, Virgil uses the device of the underworld in a slightly different way. Before he even enters the underworld, Aeneas hears the prophecies of the Sibyl, which anticipates the second half of the story.[44] Thus, in contrast to the account in the *Odyssey*, this is not the reason why he goes to the underworld. Instead, the underworld episode in the *Aeneid* serves the function both of allowing Aeneas to be reunited with his dead father Anchises and, more importantly, of permitting him to catch a glimpse of the glorious subsequent history of Rome, which vindicates all of his sufferings and self-sacrifice. In both cases, important knowledge is gleaned. Moreover, the respective underworld scenes provide an occasion for the presentation of a kind of cosmology that reflects the world-view of the time.

There is an important shift that takes place in the protagonists in the three epics. In Homer, it is the great warrior Odysseus, who makes the trip to the underworld. Likewise, in Virgil, it is the hero Aeneas, the man responsible for the beginnings of Rome, who undertakes the journey. Both of these men have accomplished heroic acts and are esteemed as great leaders by their peoples. The trips to the underworld are just one episode among others in their eventful lives. By contrast, Dante is a more ordinary person. He is not a great military hero. But yet he too must undertake a similar journey. He contrasts himself with Aeneas and with St. Paul, who is also reputed to have made such a visit to the underworld.[45] Dante asks, "But why am I to go? Who allows me to? / *I* am not Aeneas. *I* am not Paul, / neither I nor any man would think me worthy."[46] This is important since it shows that the spiritual struggles of the individual are now the main human focus and not the outward exploits such as military

---

42   *The Odyssey of Homer*, Book x, lines 488–95, p. 165.

43   Ibid., Book xi, lines 90–149, pp. 170–2.

44   Virgil, *The Aeneid*, Book 6, lines 83–7, p. 117.

45   See 2 Corinthians 12:2–4, which is the basis for the apocryphal work, the *Apocalypse of Saint Paul* or the *Visio sancti Pauli*. Although the text of this work has been mostly lost, it seems to have contained a description of Heaven and Hell.

46   *Dante's Inferno*, Canto ii, lines 31–3, p. 28.

conquests or long journeys on the sea. The inward struggle of the individual makes us all in a sense play the role of hero in our own epic. As individuals, we are now important, regardless of the fact that we have not fought great battles, defeated monsters, or ruled as famous kings.

One can also see an important change in the nature of the underworld as it is presented by the three epic poets. In Homer, the underworld is more or less simply a kind of residence for the dead. Only in a few instances is there mention of punishments, and, as we have noted, for the most part, the dead souls are merely whiling away the time there, with no real occupation or activity. Moreover, in Homer there are no real distinctions made among the different kinds of dead souls. Hades seems to be a place for everyone. By contrast, in Virgil, there is a clearer distinction made among the different souls and their fates. They are separated into two places, one Elysium, which is the home for the virtuous souls, and the other, Tartarus, where the evil ones go. Here there is a much clearer sense of rewards and punishments based on the actions of people in their lives. Moreover, Virgil has recognized and addressed the problem in Homer about the lack of activities of the dead and has given the departed souls things to do: those in Elysium engage in physical exercise and pleasant pastimes, while those in Tartarus suffer terrible punishments. In Dante, the conception of divine justice is worked out in great detail with an elaborate scheme of rewards and punishments.

The *Divine Comedy* thus represents a kind of theodicy that explains God's justice. Although the mundane world is full of apparent injustices, these will all be punished in the afterlife. This is demanded by God's power and wisdom. On the inscription of the gates of Hell, it is written, "Justice moved my heavenly constructor; / divine omnipotence created me, / and highest wisdom joined with primal love."[47] Thus, Hell was created by the demands of justice to punish the sinful. God's infinite power has made this possible, and his infinite wisdom has ensured that justice is done in the case of each and every individual.

Dante thus takes upon himself the enormous task of developing a detailed and systematic theory of divine justice in his account of the punishments in Hell. He portrays the entire spectrum of sin and thus develops a corresponding theory of justice and punishment to fit the different levels of guilt and culpability. Needless to say, this is a tremendously ambitious undertaking. Just recall that in some of the other works that we have discussed, the idea of divine justice was a mysterious matter. It was impossible to make sense of why the evil people seemed to profit and the good seemed to be punished. This was the

---

47   Ibid., Canto III, lines 4–6, p. 34.

question that Job asked with some urgency. For the Mesopotamians, there was only a vague sense of divine justice, whereas most of the time the gods seemed spiteful and impetuous. Similarly, the Greek gods were quickly offended and behaved like children. Given this background, it is now a major undertaking that Dante sets for himself to paint a vivid picture of the nature of divine justice in its finest details.

Dante's theory of punishment in the *Inferno* is an aspect of his work that overlaps with the field of social-political philosophy and jurisprudence. He is thus sometimes seen as a forerunner in the theory of punishment in these fields. It is easy to think that Dante's imaginative forms of punishment are simply arbitrary productions of a poet, designed for artistic effect, but there is a deeper underlying theory behind this.

For Dante, the basic principle of divine justice and punishment is referred to as "*contrapasso*" (in modern orthography, "*contrappasso*").[48] This Italian word comes from a combination of two Latin terms, "*patior*" the deponent verb for "to suffer" and "*contra*," which means something like "opposite." The idea implies that the punishment is conceived as the opposite or mirror image of the crime itself. It is thus intended as a natural inversion of the sin. This is a general principle, but it is not always applied consistently, and in some cases the punishment seems to resemble the sin itself instead of its opposite.

One example of *contrapasso* can be found in the third canto, where Dante and Virgil see the souls of those who remained forever neutral, refusing to take sides.[49] These sinners are rejected by both Heaven and Hell. They are condemned to run back and forth continuously following a banner. The idea is that the opposite of those who remain noncommittal are those flippant people who zealously throw themselves behind every new cause without any real reflection. This is represented by the idea of following a banner. The noncommittal people are thus condemned to this meaningless existence of aimlessly supporting an unknown political movement. Just as they in life failed to show any commitment by supporting something, in death they are compelled in a sense to support any arbitrary cause. Note that in both cases, the result is the same: the person who supports nothing shows no character, just as the person who supports everything and who quickly moves from one allegiance to the next indifferently. By contrast, the person with true moral character carefully reflects upon which causes to support and chooses the one that reflects his or her own values. Dante's point here is that even those sinners who choose evil

---

48   See ibid., Canto XXVIII, line 142, p. 207.

49   Ibid., Canto III, lines 35–69, pp. 35f.

at least show some moral character in contrast to those who remain forever neutral and noncommittal. Even though he is evil, Milton's devil in *Paradise Lost* can still in some sense be admired since he at least demonstrates a certain consistency of character, which is completely lacking in the case of these sinners in Dante.

Another perhaps more obvious example of *contrapasso* is the punishment of the sorcerers and fortunetellers in Canto 20.[50] These people dedicated their lives to gazing into the future. Now their punishment is that they have their heads turned around so that they are looking backwards and can thus only see what is behind them.[51] They are condemned to look only at the past and are prevented from seeing what is in front of them, the future. While in life they adopted the one principle in a one-sided way, that is, a fixation on the future, they are punished in death by the other side of the same principle, that is, the past, which they neglected.

One might argue that we can see in this conception of justice an echo of Aristotle's principle of *sophrosyne*. For the Greek philosopher, the goal was to find the appropriate middle way between two extremes. Here the extremes are a fixation with the future and with the past. While the sorcerers and fortunetellers were guilty of the one in life, they are punished with the other in death, just like a pendulum swinging from one side to the other. But the proper disposition is one in the middle, that is, one that is occupied primarily with the present and limits the concern with the future and the past in an appropriate manner.

Here in Canto 20 we see the familiar figure of Tiresias,[52] who connects the *Divine Comedy* with Book XI of the *Odyssey*. But while Tiresias was a sympathetic figure in Homer (and, it should be noted, also in Sophocles), here he is presented as one of the sinners wallowing in Hell. This clearly demonstrates the radical inversion of values that Christianity has effected on the pagan world. For the ancients, the ability to see into the future was a legitimate and valuable skill that was honored. By contrast, in the Christian world this is merely a sign of superstition.

The idea with *contrapasso* is that when the evil will commits a sin, it rejects the divinely ordained order of things and embraces a different principle. The person thus shows a blindness by adopting a one-sided principle. The punishment is intended to bring this to light by making the sinner suffer the opposite principle. In a sense this can be thought of as giving the sinner exactly

---

50   Ibid., Canto XX, lines 1–60, pp. 148f.
51   Ibid., Canto XX, lines 10–5, p. 148.
52   Ibid., Canto XX, lines 40–5, p. 149.

what he wants, and when the negative implications of this are shown, the one-sidedness of the principle is exposed. In this way the punishment is in a sense a reflection of the will of the sinner himself.

As noted, not all of the punishments follow the principle of *contrapasso*, strictly speaking. In Canto 28 the sinners who are guilty of having caused schisms and divisions among people are punished by having their bodies severed from the head to the midsection.[53] They wander around until they grow together and are then cut open again. With this grotesque punishment, the split that they have caused to happen among peoples is replicated on their own bodies. They have not respected the unitary whole of a community or a people, and so the unity of their own bodies is destroyed. This form of punishment seems to deviate from the principle of *contrapasso* since it is not the opposite of the sin but rather a kind of repetition or reduplication of it. This punishment takes the will of the sinner as the point of departure. Since the sinner wanted to cause division, this will is generalized to include the person's own body. Thus, in a sense the sinner has willed his own punishment, which is simply an extension or magnification of the same principle instead of some version of the opposite.

6   Conclusion

The model for religious knowing is often thought to be that of revelation. According to this view, God provides humans with knowledge that is already fixed, finished and unchangeable from the start. However, even the most cursory understanding of the history of religion shows that religious ideas are in fact mutable. Like all other ideas created by the human mind, religious ideas also change and develop over time. Some ideas are better than other ones in the sense of being more intuitively satisfying or internally consistent. One might conceive of this as a kind of evolution of ideas by natural selection. Over time new ideas arise which improve upon shortcomings of earlier conceptions.

Historians of technology and science can trace the many steps over a long period of time that led from the invention of the wheel to the development of, for example, computers. Many different ideas had to be developed and applied before complex machines were possible. So also with religious ideas. Complicated systems of belief or practice did not arise all at once. They

---

53   Ibid., Canto XXVIII, pp. 203–7.

represent ideas that developed over an extended period of time and which were constantly refined and improved as specific shortcomings became visible.

Another analogous model can be found in the development of legal thinking. Initially early peoples began by establishing the most basic laws required for civilized life to exist. Examples of this can be seen in the Ten Commandments or Hammurabi's Laws. Then over the course of time these basic laws proved to be incomplete since cases arose which were not unambiguously covered by them. Thus, new laws had to be created in order to close the legal loopholes and extend the legal framework to cover the maximal number of possible cases. Over time this resulted in the highly complex legal systems that we know today. Basic human intuitions that we would today call religious began and developed conceptually in the same way.

Early humans presumably wished that their deceased loved ones would continue to live in some form or another. But from this vague intuition, it took a long time to develop a conception of heaven or hell with all of the finely tuned features that these ideas imply. In the sequence of accounts of the underworld traced here, we can clearly see key ideas changing and becoming more refined. Perhaps most importantly, the idea of individuality and human subjectivity changes. The value of the individual increases. At first, the individual was not taken into account and did not seem to have any great significance. But then over the course of time this came to be recognized. Each person was regarded as important and needed to be understood and evaluated individually.

This new idea of human subjectivity brings with it new conceptions of the afterlife and divine justice. At each stage innovations are introduced that are intended to overcome the shortcomings of the earlier conceptions. This implies that as the concepts of individuality developed, the older conceptions of the afterlife and divine justice became unsatisfying. Thus the new concept of the individual demanded a new and updated version of the other concepts in order to keep step with people's moral intuitions. It is probably meaningless to ask which concept came first since it seems clear that we are talking here about a constellation of concepts that belong together. In any case, it seems indisputable that a huge amount of conceptual progress has been made when one compares the rather vague conceptions of the Mesopotamians and the Hebrews with the much richer conceptions found in Virgil and Dante.

Bibliography

Bernstein, Alan E., *The Formation of Hell: Death and Retribution in the Ancient and Early Christian Worlds*, London: University College London Press 1993.

Bottéro, Jean, "The Mythology of Death," in his *Mesopotamia: Writing, Reasoning, and the Gods*, trans. by Zainab Bahrani and Marc Van De Mieroop, Chicago and London: University of Chicago Press 1992, pp. 268–86.

Burkert, Walter, *Greek Religion*, trans. by John Raffan, Cambridge: Harvard University Press 1985.

[Dante Alighieri], *Dante's Inferno*, trans. by Mark Musa, Bloomington and Indianapolis: Indiana University Press 1995.

Edmonds III, Radcliffe G., *Myths of the Underworld Journey: Plato, Aristophanes, and the 'Orphic' Gold Tablets*, Cambridge: Cambridge University Press 2004.

The Epic of Gilgamesh, trans. by N.K. Sanders, Harmondsworth: Penguin 1960.

[Homer], *The Odyssey of Homer*, trans. by Richmond Lattimore, New York: Harper Collins 1965.

Johnson, Philip, *Shades of Sheol: Death and Afterlife in the Old Testament*, Downers Grove: InterVarsity Press 2002.

Kramer, Samuel Noah, *History Begins at Sumer*, Philadelphia: University of Pennsylvania Press 1956.

Louden, Bruce, "Catabasis, Consultation, and the Vision," in his *Homer's Odyssey and the Near East*, Cambridge and New York: Cambridge University Press 2011, pp. 197–221.

Moreira, Isabel and Toscano, Margaret (eds.), *Hell and Its Afterlife: Historical and Contemporary Perspectives*, Farnham and Burlington: Ashgate 2010.

Plato, *Gorgias*, trans. by Walter Hamilton and Chris Emlyn-Jones, London: Penguin 2004.

Plato, *Phaedo*, in *The Last Days of Socrates*, trans. by Christopher Rowe. London: Penguin 2010.

[Plato], *The Republic of Plato*, trans. by Allan Bloom, New York: Basic Books 1968.

Ravndal Hauge, Martin, *Between Sheol and Temple: Motif Structure and Function in the I-Psalms*, Sheffield: Sheffield Academic Press 1995 (*Journal for the Study of the Old Testament*, no. 178).

Snell, Bruno, *The Discovery of the Mind: The Greek Origins of European Thought*, trans. by T.G. Rosenmeyer, Cambridge, MA: Harvard University Press 1953.

Sourvinou-Inwood, Christiane, "Crime and Punishment: Tityos, Tantalos and Sisyphos in *Odyssey* 11," *Bulletin of the Institute of Classical Studies*, no. 33, 1986, pp. 37–58.

Sourvinou-Inwood, Christiane, "To Die and Enter the House of Hades: Homer, Before and After," in *Mirrors of Mortality: Studies in the Social History of Death*, ed. by Joachim Whaley, New York: St. Martin's Press, 1981, pp. 15–39.

Sourvinou-Inwood, Christiane, *'Reading' Greek Death to the End of the Classical Period*, Oxford: Clarendon Press 1995.

Taylor, Charles, *Sources of the Self: The Making of Modern Identity*, Cambridge, MA: Harvard University Press 1989.

Virgil, *The Aeneid*, trans. by David West, London: Penguin 1990.

Weir Smyth, Herbert, "Conceptions of Immortality from Homer to Plato," in *Harvard Essays on Classical Subjects*, ed. by Herbert Weir Smyth, Boston and New York: Houghton Mifflin 1912, pp. 239–83.

PART 3

The Myth in Action

∵

Oedipus and Perceval

The Enigma as a Hermeneutical Principle

Ethel Junco

Abstract

Based on two sources, one Greek and the other medieval, I underscore the consonances presented by the enigma, a construction of discourse that speaks and omits simultaneously. In both narrative treatments I ponder the principle of unity. I start with the enigma as the motive of action and stop with the particular answers—word and silence—as axes of self-knowledge. To support this claim, I examine the story of Oedipus in the Theban cycle, according to the dramatization of Sophocles in *Oedipus the King* and *Oedipus at Colonus*, and *Perceval* or *The Tale of the Grail* by Chrétien de Troyes; in each piece I focus on the core of the enigma, namely, the test of the Sphinx at the gates of Thebes and the procession of the Grail in the castle of the Fisher King. The two cases are resolved according to the worldviews of each age, supported on the Greek rational resourcefulness and the path of medieval mystic silence.

> The tragic man becomes enigmatic for himself.
>
> J.P. VERNANT

∴

1 Introduction

The starting point for this interpretation is Claude Lévi Strauss' well-known concept of binary narrative structures, the components of which are related by inversion. This is exemplified by the narratives of Oedipus and Perceval, and their opposite treatment of the enigma. Their adventures are built in symmetry with respect to the motive of action: Oedipus is questioned and presents a confident response; Perceval is questioned and is unable to ask. Thus, Lévi Strauss underscores "the dilemmatic character of human existence."[1]

---

1 See Lluís Duch, *Mito, interpretación y cultura*, Barcelona: Herder 2002, p. 341.

© ETHEL JUNCO, 2021 | DOI:10.1163/9789004448674_009

The anthropologist compares mythical stories referring to the prohibition of incest and claims that problems of the same type can be addressed at different levels, a fact that justifies their association in ancient Greek and native American sagas. Enigma and incest are internally related since solving an enigma involves putting together terms that were originally intended to be separated. The underlying structures of inverse resolution—Oedipus answering the question, Perceval remaining silent—show that the elements of one group can turn into the characteristic elements of another. Word and silence make the difference in the face of the enigma. We will leave the author here.[2]

Regarding this contact of sources, I would like to highlight the consonances presented by the enigma in both narrative treatments, and to ponder the principle of unity. Even though we start with the enigma as the motive of the action, I would like to focus on the particular answer—word or silence—throughout the network of images that constitute it in order to put forward the enigma as a hermeneutical principle of bidirectional resolution.

To support this claim, I will examine the story of Oedipus in the Theban cycle, according to the dramatization of Sophocles in *Oedipus the King*[3] and *Oedipus at Colonus*[4] along with Chretien de Troyes' *Perceval*.[5] In each piece I will focus on the core of the enigma, namely, the test of the Sphinx at the gates of Thebes and the procession of the Grail in the castle of the Fisher King.

2   Enigma, Narration and Image

The Oracle of Delphi is the emblematic seat of Western knowledge.[6] It is the equivalent of a philosophical altar, where the archaic knowledge is centered on Apollo, who is the paradigm of the quest for wisdom. The temple of the

---

2   In *Le regard éloigné*, Claude Lévi-Strauss establishes the opposition between the Oedipus myth and the story of Perceval. See Claude Lévi-Strauss, *Le regard éloigné*, Paris: Plon 1983. He also discusses the reason behind parallel myths in different cultures in *Paroles données*, Paris: Plon 1984.

3   Sophocles, *Antigone, Oedipus the King and Electra*, trans. by H.D.F. Kitto, Oxford: Oxford University Press 1998.

4   Sophocles, *Oedipus at Colonus*, trans. by Eamon Grennan and Rachel Kitzinger, Oxford: Oxford University Press 2005.

5   Chrétien de Troyes, *Perceval. The Story of the Grail*, trans. by Burton Raffel, New Haven and London: Yale University Press 1999.

6   On the prestige of the Oracle of Delphi from Plutarch onwards, see Herbert B. Huffmon, "The Oracular Process: Delphi and the Near East," *Vetus Testamentum*, vol. 57, no. 4, 2007, pp. 449–60.

god holds the maxims "Nothing in excess" [μηδὲν ἄγαν] and "Know thyself" [γνῶθι σεαυτόν], connected with the teachings of the Seven Sages.[7] The god of Delphi communicates messages that are not treated as religious statements, i.e., as dogmatic. Even if these are considered as an expression of the divinity addressed to man, they become a philosophical impulse: ambiguous words demand a search for meaning. In the relation between myth and logos a search for meaning is established.[8]

The oracular mode is built upon a statement of implicit reference. The formulation, which presents an image without naming the thing itself, does not expose; rather, it opens up a possibility: the hermetic language contains an inevitable provocation for the intellect.[9] The formula of the oracle enigma connects three levels: 1. Reception/perception of a message, 2. complex enunciation, and 3. need for interpretation. In the first two there is an intention: what is given in the experience of the world tries to say something. The third one is the cognitive mode that moves philosophy and survives in the subsequent scientific attempts to interrogate the world, preserving the hermeneutical relationship.

In the first two, the arrival of a message and the characteristics of its language, there is an intention: what is given in the experience of the world means that something tries to say something. The third one is the cognitive mode that moves philosophy and survives in the subsequent scientific intentions that interrogate the world, preserving the hermeneutical relationship.

This reflective position is nostalgic and binding. I will try to justify the use of these terms. It is nostalgic because it acknowledges information that comes from an ancient wisdom; the access to this is indirect and incomplete for the contemporary receiver. The thinker is not the wise man, but the one who leans towards knowledge. Wisdom—or the part of it that is possible—is not within reach. Philosophy and the forms of knowledge connected to its condition will always be a deferred communication.

On the other hand, it is binding because the reflective position is able to articulate the word or image with the source of meaning through the mediating language: oracle, *gnome* or imaginary narration. It is clear that the source,

7   Hugh Lloyd-Jones, "The Delphic Oracle," *Greece & Rome*, vol. 23, no. 1, 1976, p. 65.

8   "But perhaps the most extraordinary example of mythos persisting, century after century, side by side with ever-more-refined logos, is the oracle of Delphi." Peter Green, "Possession and Pneuma: The Essential Nature of the Delphic Oracle," *Arion: A Journal of Humanities and the Classics, Third Series*, vol. 17, no. 2, 2009, p. 27.

9   See W.K.C. Guthrie, *A History of Greek Philosophy*, vol. 3, *Socrates*, Cambridge: Cambridge University Press 1971, p. 151.

as the point of departure, also establishes interpretive guidelines. This relation of nostalgic and binding knowledge has a renewing effect in the evolution of cultures.

In the reflective position, there is a convergence of texts, the morphology of which is later systematized according to a number of disciplines: historical, literary, religious, philosophical. It is important to underscore that even though languages are restricted by the limits of the different genres, such categories are arbitrary to the mindframe of the archaic texts; the distinction between religion and poetry, or philosophy and literature, for example, is a methodological obstacle to the access to ancient sources.[10] Event though the philosophical form becomes predominant from the sixth century onwards, such philosophy integrates not only the epic and cosmogonic tradition discourse, but also lyric and tragic formats that complement its worldview.

In order to analyze the relation between the message and its interpretation, we shall refer to the notion of enigma—narration through images—and apply it to the reference texts. As an arcane message of the divine realm, the enigma acquires a bodily form in the image.[11] This image is made up of a set of linguistic, visual and auditory elements with a compositional order, which are received according to the subjective state of the character. Whereas the enigma is useful for the understanding of the stories, the images further the internal understanding of the enigma. The representation contains a symbol for the reflection.

The symbolic conception of ancient cultures presents the analogy as an intellectual guide; in the analogy there is a correspondence between proportional parts, the similarity of which transposes relations between different areas.[12] In the similarity—which is not identity—we find the power to refer to something beyond its first meaning, to another realm of meaning that is not revealed. Thus, the expressive elements that are associated by means of implicit connections, communicate a unity that is not comprehensible at first sight.

In the archaic stories, or those which are close to an original state, as is the case of the folkloric or fantastic narrations, we see a writing in reflection (enigma-image) that works as a guide to access a previous and secret

---

10   Claudio Calabrese, "Los supuestos hermenéuticos de Agustín de Hipona. Desentrañar la palabra y transmitir su misterio," *Espíritu LXIV*, vol. 150, 2015, pp. 227–43.

11   George Steiner, *Real Presences: Is there Anything in What We Say?*, London: Faber and Faber 2010, pp. 12–3.

12   See Hans-Georg Gadamer, *Truth and Method*, trans. by Joel Weinsheimer and Donald G. Marshall, New York: Continuum 2004, p. 429.

meaning; that character of vestige or memory is key to activate the current meaning. In this manner, in the stories of Oedipus and Perceval, the communication of the message proceeds according to the form of the enigma. Whether it is an oracle, a question or a strange phrase, the sign is received as a linguistic representation: brief and dense; it is an incipient information, but it is sufficient. It is a test of wisdom that offers the passage from one state to another: a key discovery or the acceptance in a group.[13] The enigma is enunciated as a type of questioning: 1. *Imperative and challenging*: its lack of resolution cannot be tolerated. 2. *Personal*: it questions a heroic prototype that is yet to be manifested. And 3, *restoring through suffering*: its resolution implies paying a price in life.

The enigma requires two conditions in order to appear. First, a question, presented by an external source or coming from within; it implies a fall or the loss of a favorable state of affairs, and the affirmation of a guilt. Then, this guilt becomes visible through a personal and cosmic shortcoming. Although this burden falls on the back of the king/hero, who is responsible for the community, it also affects the other people and nature. The existence of such state is not known until the appearance of the enigma, which starts the process of entering the meaning.

Both conditions multiply the presence of an identified evil with a certain state of unacceptable ignorance; before this ignorance, the enigma fulfills the role of restoring the insufficiency through the stimulating effect of the intellectual paradox: the obscure clarifies. Within the Greek cultural context, the polysemy is addressed to a receiver who is used to the agonistic mode of resolution that must seek and discover the meaning through the confrontation of discourses.[14]

A similar method is applied by Socrates when the god of Delphi claims that he is the wisest of all men. The philosopher does not simply accept this flattering statement, but raises it as a problem, confident that he will be able to grasp the meaning behind the enigma of Apollo: "I go from one side to another investigating and ascertaining in the sense of the god."[15] This philosophical perspective links the practical function used in the private and community spheres

---

13   Roberta Ascarelli, Ursula Bavaj and Roberto Venuti (eds.), *L'Avventura della conoscenza: momenti del Bildungsroman dal Parzival a Thomas Mann*, Naples: Guida Editori 1992, p. 9.

14   See Elton Barker, "Paging the Oracle: Interpretation, Identity and Performance in Herodotus' 'History,' " *Greece & Rome*, vol. 53, no. 1, 2006, p. 3.

15   Plato, "Apology," in *Dialogues of Plato*, vols. 1–2, trans. by R.E. Allen, New Haven and London: Yale University Press 1989, vol. 1, 23b: ταῦτ᾽ οὖν ἐγὼ μὲν ἔτι καὶ νῦνπεριιὼν ζητῶ καὶ ἐρευνῶ κατὰ τὸν θεόν.

with the speculative dimension, because the philosopher submits the oracular affirmation to rational analysis. Socrates' task is focused on self-inquiry, and he neglects worldly affairs; a *logos* applied to discovering oneself leads to the comprehension of the universal order. With this argument, Socrates presents himself to the judges; he insists that his actions are guided by the oracle of the god,[16] and adds that they have consequences for the other citizens. The oracular form, reinforced in the *Apology* by the image of the daimon, supports the principle of authority adopted by the philosopher.[17]

To answer (which is balancing the distance between languages) is to eliminate the source of evil and the insufficiency. There is a vital process involved. The enigma implies the existential experience within the condition of intelligibility. The way in which the enigma is answered can be found in the manner of living it, inasmuch as the enigma contributes to forming the personality of the apprentice.[18]

The question-enigma moves the virtuality of the answer. The divine problem cannot be solved without a human solution. With the descent of the god to man there is an intentional connection between worlds. The intrinsic ambiguity remains as a sign of the distance between the two realms. It is similar to the translation between two languages that are saying something in their own way. In mythical terms, it is the test posed by the god, the distance between the Apollinian archer and his target. Apollo, the god of the enigma, does not provide orders to be obeyed, but suggestions to be interpreted.[19] Sophocles confirms this direction: Apollo offers principles for human action, not mechanisms to control it. In this way, divine guidance can be seen in the laws of nature.[20]

---

16   See Thomas C. Brickhouse and Nicholas D. Smith, "The Origin of Socrates' Mission," *Journal of the History of Ideas*, vol. 44, no. 4, 1983, p. 659.

17   See David D. Corey, "Socratic Citizenship: Delphic Oracle and Divine Sign," *The Review of Politics*, vol. 67, no. 2, 2005, p. 203.

18   Jens Høyrup, "Sub-Scientific Mathematics: Observations on a Pre-Modern Phenomenon," *History of Science*, vol. 28, no. 1, 1990, p. 67.

19   Tom Harrison, *Divinity and History: The Religion of Herodotus*, Oxford: Oxford University Press 2000, p. 149: "The Ethiopians, Herodotus reports, obey their oracle to the letter and march wherever and whenever their god tells (2.29.7). How, we may wonder again, could any system of belief so inflexible be sustained? Greek oracles and prophecies, by contrast, are frequently equivocal—and so require interpretation."

20   Humphrey D.F. Kitto, "The Idea of God in Aeschylus and Sophocles," in *La Notion du Divin depuis Homère jusqu'à Platon, Entretiens sur l'antiquité classique, I*, ed. by Herbert Jenning Rose, Pierre Chantraine, Bruno Snell, Olof Gigon, Humphrey D.F. Kitto, Fernand Chapouthier and Willem Jacob Verdenius, Vandoeuvres: Fondation Hardt 1954, p.179.

The enigma speaks, but it does not finish what it says. It proceeds by concealing.[21] In a phenomenological sense, it is faithful to the ways of reality, which appears approximately in palimpsest. However, it demands the total expression of reality. By concealing, the enigma is able to make the illusion disappear while preserving the essential, providing access to a closed domain.[22]

The image is a trope characterized by the union of the apparently distant and the dissimilar; the resource is sustained in an internal relationship, which affirms virtual qualities above the limits of visible actuality. The perception of the image mobilizes reflection. Image and imagination can shape ideas. The process of making the image intelligible requires breaking down the parts in order to find the similarity, in which a new relation of meaning is introduced. This activity, which is essential to poetry, provides depth and expansion to language. A new relation is not just another version of one name, but an increase in meaning, which is contained in the tension between the extremes. Knowledge acquired by means of imagination expands the signified thing using its implicit wealth. Octavio Paz suggests that "poets insist on saying that the image reveals what the thing is, not what it could be," claiming that therein resides its "philosophical dignity."[23]

3   Oedipus and Perceval: In Search of an Answer

The chosen paradigms present an enigma through a network of images that operate as semantic cores, giving an internal logic to the texts. In the following I will discuss the context of both cases.

3.1   *Oedipus or the Crossroads of the Enigma*
Sophocles' treatment of the hero's misadventures in *Oedipus the King* (429 BC) and *Oedipus at Colonus* (401 BC) makes it possible to observe the tragic framework that originates with the enigma.[24]

The misfortune of the house of the Labdacids begins with Pelops cursing Laius, a curse that is taken up by Zeus, the enforcer of justice. In the origin, violence falls upon the family. As a guest of Pelops, Laius falls in love with his

---

21   Gadamer points out that in the ambiguity of the oracles and the poetic expression resides his "hermeneutic truth": "It is not the weakness but the strength of the oracle that it is ambiguous." Gadamer, *Truth and Method*, p. 482.
22   André Jolles, *Formes simples*, Paris: Éditions du Seuil 1972, p. 110.
23   Octavio Paz, *El arco y la lira*, Mexico City: Fondo de Cultura Económica 2006, p. 99.
24   Karl Reinhardt, *Sófocles*, Barcelona: Destino 1991, p. 209.

son, Chrysippus, but he rejects his advances. Laius rapes Chrysippus, and the young man commits suicide. Thus, the lineage is broken. A curse will doom the children of Cadmus: Laius will die at the hands of his descendant. In spite of this, he marries Jocasta and begets a son. To avoid the fulfilment of the prophecy, the child must die. However, the person in charge of this task shows mercy and leaves the boy with a Corinthian pastor, where he grows up unaware of his story. The kings of the region raise him as their own, and thus he becomes a teenager. An accident occurs that makes him raise questions about his birth, and so he goes to Delphi in order to find out about his origin. The response of the oracle prevents him from returning to Corinth, as it claims that he will kill his father and marry his mother. When he is going home, he meets the royal entourage at a crossroads. After a heated discussion, he becomes enraged and kills the king, his father.[25] He goes to Thebes, and at the gates of the city he finds the Sphinx, who torments the Theban people with riddles that are impossible to solve. Oedipus overcomes the beast, and the grateful Thebans offer him the throne and the hand of their queen, his mother. From this point, the one who seems to have solved the enigma becomes the enigma himself.[26]

It is at this point that Sophocles begins the first tragedy, in which he develops the key element to recognize the strength of the enigma. A plague strikes Thebes. The priests and the people seek help from their savior king. Oedipus sends his brother-in-law, Creon, to the Oracle of Delphi to find what the cause of the plague is. The god reveals that the epidemic is the result of Laius' murderer being unpunished. Oedipus curses the malefactor and goes to Tiresias to learn more. The latter appears to be reluctant, but he finally reveals the truth: regicide, parricide and incest. Oedipus does not accept this, and thinks the priest is plotting with Creon. Such reaction shows that the totality of the enigma cannot be assimilated in a natural manner.[27] Jocasta questions Tiresias and the interpretations offered by the priests, but acknowledges the truth of

---

25   Charles Segal says: "… the importance of the bestial, unnatural atmosphere of the place and the encounter." Charles Segal, *Tragedy and Civilization: An Interpretation of Sophocles*, Cambridge: Harvard University Press 1981, p. 221.

26   Carlos García-Gual, *Enigmático Edipo. Mito y tragedia*, Madrid and Mexico City: Fondo de Cultura Económica 2012, p. 9: "En una de las más atrevidas recreaciones modernas del mito, *La máquina infernal* de J. Cocteau, una obra de título muy significativo, la espantosa y astuta Esfinge, medio leona, medio mujer alada, no se suicida una vez que Edipo ha acertado la respuesta al enigma—pues en esta versión dramática ella misma le ha sugerido la solución—sino que se asombra de la ingenuidad del joven héroe, al verle alejarse rumbo a Tebas, ufano e inconsciente de su destino, que no es sino una trampa trágica urdida acaso por los dioses."

27   A.D. Sertillanges, *Le problème du mal, L'Histoire*, Paris: Aubier 1984, p. 88.

the oracles.[28] She recalls that Laius was killed at the crossroads. The tragedy becomes clear. Hearing this, Oedipus begins a process of recognition from which there is no turning back. He realizes that he is not the son of the kings of Corinth, although he was raised as such. Jocasta understands everything and takes her own life. Finally, the shepard who saved his life confirms his identity. Oedipus takes out his own eyes with Jocasta's pin. The play ends with the blind king on stage. Becoming aware of his misfortune, he goes into exile.

We see the conclusion of Sophocles' interpretation of the myth in *Oedipus at Colonus*, a play that appeared posthumously. This second tragedy inverts the elements presented in *Oedipus the King* and shows the story of the exiled blind man who turns into savior. The scholars suggest that this not a simple transformation of an individual, but a heroic ascent.[29]

Oedipus at Colonus shows the path from a guilty consciousness to purification. Past and present unfold according to the oracles, and Oedipus advances with the certainty of being guided: "the sign of my destiny."[30] He is able to understand the image of Zeus: "An earthquake, a thunder or the bolt of Zeus."[31] In the sacred forest—and against the judgement of the citizens of the region— he turns from supplicant into offering, from victim into the chosen one: "I've come / in reverence, under the god's protection, to bring / a gift to the citizens of this city."[32] However, this helpless supplicant possesses a quality that makes him unique, and this lies in his connection to the mystery: "There / is nothing left for me to say."[33] The enigma belongs to the gods, but now the victim of the oracle turns into administrator and, therefore, communicator.

---

28   S. Wiersma, "Women in Sophocles," *Mnemosyne, Fourth Series*, vol. 37, nos. 1–2, 1984, pp. 25–55.

29   Let us consider three ideas. The first argues that "Oedipus at Colonus is a mystery play which deals with the transition of Oedipus from human to heroic stature." See B.M.W. Knox, *The Heroic Temper: Studies in Sophoclean Tragedy*, Berkeley and Los Angeles: University of California Press 1964, p. 58. The second, on the other hand, focuses on "the passing of Oedipus from a human to a heroic state." See A.J.A. Waldock, *Sophocles the Dramatist*, Cambridge: Cambridge University Press 1951, p. 219. Finally, see Cecil Bowra, *Sophoclean Tragedy*, Oxford: Oxford University Press 1944, p. 309: "the apotheosis of Oedipus is what the play is about."

30   This is the only line in which I follow the translation proposed by Melissa Mueller, because it better reflects the struggle of determinism developed by Sophocles in this play. Melissa Mueller, *Objects as Actors*, Chicago: Chicago University Press 2016, p. 160. The translation I consulted by Eamon Greennan and Rachel Kitzinger proposes the following: "The password for what's to come." Sophocles, *Oedipus at Colonus*, v. 52. The original is as follows: ξυμφορᾶς ξύνθημ᾽ ἐμῆς, v. 47.

31   Sophocles, *Oedipus at Colonus*, v. 109: ἢ σεισμὸν ἢ βροντήν τιν᾽ ἢ Διὸς σέλας, v. 95.

32   Sophocles, *Oedipus at Colonus*, vv. 305–7: ἥκω γὰρ ἱερὸς εὐσεβής τε καὶ φέρων, / ὄνησιν ἀστοῖς τοῖσδ᾽, vv. 287–8.

33   Sophocles, *Oedipus at Colonus*, vv. 633–4: ἀλλ᾽ οὐ γὰρ αὐδᾶν ἡδὺ τἀκίνητ᾽ ἔπη, v. 624.

Theseus, the ruler, is the chosen recipient, but the condition is that he has to keep the secret.[34] After the second crossroads ("Whether things go one way or the other"),[35] Oedipus enters the sacrosanct zone of mystery (the forest, the Eumenides, the thunderbolt of Zeus).

Let us go back to the starting point. Oedipus enters Thebes after answering the Sphinx's riddle. His victory endows him with a certain infallibility in terms of knowledge. The premise of the myth[36] is given by the text of the enigma:

> There is a biped and quadruped being on the earth, who has only one voice, and who is also a tripod. It is the only one who changes its aspect of all the many beings that move on land, in the air or in the sea. But, when it stands on more feet, then the mobility of its limbs is much weaker.[37]

The life of Oedipus is organized between two crossroads: the first, in *Oedipus the King*, is "where three ways meet,"[38] in which he does not see and makes a mistake; but in *Oedipus at Colonus* we read: "one way or the other,"[39] and this is the end point of the pilgrimage, where he performs the purificatory rites and hears the thunder of Zeus: "... destiny itself reaching its end here ... Thunder in the air! Ah Zeus!"[40]

Oedipus has responded to the oracle with the constant self-determination that is characteristic of the heroes of Sophocles; at the end of his journey, he recognizes

---

34   About this, M. Dolores Jiménez points out that: "Sófocles ha moldeado el mito para esta-blecer un nexo con su realidad contemporánea: Atenas, inmersa en una larga y devas-tadora guerra en la que se enfrenta a Tebas, siente así la protección benéfica de Edipo y la esperanza que representa su promesa de mantener a salvo su ciudad (*Edipo en Colono*, 1764–1769)." M. Dolores Jiménez, "Edipo: el que solucionó los famosos enigmas y fue hombre poderosísimo," in *Espacios míticos: historias verdaderas, historias literar-ias*, ed. by María Dolores, María del Val Gago, Margarita Paz and Verónica Enamorado, Madrid: Centro de Estudios Cervantinos 2014, p. 165.

35   Sophocles, *Oedipus at Colonus*, v. 1599: ἐν πολυσχίστων μιᾷ, v. 1592.

36   Mauricio-Guilio Guidorizzi Bettini, *El mito de Edipo. Imágenes y relatos de Grecia a nues-tros días*, Madrid: Akal 2004, p. 93. "Un hombre de pies hinchados, es decir, un tullido. Esta marca física le da el nombre y le permite, por lo tanto, poseer una identidad."

37   It is important to remember that the content of the riddle is never specified in the play; however, we find some verses in which the chorus stated this fact: "I saw myself how the Sphinx challenged him: / He proved his wisdom; he saved our city," vv. 505–10: "φανερὰ γὰρ ἐπ᾽ αὐτῷ, πτερόεσσ᾽ ἦλθε κόρα / ποτέ, καὶ σοφὸς ὤφθη βασάνῳ θ᾽ ἁδύπολις τῷ ἀπ᾽ ἐμᾶς."

38   Sophocles, *Oedipus the King*, v. 716: ἐν τριπλαῖς ἁμαξιτοῖς.

39   Sophocles, *Oedipus at Colonus*, v. 1592: ἐν πολυσχίστων μιᾷ.

40   Ibid., vv. 1606, 1612. κτύπησε μὲν Ζεὺς χθόνιος, v. 1606.

the presence of Apollo.[41] Apollo's prediction indicated that Oedipus would die in a forest and that the land that welcomed him would be blessed.[42]

The enigma defines its existential format, first by following it involuntarily, then in salvation. Kitto expresses it as a movement that confirms "a strange appointment with heaven."[43]

3.2 Perceval and the Procession of the Enigma

At the court of Mary of Champagne, in the year 1190, Chrétien de Troyes offers the first written testimony of the myth of the Grail with his work *Perceval or The Tale of the Grail*. The theme had a strong influence during the period that runs from 1180 to 1230, in the context of the Third Crusade. Victoria Cirlot argues that this period is the stage of the "construction of the myth,"[44] which goes from the work by Chrétien de Troyes to the novel *The Quest of the Holy Grail*,[45] which deals with the central theme of chivalric literature. Their continuations were written during the end of the twelfth century and the first half of the thirteenth century at a crucial moment in the structuring of the medieval world.[46]

The action of *Perceval or The Tale of the Grail* presents the protagonist on a trip, following the narrative scheme of the *queste*.[47] It complies with the standards of this genre: the relation with Arthur's court, the quests, the goal of

---

41   M. Dyson, "Oracle, Edict, and Curse in Oedipus Tyrannus," *The Classical Quarterly*, vol. 23, no. 2, 1973, p. 211.

42   Avi Sharon explains that: "At the play's end, Sophocles has Theseus, king of Athens, lead the desolate Oedipus, who has become a kind of oracular priest, to a mysterious burial spot in the wooded precinct, where he will achieve cult status and become patron of Athens." Avi Sharon, "The Oak and the Olive Oracle and Covenant," *SiteLINES: A Journal of Place*, vol. 13, no. 2, 2018, p. 3.

43   H.D.F. Kitto, *Greek Tragedy: A Literary Study*, New York: Barnes & Noble 1961, p. 386.

44   In this regard, Victoria Cirlot says the following: "Se trata de la etapa creativa: medio siglo de diálogo ininterrumpido entre los autores, de escritura febril, y de imaginación. Pero esto no significa que el mito del grial desapareciera del horizonte literario europeo, ni mucho menos. Después de la *Queste* el mito aparece una y otra vez, aquí y allá: en la *Estoire del Saint Graal* que cierra el inmenso *Lancelot-graal*, en las distintas versiones del *Tristán en prosa*; en los siglos XIV y XV se traduce a muchas lenguas europeas, y por supuesto, fue introducido por Sir Thomas Malory en su gran compendio artúrico." Victoria Cirlot, *Grial. Poética y mito (siglos XII-XV)*, Barcelona: Siruela 2014, pp. 15–16.

45   *The Quest of the Holy Grail*, trans. by Pauline M. Matarasso, Harmondsworth: Penguin 1969.

46   Massimiliano Gaggero, "Verse and Prose in the Continuations of Chrétien de Troyes' 'Conte du Graal,'" *Arthuriana*, vol. 23, no. 3, 2013, p. 3.

47   For a exhaustive historical-literary presentation, see Carlos García-Gual, *El descubrimiento de la sensibilidad en el siglo XII: el amor cortés y el ciclo artúrico*, Madrid: Akal 2014.

restoring honor and presenting the deeds of bravery to maidens who are cho-sen as tributaries of their love.[48] In addition, in the configuration of the young Perceval, his family, education and religiosity are shown as necessary compo-nents for his psychological constitution.

Perceval ignores the conventions of chivalry because his widowed mother has preserved him from this knightly world so as not to lose him like she had lost her husband and her two other sons. The young man, ignorant of his her-itage and kinship, leaves the Welsh homeland against the will of his mother, fascinated by a group of knights coming from the court of King Arthur. After being knighted and experiencing the corresponding adventures—his victory over the Red Knight and the encounter with lady Blanchefleur—he arrives at a deserted and lifeless land where he finds the castle of the Maimed King or Fisher King. The host receives him; he will participate in a peculiar banquet and spend the night there.

The manifestation of the enigma takes place before the banquet, after the entrance of a procession formed by a page with a bleeding lance, a maiden with a grail and, finally, another page with a silver tray.[49] The shine of the grail overshadows the light of the torches. The procession repeats its passage and moves to the next room. Finally, the king withdraws.

Although Perceval is puzzled and would like to ask about the vision, he does not say anything; he remembers the advice of his master in arms, Gornemant, who has instructed him not to talk too much, which is a trait of vulgar people. He simply goes to sleep. The next day, he discovers the castle is empty. Nothing remains of the previous night and his horse is waiting, ready to depart. The knight must leave without inquiring about the nature of the grail and whom it serves. In later renditions of the legend, this ambiguous object will be trans-formed into the Holy Grail of Christian symbolism.

On his way through the forest, he meets a maid who tells him that he has encountered the Fisher King, who was maimed by a lance. Perceval could have healed him if only he had asked about the grail. With the king back to health, the land would have become prosperous again. Furthermore, he learns that his mother has died of grief as a result of his departure. Having failed in his

---

48   In his edition of the story of Perceval, José M. Lucia suggests: "Lo que interesa ahora resal-tar es cómo Chrétien, dentro de ese mismo mundo cortesano que ha terminado por dom-inar, cambia el motivo central de su obra (el debate sobre el fin amor) para acercarse a un nuevo tema que, por no haber sido completado, resulta más difícil de precisar, pero que parece que tiene en la superación de la caballería terrenal su punto de referencia." José M. Lucia, "Introducción," in Chrétien de Troyes, *El libro de Perceval (O El cuento del Grial)*, ed. by J. Manuel Lucia, Madrid: Gredos 2000, p. 16.

49   De Troyes, *Perceval. The Story of the Grail*, vv. 2976–3231.

mission, his name must change; he cannot be "Perceval of Wales" anymore. He becomes Perceval the Unhappy, the Miserable, the Unfortunate.[50]

The adventures continue under the tone of personal disorientation. Every step of the way, he receives a confirmation about his origin and his destiny as a knight. Five years later, and after having forgotten the religious education received from his mother, he arrives on Good Friday at a sanctuary where he meets his hermit uncle. There he confesses and goes to mass; absolved of his sins, the secret is revealed: on the one hand, Perceval's departure caused the death of his mother and his silence in regard to the grail was caused by his guilt. On the other hand, the grail serves the father of the Fisher King, who is sustained by a host contained in it.[51] The scene with the hermit provides a lot of information about the life of Perceval, although initially it seemed to focus on the Grail Castle. After reprimanding him for not asking, the hermit reveals the awaited answer.[52] In Chretien de Troyes' version, the story of Perceval remains incomplete.[53] The following description contains the text of the enigma:[54]

> A servant entered the hall,
> Carrying—his hand at its center
> A white lance. He came out
> Of a room, then walked between
> The fire and those seated
> The white wood, and the white
> On the bed, and everyone saw
> The white wood, and the white
> Spearhead, and the drop of blood
> That rolled slowly down
> From the iron point until
> It reached the servant's hand
> …
> And then two other servants

---

50   Ibid., vv. 3576; 3583–4.

51   Ibid., vv 6217 518.

52   Ibid., vv. 6341–5.

53   The following idea is suggested by Rupert Pickens: "The incomplete nature of Perceval's quest is reinforced by the fact that the second of the Grail Castle's mysteries—why the lance bleeds—has not yet been resolved. Nonetheless, scholars question whether or not *Le Conte du Graal* is finished." Rupert Pickens, "Le Conte du Graal: Chrétien's Unfinished Last Romance," in *A Companion to Chrétien de Toyes*, ed. by Norris J. Lacy and Joan Tasker Grimbert, Cambridge: D.S. Brewer 2005, p. 171.

54   Carlos García-Gual, *Primeras novelas europeas*, Madrid: Istmo 1990, vv. 2976–3231.

Entered, carrying golden
Candleholders worked
With enamel. They were wonderfully handsome
Boys, and the candleholders
They each clasped in their hands
Bore at least ten Burning candles. A girl
Entered with them, holding
A grail-dish in both her hands
A beautiful girl, elegant,
Extremely well dressed. And as
She walked into the hall,
Holding this grail, it glowed
With so great a light that the candles
Suddenly seemed to grow dim
Like the moon and stars when the sun
Appears in the sky. Then another
Girl followed the first one,
Bearing a silver platter[55]

It is in the presence of a crippled king that Perceval sees the procession, which parades between two hidden chambers suggesting that it serves someone important. At the banquet table, life and thought are wounded, and it is the latter that initiates the path of transformation; the wound is a preparation for consciousness. The present evil also involves an invocation of health.[56]

The loss of the sovereign zone, represented in the malaise of the king,[57] is transferred to the guest, Perceval, who is not ready to ask. The Fisher King's wound, described as a mutilation by a lance that pierced his thighs, establishes

---

55   De Troyes, *Perceval*, vv. 3192–3233. Leonardo Olschki emphasizes the secular nature of the grail, insisting that "The whole 'procession' … takes place in a completely secular setting. There is no cross, no liturgical gesture, not one single religious figure, to accompany the supposed relics of Christ's Passion." Leonardo Olschki, *The Grail Castle and its Mysteries*, Manchester: Manchester University Press 1966, pp. 12–3.

56   Erich Köhler, *L'aventure chevaleresque, Idéal et réalité dans le roman courtois*, Paris: Gallimard 1974, p. 61.

57   About this, Ernst R. Curtius points out: "¿En qué consiste la enfermedad? Algunas versiones la encubren con eufemismos, otras la revelan abiertamente: es la pérdida de la virilidad … la curación del rey-sacerdote salvará a la tierra agonizante, porque su enfermedad es la causa de que la tierra se haya secado. Ciertos cultos antiguos de la vegetación parecen haberse fundido en la tardía Antigüedad con el simbolismo de la Eucaristía y parecen haber perdurado de manera esotérica hasta la Edad Media." Ernst R. Curtius, *Literatura

a connection with Perceval's father, who was also wounded in the same manner during a battle.[58]

As we have seen, Oedipus (the crippled) and Perceval (the unfortunate) are mythical models who begin their path disconnected from the sacred, and therefore mutilated. Both etymologies refer to the tendency to a fall caused by a wound. In such conditions, however, both are guides: as king and knight they must resume the course of human existence. Paul Ricoeur argues that "... it is the great penitent in whom the service of the gods is summarized."[59]

3.3   Enigma and Knowledge

The images of the enigma are kept in a tension of different planes, one tangible and one intangible; we will refer to the physical-sensitive identification, which allows them to be perceived, and to its psychic or intellectual aspect, which offers a symbolic possibility. The way of representing the enigma guides the interpreting process. Let us recall the characteristic elements of the enigma:

Enigma	Tangible plane	Intangible plane
Imperative character	Crossroads	Rational challenge
Personal character	Wound	Evil – Ignorance
Restoring	Pilgrimage	Suffering – Knowledge

In the enunciation of both enigmas (the riddle of the Sphinx and the procession of the banquet), the notion of a space-time crossroads is implicit. The crossroads are a place where one stops to reconsider what was hitherto routine and foreseeable. The convergence of paths in classical literature has the potential for irony as it involves a difficult choice.[60] Young Oedipus stops at

---

europea y Edad Media latina, vols. 1–2, Mexico City: Fondo de Cultura Económica 2017, vol. 1, p. 168.

58   De Troyes, *Perceval*, vv. 3417–53. William Sayers' reflection on this coincidence in both wounds is interesting: "We have noted the identical wounds, both thighs pierced by a javelin, suffered by Perceval's father and his kinsman, the Fisher King. While it is widely recognized that the thighs may be a euphemistic homology in which the genital organs are seen as the seat of procreative power." William Sayers, "An Archaic Tale-Type Determinant of Chrétien's Fisher King and Grail," *Arthuriana*, vol. 22, no. 2, 2012, p. 90.

59   Paul Ricoeur, *Philosophie de la volonté II, Finitude et culpabilité*, Paris: Aubier 1988, p. 399.

60   Stephen Halliwell, "Where Three Roads Meet: A Neglected Detail in the Oedipus Tyrannus," *The Journal of Hellenic Studies*, vol. 106, 1986, p. 187.

the crossroads as he flees from the Oracle and Corinth, trying to avoid commiting nefarious crimes, but then he is led to Thebes, precisely to commit these crimes. Perceval stops at the Castle of the Maimed King because a fisherman (who is the king himself) leads him to it. Both are forced to stop and deliberate; in both cases, a fatherly figure decides for them.

On the intangible plane, the stopping represents a state of perplexity; in each protagonist it causes an opposite reaction: Oedipus chooses the rational way and gives an immediate answer; even though he seems to be right, he is wrong, because the enigma is not made for an immediate causal relationship. In this case, the enigma is not treated as something suprarational. Perceval in turn responds to the enigma by completely suspending his discursive rationality and choosing silence. Strengthened by the awareness of his error and the succession of redeeming adventures, he starts a pilgrimage that culminates in the holy place of the hermit.[61] The separation from the world prepares him for an inner experience: solitude and contemplation require similar conditions: absence of distractions, of material preoccupations, and spatial privacy.[62]

We see two positions: the confirmation of rationality and the suspension of rationality. Oedipus moves "outwardly," achieving success in the world, an apparent temporality before the revelation; Perceval goes "inward," perplexed in silence, on a path of doubt and suffering that will lead him directly to atonement.

With the position of Oedipus, we see momentary certainty and triumph, although ultimately there is error and, consequently, a continuation of the enigma: the myth shows that human certainty is inversely proportional to divine wisdom, which rules independently of knowledge. The real Oedipus enigma unfolds after the apparent one is solved. In his life as king, in his discovery of the cause of the plague, in his investigation of the murderer, in the episodes of pilgrimage and supplication of *Oedipus at Colonus*: there is where the resolution of the legitimate enigma takes place, that is, his entire penitential life makes him responsible in the face of the true enigma. For that reason alone, he will be saved by Zeus in the forest of the Eumenides and become a benefactor of the land he once tarnished.

---

61 Joan Ramón Resina claims: "El Grial es un símbolo de la armonía que existe entre la eternidad y la historia." Joan Ramón Resina, *La sabiduría del Grial*, Barcelona: Anthropos 1988, p. 245.

62 Mari Hughes-Edwards, " 'HOW GOOD IT IS TO BE ALONE?' Solitude, Sociability, and Medieval English Anchoritism," *Mystics Quarterly*, vol. 35, nos. 3–4, 2009, p. 34.

In the position of Perceval there is uncertainty and guilt, disorientation and internal tribulation: all of these are elements that favor the internalization of the enigma. While we do not know the end of Chrétien's novel, the ambiguity of the narrative will become the basis of the "Matter of Brittany."[63]

The crossroads is an image of the rational challenge. It symbolizes the imperative decision that does not understand the facts, but has fateful consequences. In addition to its individual role, the crossroads produces the father-son generational encounter, unifies the wound with the error; the descendant has power over the solution.

Regarding the characters, the enigma reveals the existence of a wound that can be healed with the answer; both Oedipus and Perceval must become aware that they carry a wound in order to get back to health. The wound is related to the definition of identity and its cause: the crimes of the lineage of the Labdacids and the death of Perceval's mother. It affects man and cosmos: the wound of the man is the infertility, the condemnation of the lineage of Laius and the deficiency of the Fisher King. The correlative cosmic wound is the wasteland and the negation of natural life: the mortal perspective of the Theban plague, which ends all forms of life, and the desert landscape and the disappearance of the castle before Perceval's eyes.[64] The persistence of drought and winter as states of paralysis in nature indicates the actuality of the crossroads and its pending resolution.

On the intangible plane, the wound is an evil that operates under the form of a generational curse, or under the form of ignorance of a personality not yet aware of itself. Both characters are young people in the process of learning, distanced from their respective homes and guided by heroic desires with incipient resources; they are both unable to heal the wound. Their condition as pilgrims indicates the state of involuntary impiety and the state of ignorance regarding their own actions (parricide and incest, abandonment and death of the mother). It constitutes the point of suspension of identity as vagabonds, exiles or pilgrims. The restoring character of the enigma, that is, the passage from wound to healing, manifests itself as a sign of logical contradiction, because it responds to the ambiguity of reality.

---

63   Lucia, "Introducción", p. 25.

64   About this, Sarah Breckenridge writes the following: "I propose instead that the Grail Castle is an architectural representation of Perceval's identity. Although the grail's presence in the Conte du Graal has come to define modern readings of the text, the grail quest is repeatedly subordinated to Perceval's quest to discover who he is and where he belongs in the Arthurian world." Sarah Breckenridge, "Cognitive Discoveries and Constructed Mindscapes: Reading the Grail Castle as a Mnemonic Device," *The Modern Language Review*, vol. 106, no. 4, 2011, p. 979.

On the personal tangible plane, Oedipus' blindness and Perceval's disorientation represent the passage from wound-ignorance to health-certainty. While Oedipus can see, he is ignorant; when he becomes blind, he learns the truth. Perceval advances with determination, until the grail paralyzes him. When life is in the stage of tribulation, there is a process of knowledge. Pain and healing are connected.

In the physical-natural order, the favorable environment for Oedipus' health is his exile from Thebes; the loss of his city will lead him to the forest of the Eumenides in Colonus. The separation from the known order is necessary, a distancing from the civilization that establishes a model of knowledge. The external distance favors the internal voice. Equally, Perceval, after his disorientation, enters the forest and arrives at the hermit's cave, the principle of healing.[65] Forest and cave, after the escape from the world, are sacred spaces which unify the instances of suffering, penance and self-knowledge in the intangible plan.

The enigma asks about a singular ("There is a being on the earth," "Whom does the grail serve?"), but its meaning is universal. Oedipus knows that "he is" the plague of Thebes and must heal the city with the truth, by abandoning it. His arrival at the forest of Colonus, forbidden to others and reserved for him, shows the confirmation of the gods. Perceval understands the meaning of the courtship of the grail in the cave of the hermit,[66] but returns to the castle because he knows that "he must" ask the question and restore the king's health. The encounter with the hermit completes his inner encounter, indispensable to close the process that justifies the story of Perceval in the Grail Castle.[67]

---

65   I have considered the suggestion of J. Rayner, which reminds us: "The ancient forest woodlands strip away the past and bring Lancelot to the chapel where he too becomes accepted into the hermit's small religious community." J. Rayner, "Lost in the Woods: Grey Areas in Malory and the Stanzaic 'Morte Arthur,' " *Arthuriana*, vol. 22, no. 2, 2012, p. 80.

66   Sylvester G. Tan, claims: "Though Perceval's unknown sin bears serious consequences for both himself and those around him insofar as it impedes him from completing his mission at the Grail Castle, the sin is no more obvious to the reader than it is to Perceval himself. Only when Perceval meets his hermit uncle, over six thousand lines into the work, does the audience learn—along with Perceval—what sinful act led to such dreadful consequences." Sylvester G. Tan, "Perceval's Unknown Sin: Narrative Theology in Chrétien's Story of the Grail," *Arthuriana*, vol. 24, no. 3, 2014, p. 130.

67   Donald Maddox writes that: "... the very essence of [Perceval's] quest is not primarily a tangible object or a special place, but above all a cognitive discovery." Donald Maddox, *The Arthurian Romances of Chretien de Troyes. Once and Future Fictions*, Cambridge: Cambridge University Press 1991, p. 111.

The arrival at the final space shows an interior journey, which complies with the laws of oracular ambiguity: those who walk with wounds, like beggars, will end up as heroes, reconciled with their identity.

Through the enigma that is addressed to the king/knight there is a transfer from the deficiency state to the donation state, from ignorance to knowledge, not as an intellectual affirmation, but as a natural phase of health. The guilt-healing relation is distributed among the characters and establishes an intergenerational and interpersonal connection. The illness-remedy demands reciprocal dependence, not only because one has the need and the other the solution, but because the attributes are provisional and interchangeable. Oedipus contaminates and sickens the people, but redemption will make him a protector; the health of the Fisher King is Perceval's health, but neither one can reach it without the other.

The enigma is the principle of paradoxical knowledge: to answer it is to remain ignorant and to be silent is to begin to know. It is to the intellect what the labyrinth is to space: the output cannot be linear, but ascending. The enigma continues to apply the Apollinian exhortation of "knowing yourself." The immutability of the divine sustains the human constancy.

3.4   *The Enigma in Time*

We have to take into account another element: the answer to the enigma requires life. Time is the melting pot for the process in the inner and outer space. The passage of time allows the preparation to receive the message. The starting point of both characters is heroic insufficiency; although they are determined to dominate the world, their resources are chaotic: Oedipus is arrogant and vain; Perceval is a rustic who does not know the rules of civilization. Both lack an educational relationship with a father. The journey will provide the educational trials. As the enigma arises in uncultivated conditions, their answers will be inadequate; the desolateness they unleash around them is connected to their ignorance.

Time also acts to overcome the original guilelessness and transform it into a restored Innocence. The mistakes of both lives determine the loss of an ignored innocence; the pain leads to the recovery of another kind of innocence, which is stable and definitive. Oedipus lives confidently thinking of himself first as the son of the kings of Corinth, and then as the legitimate sovereign of Thebes, a good husband and father. Perceval has remained in a situation of artificial upbringing, oblivious to the fate he deserves by his condition. One hides behind his rationality; the other, behind his emotivity; they both remain ignorant of themselves. All their naivete is crushed by the enigma, which, by revealing their identities, opens the way to a second innocence, restoring the purity. The second and definitive birth occurs thanks to this self-acquired iden-tity. Time clears the outward crossroads and transforms it into a sacred space, making the path circular: the god establishes the enigma and then closes it.

Historical temporality only works for human interpretation; what seems like an early announcement of the possibility of understanding, is favorable for a total learning. For Oedipus the final point is the temple of the Eumenides, divinities of reconciliation. The blind man enters there as a supplicant; he is purified, and he is received in his death. His tomb will be a place of pilgrimage and protection. Perceval, after having forgotten the advice of his mother and his mentor, arrives on Good Friday at the hermitage, leaves his arms, cries and confesses. The god who receives Oedipus announces himself in thunder; the God of Perceval, in communion.

Even though the form of their answers is different (immediacy and suspen-sion), the understanding of both is marked by an internal process extended in time. Likewise, the truth is clear to others and obscure to them: Oedipus receives the truth in full detail from Tiresias, but he does not accept it.[68] Perceval is informed twice of the death of his mother, by the weeping maiden and by the hermit;[69] he is informed three times of his failure to ask the proper question about the procession in the Grail Castle, by the weeping maiden, the hidden maiden and finally by the Hermit.[70] While the others know instantly, they will know through time, because what for the others is a fact, for them is identity.

Time is essential to assess the enigma. Its truth cannot manifest itself in an isolated or precipitated act, but in the succession of different experiences inte-grated in the final unity. The progression of the enigmatic method associates it with the comprehensive way of wisdom.

4   Conclusion

Before rational speculation, the chosen texts propose a mode of reflection that involves an aesthetic approach. Its formulation follows the rhythm that goes from myth to enigma, from oracle to image. If the hidden reveals itself, know-ing does not require acting, but contemplation. The examples suggest a truth that is not considered from an objective point of view; it does not precede consciousness either. Thus, to know is not the same as to identify. The purpose

---

68   Sophocles, *Oedipus the King*, vv. 408–28.
69   De Troyes, *Perceval*, vv. 3531–3, 6318–24.
70   Ibid., vv. 3521–3, 4578–90, 6335–40.

of the stories, accordingly, "does not consist in a technical virtuosity of 'understanding' everything written. Rather, it is a genuine experience ... it consists in that the interpretation does not imply understanding everything, but that it produces an encounter experience that interpellates for the truth."[71]

The enigma reinstates a pre-modern knowledge matrix. The modern pattern of understanding is the guarantee of the conscience of the subject before the statements of the truth; the enigma follows the opposite direction, because it encrypts the access to what is real in the ambiguity of the expression. It does not avoid the crossroads; it is not even close to solving it. Rather, it claims that dissonances, the "misunderstandings," are also a form of understanding. From the point of view of rational efficiency, Oedipus and Perceval are in the wrong; however, from these wrong answers the opportunity arises to reverse their lives and solve them heroically. Transparency and accuracy do not appear as hermeneutical values.

In the mythical line, the enigma complies with the laws of language in the philosophical way: whether it is Oedipus listening to the Sphinx or Perceval observing the procession—hearing and sight—we, the historical recipients, receive the message in a logically structured narrative. Consequently, one can reason about the statement because the meaning is articulated in the parts of the whole. The formal compositional rigor replicates its internal demand: since it is not a simple knowledge relation between subject and object, the answer requires the greatest intellectual tension. It is not a matter of establishing a direct correlation with a single meaning; it is about uncovering. The enigma is a premise of history and enters it through a pre-historical language, the first sign in the separation of the unity. Therefore, the answer, made from history, is transient and insufficient.

Although structurally there is divergence, hermeneutically there is convergence: word and silence correspond to the same heuristic psychological attitude; trust or distrust in one's own abilities reflect the same conviction in the cognitive value of the enigma and in its non-trivial origin. "There is a being on the earth," "Whom does the grail serve?" These are questions that connect the myth-story drama and that must be solved individually. The universality of the mythical approach is valid in the relation between the experience and the consciousness of the characters; the incomprehension of the enigma initiates the process that unravels the truth in their lives.

This offers a methodological warning: reconsider the illusory character of knowledge that contributes to the loss of the sense of the world, as our

---

71   Gadamer, *Truth and Method*, p. 483.

positivist experience indicates, and integrate the enigma as a hermeneutical principle.

Translated by Nassim Bravo

Bibliography

Ascarelli, Roberta, Bavaj, Ursula and Venuti, Roberto Venuti (eds.), *L'Avventura della conoscenza: momenti del Bildungsroman dal Parzival a Thomas Mann*, Naples: Guida Editori 1992.

Barker, Elton, "Paging the Oracle: Interpretation, Identity and Performance in Herodotus' 'History,'" *Greece & Rome*, vol. 53, no. 1, 2006, pp. 1–28.

Bowra, Cecil, *Sophoclean Tragedy*, Oxford: Oxford University Press 1944.

Breckenridge, Sarah, "Cognitive Discoveries and Constructed Mindscapes: Reading the Grail Castle as a Mnemonic Device," *The Modern Language Review*, vol. 106, no. 4, 2011, pp. 968–87.

Brickhouse, Thomas C. and Smith, Nicholas D., "The Origin of Socrates' Mission," *Journal of the History of Ideas*, vol. 44, no. 4, 1983, pp. 657–66.

Calabrese, Claudio, "Los supuestos hermenéuticos de Agustín de Hipona. Desentrañar la palabra y transmitir su misterio," *Espíritu LXIV,* vol. 150, 2015, pp. 227–43.

Cirlot, Victoria, *Grial. Poética y mito (siglos XII-XV)*, Barcelona: Siruela 2014.

Corey, David D., "Socratic Citizenship: Delphic Oracle and Divine Sign," *The Review of Politics,* vol. 67, no. 2, 2005, pp. 201–28.

Curtius, Ernst R., *Literatura europea y Edad Media latina*, vols. 1–2, Mexico City: Fondo de Cultura Económica 2017.

De Troyes, Chrétien, *Perceval: The Story of the Grail*, trans. by Burton Raffel, New Haven and London: Yale Unviersity Press 1999.

Duch, Lluís, *Mito, interpretación y cultura*, Barcelona: Herder 2002.

Dyson, M., "Oracle, Edict, and Curse in Oedipus Tyrannus," *The Classical Quarterly*, vol. 23, no. 2, 1973, pp. 202–12.

Gadamer, Hans-Georg, *Truth and Method*, trans. by Joel Weinsheimer and Donald G. Marshall, New York: Continuum 2004.

Gaggero, Massimiliano, "Verse and Prose in the Continuations of Chrétien de Troyes' 'Conte du Graal,'" *Arthuriana,* vol. 23, no. 3, 2013, pp. 3–25.

García-Gual, Carlos, *Primeras novelas europeas*, Madrid: Istmo 1990.

García-Gual, Carlos, *Enigmático Edipo. Mito y tragedia*, Madrid and Mexico City: Fondo de Cultura Económica 2012.

García-Gual, Carlos, *El descubrimiento de la sensibilidad en el siglo XII: el amor cortés y el ciclo artúrico*, Madrid: Akal 2014.

Green, Peter, "Possession and Pneuma: The Essential Nature of the Delphic Oracle," *Arion: A Journal of Humanities and the Classics, Third Series*, vol. 17, no. 2, 2009, pp. 27–47.

Guthrie, W.K.C., *A History of Greek Philosophy*, vol. 3, *Socrates*, Cambridge: Cambridge University Press 1971.

Halliwell, Stephen, "Where Three Roads Meet: A Neglected Detail in the *Oedipus Tyrannus*," *The Journal of Hellenic Studies*, vol. 106, 1986, pp. 187–90.

Harrison, Tom, *Divinity and History: The Religion of Herodotus*, Oxford: Oxford University Press 2000.

Høyrup, Jens, "Sub-Scientific Mathematics: Observations on a Pre-Modern Phenomenon," *History of Science*, vol. 28, no. 1, 1990, pp. 63–87.

Huffmon, Herbert B., "The Oracular Process: Delphi and the Near East," *Vetus Testamentum,* vol. 57, no. 4, 2007, pp. 449–60.

Hughes-Edwards, Mari, "'HOW GOOD IT IS TO BE ALONE?' Solitude, Sociability, and Medieval English Anchoritism," *Mystics Quarterly*, vol. 35, nos. 3–4, 2009, pp. 31–61.

Jiménez, M. Dolores, "Edipo: el que solucionó los famosos enigmas y fue hombre poderosísimo," in *Espacios míticos: historias verdaderas, historias literarias*, ed. by María Dolores, María del Val Gago, Margarita Paz and Verónica Enamorado, Madrid: Centro de Estudios Cervantinos 2014, pp. 152–87.

Jolles, André, *Formes simples*, Paris: Éditions du Seuil 1972.

Kitto, Humphrey D. F., "The Idea of God in Aeschylus and Sophocles," in *La Notion du Divin depuis Homère jusqu'à Platon. (Entretiens sur l'antiquité classique, I.)*, ed. by Herbert Jennings Rose, Pierre Chantraine, Bruno Snell, Olof Gigon, Humphrey D.F. Kitto, Fernand Chapouthier and Willem Jacob Verdenius, Vandoeuvres: Fondation Hardt 1954, pp. 169–89.

Kitto, Humphrey D.F., *Greek Tragedy: A Literary Study*, London and New York: Routledge 1961.

Knox, B.M.W., *The Heroic Temper: Studies in Sophoclean Tragedy*, Berkeley and Los Angeles: University of California Press 1964.

Köhler, Erich, *L'aventure chevaleresque, Idéal et réalité dans le roman courtois*, Paris: Gallimard 1974.

Lévi-Strauss, Claude, *Le regard éloigné*, Paris: Plon 1983.

Lévi-Strauss, Claude, *Paroles données*, Paris: Plon, 1984.

Lloyd-Jones, Hugh, "The Delphic Oracle," *Greece & Rome*, vol. 23, no. 1, 1976, pp. 60–73.

Lucia, José M., "Introducción," in Chrétien de Troyes, *El libro de Perceval (O El cuento del Grial)*, ed. by J. Manuel Lucia, Madrid: Gredos 2000.

Maddox, Donald, *The Arthurian Romances of Chretien de Troyes: Once and Future Fictions*, Cambridge: Cambridge University Press 1991.

Mueller, Melissa. *Objects as Actors: Props and the Poetics of Performance in Greek Tragedy*, Chicago: The University of Chicago Press 2016.

Olschki, Leonardo, *The Grail Castle and its Mysteries*, Manchester: Manchester University Press 1966.

Pickens, Rupert, "Le Conte du Graal: Chrétien's Unfinished Last Romance," in *A Companion to Chrétien de Toyes*, ed. by Norris J. Lacy and Joan Tasker Grimbert, Cambridge: D.S. Brewer 2005 pp. 169–87.

Paz, Octavio, *El arco y la lira*, Mexico City: Fondo de Cultura Económica 2006.

[Plato], "Apology," in *Dialogues of Plato*, vol. 1, trans. by R.E. Allen, New Haven and London: Yale University Press 1989.

The Quest of the Holy Grail, trans. by P.M. Matarasso, Harmondsworth: Penguin 1969.

Rayner, Samantha J., "Lost in the Woods: Grey Areas in Malory and the Stanzaic 'Morte Arthur,'" *Arthuriana*, vol. 22, no. 2, 2012, pp. 75–84.

Reinhard, Karl, *Sófocles*, Barcelona: Destino 1991.

Resina, Joan Ramón, *La sabiduría del Grial*, Barcelona: Anthropos 1988.

Ricoeur, Paul, *Philosophie de la volonté II, Finitude et culpabilité*, Paris: Aubier 1988.

Sayers, William, "An Archaic Tale-Type Determinant of Chrétien's Fisher King and Grail," *Arthuriana*, vol. 22, no. 2, 2012, pp. 85–101.

Sharon, Avi, "The Oak and the Olive Oracle and Covenant," *SiteLINES: A Journal of Place*, vol. 13, no. 2, 2018, pp. 3–4.

Segal, Charles, *Tragedy and Civilization: An Interpretation of Sophocles*, Cambridge: Harvard University Press 1981.

Sertillanges, A.D., *Le problème du mal, L'Histoire*, Paris: Aubier 1984.

Sophocles, *Antigona, Oedipus the King & Electra*, trans. by H.D.F. Kitto, Oxford: Oxford University Press 1998.

Sophocles, *Oedipus at Colonus*, trans. by Eamon Grennan and Rachel Kitzinger, Oxford: Oxford University Press 2005.

Steiner, George, *Real presences: Is there Anything in What we say?*, London: Faber and Faber 2010.

Tan, Sylvester G., "Perceval's Unknown Sin: Narrative Theology in Chrétien's Story of the Grail," *Arthuriana*, vol. 24, no. 3, 2014, pp. 129–57.

Waldock, A.J.A., *Sophocles the Dramatist*, Cambridge: Cambridge University Press 1951.

Wiersma, S., "Women in Sophocles," *Mnemosyne, Fourth Series*, vol. 37, nos. 1/2, 1984, pp. 25–55.

Reinterpreting Medieval Lore through the Modern Prism

The Myth of Robin Hood in Kierkegaard's Early Journals

Nassim Bravo

Abstract

This article offers an overview of Søren Kierkegaard's use in his early journals of a fictional figure called the Master-Thief [*Mestertyven*], a modern reinterpretation of the late medieval legend of Robin Hood. I would like to argue that this early treatment of medieval folklore in the Dane's *Nachlass* can be used as a point of departure or foundation upon which we might get a better appreciation of the crucial role played by myth in Kierkegaard's philosophy. An analysis of the figure of the Master-Thief will also reveal the way in which a myth from the Middle Ages was reinterpreted and integrated into a modern worldview.

1　Introduction

This article offers an overview of Søren Kierkegaard's use in his early journals of a fictional figure he called the Master-Thief [*Mestertyven*], a modern reinterpretation of the late medieval legend of Robin Hood. I would like to argue that this early treatment of medieval folklore in the Dane's *Nachlass* can be used as a point of departure or foundation upon which we might get a better appreciation of the crucial role played by myth in Kierkegaard's philosophy. An analysis of the figure of the Master-Thief will also reveal the way in which a myth from the Middle Ages was reinterpreted and integrated into a modern worldview.

Most scholars are aware of Kierkegaard's recurring allusions to literary or mythical figures and motifs in his authorship. In a manner similar to Plato, the writer from Copenhagen often utilized myths, literary motifs or lore in order to convey abstract or complex ideas, a practice that, as was the case with the Athenian philosopher, frequently prevented a more univocal or direct interpretation of his thought, but at the same time made his writings more attractive and approachable to the general reading public, who was able to easily recognize the references. Indeed, major works like *Either/Or, Fear and Trembling* or *Repetition* are well known for their extensive analysis of mythical or literary characters like Don Juan, Agnes and the Merman, or Job. This practice is well

© NASSIM BRAVO, 2021 | DOI:10.1163/9789004448674_010

documented, and I have had the benefit of drawing on rich scholarly work.[1] Classical mythology, both Greek and Roman, was a major source of inspiration for Kierkegaard, who was an enthusiastic admirer of antiquity, and he steadily made use of figures such as Antigone, Nemesis or Prometheus. At the time, old Nordic culture was drawing much attention, and thus Kierkegaard also utilized and commented upon characters such as Thor and Loki. Personages from modern literature, Scandinavian or otherwise, are present as well, and we read in the authorship about Hamlet or Don Quixote, but insights on Holberg's Per Degn or Oehlenschläger's Aladdin were also part of his vast repertoire.

On the whole, the frequent use of myth reveals the fact that Kierkegaard was of course a great reader and well versed in various types of literature and tradition, but this also says a good deal about his position with regard to what he called speculative thought, i.e., systematic philosophy. As is well known, Kierkegaard considered himself a poet more than a philosopher, so it was completely in order that he relied so much on literary references. However, in this paper I would like to try a different approach.

Kierkegaard's early use of mythical figures had to do more with the depiction of universal ideas or character traits. This was by no means an original interpretation. It was a very common practice of the period to understand myth in this manner, and hence we see, for example, that Faust was frequently associated with doubt, while the Wandering Jew was linked to despair. Nonetheless, whereas the European trend—especially in the German states and Denmark—was concerned with finding, with the help of the ideas represented by these characters, a national cultural identity, Kierkegaard was more interested in the development of the individual self. In an age of rising nationalism in which many Danish liberal intellectuals were striving to put an end to absolute monarchy and get a modern constitution, the young Kierkegaard's passion was devoted to the intricacies of psychology. His use of myth was oriented accordingly. Faust's doubt could represent, indeed, modern skepticism, or the despair of the Wandering Jew could be the image of Denmark's distress when the nation was on the brink of bankruptcy after the disastrous Napoleonic wars. This is true, but they could also be used to illustrate

---

1   See Niels Thulstrup and Marie Mikulová Thulstrup (eds.), *Kierkegaard: Literary Miscellany*, Bibliotheca Kierkegaardiana, vol. 9, Copenhagen: C.A. Reitzel 1981. Katalin Nun and Jon Stewart (eds.), *Kierkegaard's Literary Figures and Motifs*, Tome I, *Agamemnon to Guadalquivir*, Farnham and Burlington: Ashgate 2014 (*Kierkegaard Research: Sources, Reception and Resources*, vol. 16). Katalin Nun and Jon Stewart (eds.), *Kierkegaard's Literary Figures and Motifs*, Tome II, *Gulliver to Zerlina*, Farnham and Burlington: Ashgate 2015 (*Kierkegaard Research: Sources, Reception and Resources*, vol. 16).

certain stages in the evolution of personhood. In this sense, Faustian doubt was interpreted as the point of departure of an awakened consciousness, or the Wandering Jew's despair could be the representation of the boundary that separates that awakened consciousness from genuine religious belief. A reader might recognize in this early concern with psychology a connection with the more nuanced treatment of the so-called existential spheres in Kierkegaard's mature authorship. I believe therefore that it is important to bring into view the central role of myth, particularly medieval myth, in this discussion.

Before moving on to the analysis proper of the Master-Thief, there is one more aspect that needs to be addressed. A closer inspection of Kierkegaard's early journals reveals that he was in constant dialogue with some of his Danish contemporaries. One might find frequent references to local figures such as the poet Johan Ludvig Heiberg (1791–1860), the theologian Hans Lassen Martensen (1808–84), or the storyteller Hans Christian Andersen (1805–75). Within the more limited context of Copenhagen literary circles, Kierkegaard was indeed part of an ongoing debate about the aforementioned psychological interpretation of myth. This exchange might seem awfully parochial to the casual reader, especially since many of these names are obscure and rarely mentioned outside Denmark, but I would like to argue that an exploration of these sources is necessary to fully comprehend the finer details and reach of Kierkegaard's existential investigation of myth. Thus I will attempt to reconstruct a lost horizon of understanding. My hope is to provide the reader with a tool to help him or her to understand this discussion in its proper context.

In order to do this, first I will examine both the original sources of the myth in question, the late medieval ballads about Robin Hood, and its most influential modern reinterpretation, Sir Walter Scott's depiction of the noble bandit in his historical novel *Ivanhoe*. Here I would like to note the manner in which the modern worldview of the Scottish author refashioned the fundamental features of the medieval figure of Robin Hood. I will then turn to Kierkegaard's local context and try to offer an overview of the literary discussions in Copenhagen during the 1820s and 1830s. The literary trends of the age exerted a strong influence on Kierkegaard, who was a young student at the time, and so examining them is important to fully understand his reception and treatment of the myth. Finally, I will outline in more detail Kierkegaard's reconstruction of the medieval legend. Since Robin Hood played a social role both in his medieval and modern renditions, I will also address here the sociopolitical situation of Denmark during the early 1830s. As a young man in a time of tumult marked by the rise of nationalism and liberalism, Kierkegaard was strikingly disinterested in politics; rather, he was fascinated by the inner life of the self and the evolution of the character, an inclination that can be observed in his representation of the Master-Thief.

2   The Medieval Legend of Robin Hood and Its Modern Reinterpretation

In a loose paper from September 12, 1834, Kierkegaard wrote the following: "It amazes me that never (as far as I know) has anyone ever worked through the idea of a 'Master Thief,' an idea that certainly lends itself, in the utmost, to dramatic treatment."[2] He was mistaken.

The theme of the kind outlaw did have a dramatic treatment, as shown in the early Romantic drama from 1781 by Friedrich Schiller, *The Robbers*. Kierkegaard owned *Schillers sämtliche Werke* both from 1830 (though he presumably gave it away in 1833 to a young student called Christian Seidelin),[3] and the more recent edition from 1838.[4] Furthermore, *The Robbers* was performed in 1834 at Copenhagen's Royal Theater. It would be hard to believe that Kierkegaard, as a regular visitor of the theater—which was, after all, the center of all cultured and cosmopolitan life in Copenhagen—was not aware of this latest rendition of Schiller's play. Taking all of this into account, András Nagy goes one

---

2   *sks* 27, 118, Papir 97:1 / *kjn* 11, 119. In this article I will use two main sources when referring to Kierkegaard's *oeuvre*: the latest Danish edition, the *Søren Kierkegaards Skrifter*, edited by Niels Jørgen Cappelørn, Joakim Garff, Jette Knudsen, Johnny Kondrup and Alastair McKinnon, and the more recent English translation of Kierkegaard's posthumous writings, *Kierkegaard's Journals and Notebooks*, edited by Niels Jørgen Cappelørn, Alastair Hannay, David Kangas, Bruce H. Kirmmse, George Pattison, Vannesa Rumble and K. Brian Söderquist. In the footnotes I use the following abbreviations. For the *Skrifter*, the abbreviation *sks*, followed by the volume number, the page number, and, when quoting Kierkegaard's journals and papers, the entry number. For the English translation, I use the abbreviation *kjn*, followed by the volume number and the page number.

3   See Hans Peter Rohde, "Søren Kierkegaard som Bogsamler," in *Auktionsprotokol over Søren Kierkegaards Bogsamling*, ed. by Hans Peter Rohde, Copenhagen: Det kongelige Bibliotek 1967, pp. xvi–xvii; and Henning Fenger, *Kierkegaard, The Myths and Their Origins: Studies in the Kierkegaardian Papers and Letters*, trans. by George C. Schoolfield, New Haven and London: Yale University Press 1980, p. 37.

4   See Friedrich von Schiller, *Schillers sämtliche Werke in zwölf Bänden*, vols. 1–12, Stuttgart and Tübingen: Verlag der J.G. Cotta'schen Buchhandlung 1838; and Katalin Nun, Gerhard Schreiber and Jon Stewart (eds.), *The Auction Catalogue of Kierkegaard's Library*, Farnham and Burlington: Ashgate 2015 (*Kierkegaard Research: Sources, Reception and Resources*, vol. 20), entry 1804–1815, p. 91.

step further and suggests that Kierkegaard's Master-Thief figure was probably inspired by *The Robbers*.[5]

But there was another example of this closer to home. In 1827, the poet Steen Steensen Blicher (1782–1848), one of the main representatives of Danish realism and an author strongly admired by Kierkegaard for his talent as a novelist, published a novella titled *The Robber's Den* [*Røverstuen*].[6] The protagonist of the piece, a noble-spirited robber named Black Mads [*Sorte Mads*], was clearly inspired by the highly romanticized figure of Robin Hood as depicted in Sir Walter Scott's famous historical novel from 1820, *Ivanhoe*. Blicher was one of Kierkegaard's favorite authors—as can be deduced from his enthusiastic comments in *From the Papers of One Still Living* from 1838[7]—and therefore it was likely that he knew of or even read this novella.

The figure of the legendary outlaw stems from the English folklore of the late Middle Ages, and there we can observe some major differences from the more familiar and modernized version of Robin Hood. For example, in one of the earliest sources, the ballad written in Middle English *Robin Hood and the Monk* from the fifteenth century, the famous bandit does not display a gentle character and is shown instead as a violent and temperamental rogue who assaults Little John after refusing to pay a bet he has lost to his friend:

> A ferly strife fel them between,
> As they went bi the wey;
> Litull John seid he had won five schillings,
> And Robyn Hode seid schortly nay.
> With that Robyn Hode lyed Litul Jon,
> And smote hym with his hande;
> Litul Jon waxed wroth therwith,
> And pulled out his bright bronde.[8]

---

5   See András Nagy, "Schiller: Kierkegaard's Use of a Paradoxical Poet," in *Kierkegaard and His German Contemporaries*, Tome III, *Literature and Aesthetics*, ed. by Jon Stewart, Aldershot and Burlington: Ashgate 2008 (*Kierkegaard Research: Sources, Reception and Resources*, vol. 6), p. 173.

6   See Steen Steensen Blicher, "Røverstuen," in *Samlede Noveller og Skitser*, vols. 1–3, Copenhagen: Gyldendalske Boghandel Nordisk Forlag 1905, vol. 1, pp. 92–130. It is important to note that Kierkegaard owned a copy of the first volume of the original edition of Blicher's *Collected Novels* [*Samlede Noveller*] from 1833, in which the aforementioned novella is included. See Nun, Schreiber and Stewart (eds.), *The Auction Catalogue of Kierkegaard's Library*, entry number 1521–1523, p. 82.

7   See *SKS* 1, 24–25/ *EPW*, 69.

8   Stephen Knight and Thomas H. Ohlgren (eds.), "Robin Hood and the Monk," in *Robin Hood and Other Outlaw Tales*, Kalamazoo: Medieval Institute Publications 1997, vv. 51–8.

In this ballad there is no mention of Robin Hood's proverbial generosity towards the poor, a trait that first appears in a later ballad, *A Gest of Robyn Hode* from the late fifteenth century, in which it is said of the robber that he "was a good outlawe, and dyde pore men moch god."[9]

Even so, the medieval Robin Hood of the folklore is not yet the champion of social equality familiar to the modern reader, including Kierkegaard. In the *Gest*, he is described as a yeoman ("I shall you tel of a gode yeman, His name was Robyn Hode"),[10] and as such he held a particular social status and behaved accordingly. In the Elizabethan play by Anthony Munday, *The Downfall of Robert, Earle of Huntington* from 1598,[11] he is even presented as a nobleman, precisely the titular and disgraced Earl of Huntington. In consequence, his unselfishness was the result of medieval courtesy and chivalrousness, not of the more modern desire for social transformation.

Walter Scott presents a different figure in *Ivanhoe*. He transforms the medieval yeoman into Robin of Locksley, a dispossessed Saxon nobleman turned into the kind brigand and patriotic social fighter of modern tradition. Central in Scott's novel is the conflict between Normans and Saxons during the twelfth century, a theme that does not appear in the early ballads and might not even have existed during the period in which the story of *Ivanhoe* takes place. In fact, the struggle of the primitive Saxon locals (such as Robin himself) against the sophisticated and materialistic Norman invaders (Prince John) was probably a reflection of the modern rivalry between Scottish nationalists and the more advanced English, and the quest for reconciliation and unity in Britain, represented in the novel by the efforts of King Richard and the protagonist Wilfred of Ivanhoe. It is within this context that Walter Scott links Robin Hood to Saxon national resistance against the Norman tyranny.[12] It is clear that this nationalist element is more modern than medieval.

Regarding the famous motif of stealing from the rich and giving to the poor, Scott relied heavily on the biographical reconstruction of the bandit made by his friend, the extravagant antiquary Joseph Ritson (1752–1803), in his influential *Robin Hood: A Collection of all the Ancient Poems Songs and Ballads now extant, Relative to that Celebrated Outlaw* from 1795. Although the direct purpose of the edition was to present an unabridged collection of Robin Hood's

9   Knight and Ohlgren (eds.), "A Gest of Robyn Hode," in *Robin Hood and Other Outlaw Tales*, vv. 1823–4.

10   Knight and Ohlgren (eds.), "A Gest of Robyn Hode," vv. 3–4.

11   See Knight and Ohlgren (eds.), "The Downfall of Robert, Earle of Huntington," in *Robin Hood and Other Outlaw Tales*.

12   See Chris Worth, "*Ivanhoe* and the Making of Britain," *Links & Letters*, no. 2, 1995, p. 72.

early sources, Ritson was a democrat and an admirer of the ideals of the French Revolution, and thus his interpretation of the legend was particularly biased. In the introductory chapter titled "The Life of Robin Hood," Ritson describes the legendary robber as

> a man who, in a barbarous age, and under a complicated tyranny, displayed a spirit of freedom and independence which has endeared him to the common people, whose cause he maintained (for all opposition to tyranny is the cause of the people), and, in spite of the malicious endeavours of pitiful monks, by whom history was consecrated to the crimes and follies of titled ruffians and sainted idiots, to suppress all record of his patriotic exertions and virtuous acts, will render his name immortal.[13]

Robin of Locksley appears here as a disgraced nobleman who makes common cause with the disenfranchised. He is a revolutionary hero who abandons his privileges—a Lafayette, as Chris Worth suggests[14]—in order to fight for freedom and social justice. When asked who gave Robin Hood permission to steal from the rich and give to the poor, Ritson responded: "That same power, one may answer, which authorizes kings to take where it can be worst spared, and give it where it is least wanted. Our hero, in this respect, was a knight-errant; and wanted no other commission than that of Justice, whose cause he militated."[15]

While Scott's main aim in *Ivanhoe* was to portray the nationalistic struggle against the increasingly repressive measures adopted by the English parliament after the trauma of the Napoleonic wars and the victory at Waterloo, he welcomed and included the revolutionary generosity displayed by Robin Hood in his friend Ritson's version of the legend. It made sense to add this virtuous trait to the Saxon dispossessed, Robin Hood himself, trying to break free from the Norman yoke.

The political subtext of Walter Scott's novel shows that this modern Robin Hood had little to do with the original myth of the late medieval ballads. It was the same personage interpreted from two different worldviews, the disappearing chivalric system and modern nationalism. The very existence of

---

13   Joseph Ritson, "The Life of Robin Hood," in *Robin Hood: A Collection of All the Ancient Poems, Songs and Ballads, now extant, Relative to that Celebrated English Outlaw*, vols. 1–2, ed. by Joseph Ritson, London: William Pickering 1832, vol. 1, p. xi.

14   See Worth, "*Ivanhoe* and the Making of Britain," p. 72.

15   Ritson, *Robin Hood: A Collection*, p. xi.

Joseph Ritson's book reveals the intention of employing a figure of medieval lore in order to portray modern ideas; through his collection of poems and ballads, Ritson wanted to provide original source material so the reader could then fashion his or her own modern Robin Hood figure.

Scott's historical novels from the 1820s, including *Ivanhoe*, were promptly translated into Danish and exerted a strong influence on several local writers such as Bernhard Severin Ingemann (1789–1862), Hans Christian Andersen and the aforementioned Blicher. Of course, Kierkegaard was aware of this.

3   Copenhagen's Literary Context during the 1820s and the 1830s

In the early 1830s, Kierkegaard was enrolled at the University of Copenhagen as a student of theology, but in fact he was more interested in becoming a writer, and thus he followed closely the latest events in the literary circles of the capital city. He was still several years away from starting his authorship proper with the publication in 1843 of *Either/Or*, but that did not stop him from writing, as he spent considerable time scribbling in his journal—in reality a collection of journals, notebooks and loose papers. There he pondered the literary trends of the time.

A decade earlier, during the 1820s, one of the literary genres on the rise in Copenhagen was the novella or short novel. Many Danish authors tried their luck at this new type of prose. Blicher penned in 1824 his breakthrough masterpiece, the short novel *The Journal of a Parish Clerk* [*En Landsbydegns Dagbog*], also influenced by Walter Scott. That same year, Kierkegaard's friend and mentor, Poul Martin Møller (1794–1838), read at the Student Union of the university fragments of his incomplete novella, *A Danish Student's Adventure* [*En dansk Students Eventyr*], a historical piece that displayed Scott's imprint as well. One of the most important poets of the age, Adam Oehlenschläger (1779–1850), who had introduced literary Romanticism in Denmark, published in 1825 a Goethian novella titled *The Island in the South Sea* [*Øen i Sydhavet*]. The next year, Frederik Christian Sibbern (1785–1872), who was also Kierkegaard's professor and friend, wrote the epistolary short novel *à la* Werther, *Gabrielis' Letters* [*Gabrielis Breve*], a piece that would later become a classic in Danish literature. From 1827 to 1828, Thomasine Gyllembourg (1773–1856), who was perhaps Kierkegaard's favorite novelist, published three short novels, *The Family Polonius* [*Familien Polonius*], *The Magic Key* [*Den magiske Nøgle*], and her masterpiece, *An Everyday Story* [*En Hverdags-Historie*]. Finally, it is also important to mention Denmark's most famous writer—although at the time he was only a rising young talent—Hans Christian Andersen, who a decade later would publish three incredibly successful short novels: *The Improvisator* [*Improvisatoren*], *O. T.*, and *Only a Fiddler* [*Kun en Spillemand*].

What was attractive about the novella was that, unlike poetry, it offered the author a more ample canvas in which to render ideas or illustrate the development of characters. In this regard, the literary scene of Copenhagen was strongly influenced by two major figures, the forenamed Walter Scott and Johann Wolfgang von Goethe. With respect to the former, there were several authors like Blicher or Møller who tried to follow in the steps of Scott, whose prose, as discussed earlier, dealt with modern ideas like nationalism. As for the latter, Goethe was almost universally admired in the literary circles of Copenhagen. The renowned Kierkegaard scholar, Henning Fenger, called this burst of enthusiasm the "Goethe fever."[16] Thus, for example, one of the more influential intellectual figures of the day, the philosopher, poet and literary critic Johan Ludvig Heiberg, claimed that Goethe was one of the two greatest minds of the age (the other was Hegel).[17] In Heiberg's view, the biggest merit of the German poet was his ability to convey obscure and abstract concepts in a manner that was both attractive and understandable for the large reading public.

Kierkegaard, who as a young man was a fervent admirer of Heiberg, agreed with this opinion. In a passage of his *Notebook 3* from 1836, he praised Goethe for the way in which he managed to present a whole worldview through the development of Wilhelm, the titular protagonist of the celebrated *Wilhelm Meister* cycle:

> If I were to say in a few words what I actually regard as masterful about Goethe's *Wilhelm Meister*, I would say that it is the well-balanced governance running through the whole of it, the whole Fichtean moral world order immanently present in the totality. The novel itself develops this in a more doctrinaire fashion, gradually leading Wilhelm to the point which, if I may say so, is given in the theory. It does so in such a way that, at the end of the novel, the worldview which the poet has brought to bear now comes alive in him just as it existed prior to and beyond Wilhelm. This accounts for the consummate total impression the novel makes, perhaps

---

16   See Fenger, *Kierkegaard, the Myths and Their Origins*, p. 81.

17   See Johan Ludvig Heiberg, *Om Philosophiens Betydning for den nuværende Tid*, Copenhagen: C.A. Reitzel 1833, p. 36. Reprinted in Heiberg's *Prosaiske Skrifter*, vols. 1–11, Copenhagen: J.H. Schubothes Boghandling 1841–1843, vol. 1, p. 417. In English in *Heiberg's On the Significance of Philosophy for the Present Age and Other Texts*, trans. by Jon Stewart, Copenhagen: C.A. Reitzel 2005 (*Texts from Golden Age Denmark*, vol. 1), p. 107.

more so than any other; it is really the entire world conceived in a mirror, a true microcosm.[18]

The model of the German *Bildungsroman*, especially Goethe's, was very influential for the new Danish novella. However, whereas the former focused more on the upbringing and general development of the protagonist throughout the novel in order to show the process in which he or she acquired an integral worldview, the latter adopted the form of literary realism that, while it did not neglect the character's inner life evolution, was more interested in portraying poetically the folklore, customs and values of the local culture, including elements of daily life that were hitherto deemed trivial or unworthy from a literary point of view.[19]

At the time, Kierkegaard was more interested in the literary elaboration of the character's development than in depicting Danish folklore or discussing sociopolitical issues in the style of Walter Scott's prose. Nonetheless, he might have been intrigued by his use of medieval myth, in this case the legend of Robin Hood. It is unclear if Kierkegaard ever read *Ivanhoe* since there is not a single mention of it in the whole authorship,[20] but considering the undeniable influence of Scott on the Danish literature of the time and the fact that Kierkegaard himself was an avid reader, it would be unlikely that he was not at least aware of the novel. Even if he did not read it directly, he might have been familiar, as stated earlier, with Blicher's more recent depiction of the myth of the kind bandit in his novella *The Robber's Den*.[21]

---

18   *SKS* 19, 102, Not3:5 / *KJN* 3, 100.

19   For a more detailed discussion of Danish realism, see Joakim Garff, "Andersen, Kierkegaard—and the Deconstructed *Bildungsroman*," in *Kierkegaard Studies Yearbook*, 2006, pp. 86–7. See also Claes Kastholm Hansen, *Den kontrollerede virkelighed. Virkelighedsproblemet i den litterære kritik og den nye danske roman i perioden 1830–1840*, Copenhagen: Akademisk Forlag 1975, pp. 14ff.

20   In fact, Walter Scott is only mentioned twice in Kierkegaard's writings. See *SKS* 1, 30 / *EPW*, 74, where Kierkegaard criticizes H.C. Andersen as a novelist for imitating Walter Scott in a poor manner by focusing excessively in folklore descriptions while neglecting character development. See also *SKS* 17, 218, DD:6 / *KJN* 1, 210, where Kierkegaard makes reference to Scott's novel *The Abbot* from 1820 and its depiction of medieval festivals. Kierkegaard did not read English, and thus he quoted Scott's German translation from 1826–33. See *Walter Scott's sämmtliche Werke*, vols. 1–173, Stuttgart: Franckh 1826–1833.

21   Even though Kierkegaard makes no direct mention of the novel, in a loose paper from 1836 he makes reference to the romantic element in Blicher's descriptions of the heaths of Jutland [*den jydske Hede*]. Such a description, perhaps the most popular one in Blicher's *oeuvre*, appears precisely in *The Robber's Den*. See *SKS* 27, 129, Papir 125:1 / *KJN* 11, 131. See also Blicher, "Røverstuen," p. 108.

Both Scott and Blicher used a medieval legend, Robin Hood, the myth of the noble robber, and refashioned it in a modern way, although for different purposes. On the one hand, Scott was a more political author. As discussed, he wished to portray local patriotic fervor, embodied by the Saxon Robin of Locksley, in its struggle against the foreign oppressor, the Norman overlords. Even though Robin did not embody the idea of revolution, as in the more radical version of Scott's friend Ritson, the reinterpreted myth did represent a contemporary issue: the conflict between the nationalist, romantic Scotland and the industrialized England.

On the other hand, Blicher was the archetypical writer of Danish realism. In *The Robber's Den*, he describes the rough natural conditions of the Jutland heath, and in this manner he also illustrates the character of the local common folk. As Michael Jones says, "Blicher makes us bump along a deeply rutted road until we are enmeshed in the life of the people who dwell there, and are swallowed up by its impoverished but starkly beautiful environment."[22] By sketching a geographical landscape, the author depicts the local culture as well. The main character of the story, Black Mads, is a poor farmer. As he is unable to make ends meet, he is forced to engage in illegal activities such as poaching, and thus he has to go underground because the local authorities are looking for him in order to deliver him to Copenhagen for punishment.

Black Mads is not a dispossessed nobleman or a patriot fighter, like Scott's Robin of Locksley; he is not trying to implement social justice either. In fact, he is not even a robber. He is just an impoverished, honest Jutlander trying to survive. In the story, Black Mads helps a young nobleman get together with his lover. The couple is fleeing from the main antagonist, the manor owner, who is also the girl's father, so Black Mads helps them escape and hides them in his hideout in an ancient barrow (the titular robber's den). In the happy ending, a gathering is shown with both the nobility and the common folk fraternizing. Blicher attempts to depict the utopian harmony between the two social classes—an ideal also present in Scott's *Ivanhoe*—achieved by the efforts and the moral purity of the prototypical Jutlander, the "robber" Black Mads. Indeed, although he is considered an outlaw by the state, that is, the "established order," he is also well liked and popular with the peasants, who are often at odds with the local nobility whose hunting sorties result in the destruction

---

22   Michael Jones, "The Jutland Cipher: Unlocking the Meaning and Power of a Contested Landscape," in *Nordic Landscapes: Region and Belonging on the Northern Edge of Europe*, ed. by Michael Jones and Kenneth R. Olwig, Minneapolis and London: University of Minnesota Press 2008, p. 35.

of their farms. From the perspective of folklore, Black Mads was a righteous person.

Considering the ideas they were trying to convey, nationalism and local folklore, it seems that the novel was certainly the proper literary medium for Scott and Blicher. It offered an extended outlet that allowed a more detailed development of the worldview they wished to describe. Kierkegaard was attracted to the genre as well. He would try his luck at writing a novella in pieces such as "The Seducer's Diary" in the first part of *Either/Or*, or *Repetition*, both works from 1843, when short novels were still popular in Denmark. But in 1834, he had something else in mind. He wanted to write about the inner life of his own Robin Hood, a figure he called the Master-Thief, and he thought that the most adequate venue for this was drama, not prose.

In this he followed the literary aesthetics proposed by the aforementioned Johan Ludvig Heiberg. During the 1820s and 1830s the name Heiberg was a powerhouse in Copenhagen literary circles.[23] Many young writers, including Kierkegaard and H.C. Andersen, admired him and strived to emulate him. Heiberg first became famous in the literary scene by introducing in Denmark a new dramatic genre he had learned about while he lived in Paris: the vaudeville. An accomplished stylist and verse composer, he excelled at these light-hearted, usually one-act farces, which were extraordinarily entertaining and soon became classics in Danish literature. Jonas Collin, the director of the Royal Theater, supported his idea of creating a Danish vaudeville, and from 1825 to 1828 Heiberg penned some of his most famous comedies such as *King Solomon and George the Hatter* [*Kong Solomon og Jørgen Hattemager*, 1825], *April Fools* [*Aprilsnarrerne*, 1826], *The Reviewer and the Animal* [*Recensenten og Dyret*, 1826], and *The Elves' Hill* [*Elverhøj*, 1828]. The plays were such an incredible success at the box office that in 1829 Heiberg finally landed a permanent position as the official poet and translator of the Royal Theater.[24]

Heiberg was so invested in this that he published in 1826 a vaudeville manifesto titled *On Vaudeville as a Dramatic Genre and its Significance for the Danish*

---

23   For a more detailed account of Heiberg's life and thought see Henning Fenger, *The Heibergs*, trans. by Frederick J. Marker, New York: Twayne Publishers 1971; Morten Borup, *Johan Ludvig Heiberg*, vols. 1–3, Copenhagen: Gyldendal 1973; Jon Stewart, *A History of Hegelianism in Golden Age Denmark, Tome I, The Heiberg Period: 1824–1836*, Copenhagen: C.A. Reitzel's Publishers 2007 (*Danish Golden Age Studies*, vol. 3); Jon Stewart (ed.), *The Heibergs and the Theater. Between Vaudeville, Romantic Comedy and National Drama*, Copenhagen: Museum Tusculanum Press 2012 (*Danish Golden Age Studies*, vol. 7); and Vibeke Schrøder, *Tankens våben. Johan Ludvig Heiberg*, Copenhagen: Gyldendal, 2001.

24   See Heiberg, "Autobiographiske Fragmenter," in *Prosaiske Skrifter*, vol. 11, pp. 503. In English in *Heiberg's On the Significance of Philosophy*, p. 67.

Stage [*Om Vaudevillen, som dramatisk Digtart, og om dens Betydning paa den danske Skueplads*],[25] a text that also realized his desire to theorize about the cultural and social role of literature and drama. Indeed, Heiberg was not only a dramatist, but he was a literary critic, an aesthetician and a philosopher as well. After experiencing a sort of philosophical epiphany in 1824,[26] he became an enthusiastic follower of Hegel's philosophy and immediately devoted himself to the task of introducing Hegelianism into Denmark. In his controversial treatise from 1833, *On the Significance of Philosophy for the Present Age* [*Om Philosophiens Betydning for den nuværende Tid*], Heiberg attempted to diagnose what he saw as the cultural crisis of the age—nihilism and the social decay into bourgeois philistinism—and concluded that the remedy for this was philosophy: Hegelian philosophy. According to him, "Philosophy is nothing other than the knowledge of the eternal or the speculative Idea, reason, or truth; these different terms all designate the same substance. Philosophy presents the idea as the only cause. Consequently, in all finite effects philosophy sees nothing but the Idea."[27]

The gist of the argument was that Hegel had proved in his system that the eternal truth, what Heiberg liked to call the *speculative Idea* [*speculative Idee*], was always present in finite actuality. If people became aware of this, Heiberg argued, they would also be able to overcome nihilism, as their heretofore trivial daily lives would suddenly appear as full of meaning. However, this process was complicated by the difficulty of Hegel's obscure philosophy, "as most people openly acknowledge that they do not understand him."[28] It was precisely for this reason that Heiberg admired Goethe so much. The German poet, he claimed, was capable of conveying in an aesthetically attractive manner the spirit of the age, the Idea, within finitude. On account of this he called Goethe a *speculative poet* [*speculative Poet*], a category in which he also included Dante and Calderón

25   See Heiberg, *Om Vaudevillen, som dramatisk Digtart, og om dens Betydning paa den danske Skueplads*, Copenhagen: Ferdinand Printzlau 1826. Reprinted in Heiberg's *Prosaiske Skrifter*, vol. 6, pp. 41–111.

26   See Heiberg, "Autobiographiske Fragmenter," pp. 500–1. In English in *On the Significance of Philosophy*, p. 65. See Jon Stewart, "Johan Ludvig Heiberg: Kierkegaard's Criticism of Hegel's Danish Apologist," in *Kierkegaard and his Danish Contemporaries*, Tome I, *Philosophy, Politics and Social Theory*, ed. by Jon Stewart, Farnham and Burlington: Ashgate 2009 (*Kierkegaard Research: Sources, Reception and Resources*, vol. 7), pp. 35–76. "The Finite and the Infinite: Johan Ludvig Heiberg's Enigmatic Relation to Hegelianism," *Filosofiske Studier*, 2008, pp. 267–280.

27   Heiberg, *Om Philosophiens Betydning for den nuværende Tid*, pp. 5–6. Reprinted in Heiberg's *Prosaiske Skrifter*, vol. 1, pp. 385–6. In English in *On the Significance of Philosophy*, p. 88.

28   Heiberg, *Om Philosophiens Betydning for den nuværende Tid*, p. 37. Reprinted in Heiberg's *Prosaiske Skrifter*, vol. 1, p. 417. In English in *On the Significance of Philosophy*, p. 108.

de la Barca.[29] He also proposed a new poetic genre, the *didactic poem [Lærdigt]*, a special literary composition that would achieve the ultimate philosophical goal of reconciling the ideal (the infinite) and the actual (the finite).[30]

Thus, the remedy for the cultural crisis of the age was philosophy, and the proper medium for philosophy was poetry, i.e., the didactic poem, which Heiberg would later call *speculative poetry*.[31] That the most adequate poetic genre for this task was drama can hardly come as a surprise given the fact that Heiberg was a man devoted to the Danish stage. Nonetheless, it might be a little strange that of all the dramatic genres it was the vaudeville that he chose for this elevated mission. But Heiberg knew what he was doing. The gentle, light comedy of his vaudevilles was very popular and could draw a larger audience than a more dense type of drama, let alone a philosophical treatise. Therefore, a skillful playwright—such as Heiberg—would be capable of conveying in a subreptitious way his or her philosophical message.

But also from a purely aesthetical point of view drama occupied the highest position. In 1828, Heiberg published in the literary journal he edited, *Kjøbenhavns flyvende Post*, a series of articles in which he developed a classification of poetic genres organized in triads.[32] Following the familiar Hegelian aesthetical categories, the main triad consisted of lyric, epic, and, in the highest place, dramatic poetry. The latter unfolded into a new triad: immediate drama, tragedy and comedy. According to this classification, the superior genres were those with a higher consciousness of the universal and ideal, while the lower genres were those bound to the immediate and finite. Therefore, according to Heiberg's aesthetics, drama, and comedic drama no less, was the most adequate venue to present universal ideas.

Although this statement might seem debatable, especially at a time when prose was starting to get the upper hand in the literary circles of Copenhagen,

---

29   Heiberg, *Om Philosophiens Betydning for den nuværende Tid*, pp. 37–8. Reprinted in Heiberg's *Prosaiske Skrifter*, vol. 1, pp. 418–9. In English in *On the Significance of Philosophy*, p. 108.

30   Heiberg, *Om Philosophiens Betydning for den nuværende Tid*, p. 40. Reprinted in Heiberg's *Prosaiske Skrifter*, vol. 1, pp. 420–1. In English in *On the Significance of Philosophy*, pp. 109–10.

31   For Heiberg's development of speculative poetry, see Stewart, "Heiberg's Conception of Speculative Drama and the Crisis of the Age: Martensen's Analysis of *Fata Morgana*," in *The Heibergs and the Theater*, pp. 147–58. See also Nassim Bravo, "Heiberg's 'A Soul after Death': A Comedic Wake-Up Call for the Age," in *The Crisis of the Danish Golden Age and its Modern Resonance*, ed. by Jon Stewart and Nathaniel Kramer, Copenhagen: Museum Tusculanum Press 2020 (*Danish Golden Age Studies*, vol. 12), pp. 30–49.

32   See Heiberg, "Svar paa Hr. Oehlenschlägers Skrift: 'Om Kritiken i *Kjøbenhavns flyvende Post*, over Væringerne i Miklagard,'" in *Prosaiske Skrifter*, vol. 3, pp. 194–284.

Heiberg's classification of genres was very influential. Kierkegaard, who would arguably become the greatest prose writer in the history of Danish literature, was probably paying heed to the poet's theory, because he copied Heiberg's scheme in his *Journal BB*.[33] This is perhaps one of the reasons why Kierkegaard was attracted to the idea of tackling the Master-Thief subject through drama when apparently all other young authors were busy writing short novels.

4   Kierkegaard's Use of a Medieval Myth: The Master-Thief

It should be noted from the start that the so called Master-Thief project never came to fruition, and as such it is part of Kierkegaard's posthumous writings. Regarding these, when he died on November 11, 1855, "everything in his room was found to be in order, as if he were going to travel, to take a trip to the country," according to the testimony of his secretary, Israel Levin.[34] Indeed, Kierkegaard's *Nachlass* reveals a high degree of systematization, as he labeled and categorized his manuscripts into various journals (*AA* through *KK*) and notebooks (*1* through *14*). Nonetheless, there was a group of writings that resisted a more strict classification, material Kierkegaard himself called the "loose papers" [*løse Papirer*], consisting of scraps of paper, loose sheets and even pieces of cardboard. The project about the Master-Thief belongs to this group, specifically to the portion of papers designated as "Aesthetica. Older" [*Æsthetica. Ældre*], which was found in "a large cardboard box marked 'A' and with the inscription 'Journals and other such from an earlier period [*Journaler og andet Sligt fra en ældre Tid*].'"[35]

In reality, the "project"[36] consists of only three loose papers (97, 98 and 123) divided into eight entries.[37] The first entry is dated on September 12, 1834.

---

33   See *SKS* 17, 113, BB:23 / *KJN* 1, 106–7.

34   Bruce H. Kirmmse, ed. and trans., *Encounters with Kierkegaard: A Life as Seen by His Contemporaries*, Princeton: Princeton University Press 1996, p. 212.

35   Niels Jørgen Cappelørn, Elise Iuul, Stine Holst Petersen and Steen Tullberg, "Critical Account of the Text," in *KJN* 11, 412.

36   For more detailed accounts about the Master-Thief project, see Henning Fenger, "Mestertyven. Kierkegaards første dramatiske forsøg," *Edda*, no. 71, 1971, pp. 331–9. Sara Katrine Jandrup, "The Master Thief, Alias S. Kierkegaard, and his Robbery of the Truth," *Søren Kierkegaard Newsletter*, no. 43, 2002, pp. 7–11; Nassim Bravo, "The Master-Thief: A One-Man Army against the Established Order," in *Kierkegaard's Literary Figures and Motifs*, Tome II, pp. 111–20; Nassim Bravo, "Kierkegaard y el proyecto sobre el ladrón maestro (1834–1835): El rebelde marginado frente al orden establecido," *Eidos*, no. 32, 2020, pp. 281–308.

37   See *SKS* 27, 118–21, Papir 97:1–6 / *KJN* 11, 119–122. *SKS* 27, 121, Papir 98 / *KJN* 11, 122. *SKS* 27, 123, Papir 103 / *KJN* 11,124.

While there are loose papers from as early as 1830, most of this material consists of excerpts from books about history of the Church or notes from theological courses at the University of Copenhagen. This means that the Master-Thief
idea was Kierkegaard's first literary project. In that first entry Kierkegaard discusses the folkloric background of the Master-Thief figure:

> We should note that nearly all nations have had such an idea and that the
> ideal of the thief has hovered before them. We see that however differ-
> ent a Fra Diavolo is from a Peer Mikkelsen or a Morten Frederiksen, they
> nonetheless have certain traits in common. Many stories about thieves
> are in circulation. These are attributed by some to Peer Mikkelsen, by oth-
> ers to Morten Frederiksen, and by still others to a third, etc., without it
> being possible to determine definitely their ultimate source, which shows
> precisely that people have fabricated a certain ideal of a thief as charac-
> terized by certain broad traits, and that these traits have been attributed
> by them to this or that actual thief.[38]

It is interesting to see how he first connects the ideal traits of the Master-
Thief to actual, contemporary and local criminals like Peder Mikkelsen and
Morten Frederiksen. But this relation is in fact indirect. Kierkegaard argues
that the ideal of the good thief, including his romanticized features, is shared
by many nations. He states that it is the folk that fabricates the myth of the
thief, although it is difficult to establish if this myth is rooted in a historical
thief. Since the original sources are obscure, people tend to link this mythical
knowledge to a more concrete and immediate figure, i.e., popular real thieves.

Kierkegaard did some research on these real-life outlaws. He presumably
learned of Morten Frederiksen from two sources. The first one, based on actual
criminal records, associates the alias "Master-Thief" with Frederiksen. The
work, whose author and date is unknown, is pompously titled *The Infamous
Master Thief and Rasping House Prisoner Morten Frederiksen's True Life Story
[Den berygtede Mestertyv og Rasphuusfange Morten Frederiksens sandfærdige
Levnetshistorie]*.[39] Peder Mikkelsen (1762–1809) was in fact also known as the

---

38 *SKS* 27, 118, Papir 97:1 / *KJN* 11, 119.
39 See *Den berygtede Mestertyv og Rasphuusfange Morten Frederiksens sandfærdige
    Levnetshistorie; hvorledes han nemlig, efter at have taget Tjeneste ved det Militaire, flere
    Gange blev afstraffet som Tyv og Deserteur baade her i Danmark og i Udlandet; hvorledes
    han herpaa blev hensaat i Slaveriet og senere i Rasphuset, hvorfra han brød ud, for at
    begaae nye Forbrydelser, indtil han endelig efter mangfoldige sælsomme Eventyr blev
    hensat i Citadellet*, Copenhagen: no year. The second source was a lecture given by P.L.

Master-Thief, and Kierkegaard might have read about him from War Minister T.P. Hansen's *Archive for Danish and Norse Criminal Stories* [*Archiv for danske og norske Criminalhistorier*],[40] a collection of biographies of criminals—most of them murderers—based on official judiciary records.

Admittedly, both Frederiksen and Mikkelsen were, according to the sources, little more than common criminals and could hardly be qualified as "ideal thieves," at least compared to either the medieval or modern traditions. In spite of this, Kierkegaard mentions that Mikkelsen was depicted "as stealing from the rich in order to help the poor, which bespeaks nobility, and that he does not steal for his own use."[41] Such generosity of spirit was presumably attributed to Mikkelsen by the people, who might have felt inclined to associate grandiose qualities to an otherwise regular thief who had acquired some notoriety for escaping a couple of times from prison. Frederiksen was similar in this regard since he had become famous for escaping in a spectacular fashion from the Roskilde prison, an anecdote that was well known in Copenhagen. They had become "Master-Thieves" because of their cunning, and only then acquired the rest of the ideal traits of the noble robbers.

At this point, Kierkegaard jumps from the actual to the ideal, and proceeds to describe the familiar and romanticized characteristics of the Master-Thief:

> We should keep in mind that wickedness, thievishness, etc., are by no means the sole basis for this. No, on the contrary, the master thief is also thought to be endowed with goodness, amiability, charity and also with surpassing tact, cunning, and cleverness; he has been imagined, moreover, as someone who actually does not steal for the sake of stealing, that is, to appropriate another's property, but for some other reason. Often we may think of him as someone who is dissatisfied with the existing order and who then expresses his dissatisfaction by violating the rights of others and in so doing gains the opportunity to mock and confront the authorities.[42]

Benzon on February 11, 1826, and later published in 1827. See Peter Lorentz Benzon, "Kort Omrids af Morten Frederiksens Levnetsløb," in *Criminalhistorier uddragne af Danske Justits-Acter*, Copenhagen: Andreas Seidelin 1827, pp. 46–60. See also Karl Peder Pedersen, "Forbryderhistorier. Om trykte kilder til kriminelles historie ca. 1800–1850," *Personalhistorisk Tidsskrift*, no. 2, 2010, pp. 218–32.

40   See T.P. Hansen (ed.), *Archiv for danske og norske Criminalhistorier, eller mærkværdige Domfældtes Levnet, Forbrydelser og Straf,* Copenhagen: published by the editor 1834, pp. 85–90.

41   *SKS* 27, 118, Papir 97:1 / *KJN* 11, 119.

42   *SKS* 27, 118, Papir 97:1 / *KJN* 11, 119.

We note in this passage that Kierkegaard combines the mischievous shrewd-
ness of the actual criminals (Mikkelsen, Frederiksen) with the generosity of
the ideal thief shared by both the chivalric medieval Robin Hood tradition
or the more modern and political version by Walter Scott. Finally, the Dane
adds a "political" quality, the true reason behind the Master-Thief's criminal
ways, interpreted here as a dissatisfaction with the existing order. It seems
Kierkegaard's thief does not oppose the established authorities in order to
reclaim his honor, as the medieval bandit would do, or to encourage national
revolutionary resistance, like the Saxon hero of Walter Scott, but to "mock and
confront the authorities," i.e., he has a satirical motive.

Also unlike the courteous Robyn Hode from the late medieval ballads or the
gregarious Robin of Locksley of *Ivanhoe* who feels at home with his comrades,
for he is a man of the people, Kierkegaard's Master-Thief is a loner who "cannot
find any comfort or encouragement among other thieves, for they are situated
altogether too far below him, and vice prevails among them."[43] Therefore, he is
not a popular hero, because he despises his bandit fellows; his grievance with
the established order seems to be of a personal nature and probably has little to
do with a pursuit of social justice, as was the case with Scott's or even Blicher's
kind outlaw. In a later entry dated on March 15, 1835, Kierkegaard writes:

> When one compares the master thief with the Italian robber, one will see
> an essential difference: in the latter, the social element is dominant. We
> cannot picture him other than at the head of a band of robbers among
> whom, once the dangers and difficulties of the robbery are past, he sur-
> renders himself to jubilation, while with the master thief something
> much more profound asserts itself, a certain streak of melancholia, a self-
> encapsulation, a dark intimation of life's circumstances, a deep-seated
> dissatisfaction.[44]

The "Italian robber" was Michael Pezza (1771–1806), also known as Fra Diavolo
("Brother Devil"), who was already mentioned by Kierkegaard in the first entry
of the project. Like Mikkelsen and Frederiksen, Pezza was a real bandit. In a
way that resembled Scott's Robin of Locksley, he combined his activities as
a brigand with the organization of a local Neapolitan resistance against the
forces of a foreign power, in this case revolutionary France, a fight he continued until he was captured and executed in 1806. Also similarly, Fra Diavolo

---

43   *SKS* 27, 119, Papir 97:1 / *KJN* 11, 120.
44   *SKS* 27, 123, Papir 103 / *KJN* 11, 124.

represented a traditional local culture in its struggle with a more advanced and cosmopolitan invader. It should be noted that Kierkegaard probably learned of Fra Diavolo not from any historical records, but from the opera by Daniel François Esprit Auber (1782–1871), *Fra Diavolo, ou L'hôtellerie de Terracine*, performed at the Royal Theater of Copenhagen on January 29, 1835, the very same day he wrote three entries about the Master-Thief. With lyrics by the French vaudeville author Eugène Scribe (1791–1861)—who was, by the way, one of Heiberg's favorite dramatists—it goes without saying that in this piece Fra Diavolo, a guerrilla rebel against French rule, is not shown in the best light possible. Nonetheless, Kierkegaard observes correctly that here the social element is dominant: Fra Diavolo was a popular hero, a patriot and a liberator.

In order to understand the gap between Scott's socially oriented interpretation of the Robin Hood myth and Kierkegaard's heavy subjectivization of the legend it might be important to pay attention to the context of Copenhagen during the first decades of the nineteenth century. The period in question, the so-called Golden Age of Denmark, was paradoxically a time of economic bankruptcy, social turmoil and religious crisis. It was in part due to this outward impasse that Danish intellectuals sought a solution in culture itself, and thus we have come to know this period as a Golden Age of artistic, literary and philosophical production. In this manner, for example, when in 1833 Heiberg attempted to diagnose the crisis of the age in the aforementioned *On the Significance of Philosophy for the Present Age*, he claimed that the answer to Denmark's troubles was cultural and philosophical, not social and revolutionary. Unlike France, where the intelligentsia formed a vanguard elite, Danish intellectuals, such as Heiberg, were essentially conservative.

In the early 1830s, Denmark was going through a period of political effervescence and several members of this cultural clique in Copenhagen tried to resist the surge of liberalism inspired by the July Revolution of 1830. Indeed, on November 28, 1835, the same year of the Master-Thief project, Kierkegaard himself delivered a lecture in the Student Union in which he criticized liberal journalism and suggested that Denmark did not necessarily have to follow the revolutionary path established by France.[45] In this situation, a figure like Fra Diavolo—a local patriot fighting foreign influence—might have been attractive to a conservative writer. However, Kierkegaard was convinced, like Heiberg, that the answer had to do more with inwardness and a reflection on the self than with political journalism, social struggle or, in the case of Fra Diavolo, guerilla warfare.

---

45   See *SKS* 27, 189–204, Papir 254 / *KJN* 11, 194–209.

This might raise the question of why Kierkegaard chose a figure modeled on the legend of Robin Hood, an obviously popular hero, if he was not interested on the social aspect of the myth. But then we ought to remember that the Master-Thief did have a profound dissatisfaction with the established order and wanted to confront and ridicule the authorities. In Kierkegaard's view, this estrangement with the way actuality works did not imply social activism. That feature was in fact introduced into the noble bandit myth by Walter Scott's modern worldview, for the source of the medieval Robin Hood's defiance, as has been discussed earlier, was not an unquenchable thirst for social justice, but chivalric tradition: his struggle was for honor's sake, a different kind of justice.

Likewise, Kierkegaard's hero is not a social fighter and he only allies himself with other criminals in order to "make use of them in the attainment of his aims; in other respects he must despise them."[46] What are these aims? He is unhappy with the existing order and the injustices of the authorities, but instead of fighting headlong against a tyrant, he wants to expose this overall malfunction through humor and ridicule. In the third entry of the project, dated on January 29, 1835, Kierkegaard explains:

> He is, of course, to be thought of as in possession of an excellent sense of humor, which may easily be combined with his sense of dissatisfaction, which in turn, makes him prone to satire—even if he is not always to be conceived of as discontented—this is nonetheless easily reconciled with his origin among the lower classes, the roots of the nation. In some cases he will resemble a Till Eulenspiegel.[47]

Kierkegaard alludes here to another mythical figure from the Middle Ages, the Germanic Till Eulenspiegel. In a loose paper dated on March 16, 1835, he writes: "Eulenspiegel would seem to represent the satirical element in the Scandinavian."[48] Later, on October 1, 1835, we read the following: "It is also remarkable that Germany has its Faust, Italy and Spain their Don Juan, the Jews (??) the Wandering Jew, Denmark and northern Germany Eulenspiegel, etc."[49] Like Robin Hood, the sources on the legend of Till Eulenspiegel—or Till Ugelspegel in Danish—stem from the late Middle Ages and speak of an itinerant prankster who roamed Northern Germany exposing and mocking the

---

46   *SKS* 27, 119, Papir 97:1 / *KJN* 11, 120.
47   *SKS* 27, 119, Papir 97:3 / *KJN* 11, 120.
48   *SKS* 27, 123, Papir 104 / *KJN* 11, 124.
49   *SKS* 27, 185, Papir 253 / *KJN* 11, 191.

stupidity of the nascent bourgeoisie. A satirist, Eulenspiegel revealed the inadequacies of a corrupt society through parody and humor. The idea behind this approach, in Kierkegaard's view, was that by exposing the inner contradictions of actuality, the satirist or humorist would be able to raise the awareness of his or her contemporaries, thus helping to solve the problems of the age. This is the main reason why Kierkegaard would later become so passionately interested on the figure of Socrates—the prototypical ironist—and now wanted to depict his bandit as a humorist. After doing his duty, the Master-Thief would surrender himself to the authorities:

> Such a master thief, brazen and forthright (Kagerup, for example), will confess his crime and suffer the punishment for it like a man who knows himself to have lived for an idea, and precisely by doing so he acknowledges the reality of the state and does not deny it—as one perhaps could say—with his life; he only opposes injustices. We certainly might understand him as someone who wants to taunt the law, but in this we must then see a sort of mockery of everything and, in his deed, an expression of a vanity that is entirely part of his idea. He will never forget open-hearted cheerfulness, and he will come forth with his own confession after he has shown how he *could* evade the law.[50]

Søren Andersen Kagerup (1811–1832) was another Danish thief. He was arrested when he committed a petty robbery and, in a harsh turn of events, he was sentenced to life imprisonment and, after killing an inmate, was beheaded in 1832. According to the pastor Carl Holger Visby (1801–1871),[51] who worked as the chaplain of Copenhagen's prison from 1826 to 1842 and presumably interviewed Kagerup in person, the young criminal remained calmed when he was about to be executed and displayed a strong sense of justice, admitting he deserved to lose his life for his crime.[52]

In a way that reminds us of Socrates, the Master-Thief also accepts with serenity his ultimate fate. This indifference towards his own life shows that the satire was aimed not only at the "vanity" of the established order, but also

---

50   *SKS* 27, 119, Papir 97:2 / *KJN* 11, 120.
51   Kierkegaard knew and respected Visby, and learned of Kagerup from a series of articles published by the pastor. See Carl Holger Visby, "Psychologiske Bemærkninger over den, med Øxen henrettede, Morder Søren Andersen Kagerup," *Borgervennen*, nos. 20–25, 1832, pp. 141–87; see also, Hansen (ed.), *Archiv for danske og norske Criminalhistorier*, pp. 220–55.
52   See Visby, "Psychologiske Bemærkninger over den Morder Søren Andersen Kagerup," p. 170.

at himself. This early treatment of the concept of satire would set the founda-tion for the development of the important Kierkegaardian notions of irony and humor. Thus, in a later entry Kierkegaard would claim: "Irony's standpoint as such is *nil admirari*, when it kills itself, has through humor *despised* everything, itself included."[53]

5   Conclusion

The Master-Thief project was brief, vague and fragmentary. The last entry, the one about the melancholic character of the hero, was dated on March 15, 1835. After that, Kierkegaard lost interest and dropped the idea, and would later recall with candor his juvenile obsession with the thief.[54] He probably realized that the Robin Hood myth did not fit well after all with the kind of figure he wanted to develop, that of the isolated individual with a deep inner life and a high degree of self-awareness that clings to a personal idea and defies the established order. Such a role was better represented by characters that would later capture Kierkegaard's attention: Till Eulenspiegel, Faust, the Wandering Jew, Socrates and even Abraham. This, however, does not mean that the Master-Thief project was unimportant.

The use of medieval legends was a trend during the age and intellectuals constantly drew on medieval lore in order to convey modern ideas. They were certainly aware that they were transforming the original myths, but saw in this an effective way of connecting a remote mythical national past with their con-temporary issues. In this sense, Kierkegaard was a man of his time, and this is perhaps the reason why he initially attempted to use a more "local" myth, i.e., a Northern European legend like the Anglo-Saxon Robin Hood or the Germanic Till Eulenspiegel.

Local folklore was so important to him that he went out of his way to inves-tigate real Danish thieves like Mikkelsen, Frederiksen and Kagerup in order to see what the connection was between the ideal (the myth) and the actual (the local ethos). In the spirit of Hegel's philosophy—something he probably learned from Heiberg—Kierkegaard might have thought that folklore, literature and philosophy expressed the same ideas, although through different venues. The exercise of drawing parallels between his local contemporary folklore and literary myths would later become a constant practice in his future authorship.

---

53   *SKS* 27, 157, Papir 209 / *KJN* 11, 164.
54   See *SKS* 17, 134–5, BB:42 / *KJN* 1, 128.

Naturally enough, the Dane's interpretation of medieval myth, in this case the legendary figure of Robin Hood, was permeated with the modern world-views of his contemporaries. The good robber familiar to him is not the chivalrous Robyn Hode from the Middle Ages, but the socially inclined Robin of Locksley of *Ivanhoe*. But even then we have observed that Kierkegaard introduced in his project some features that reflected the more local literary discussions held by his Danish contemporaries, especially Johan Ludvig Heiberg. It is not accidental that instead of fighting the established order through revolutionary action, like the hero depicted by Walter Scott, the Master-Thief uses humor and satire, much in the spirit of Heiberg's attempt to tackle the crisis of the age with his philosophical vaudevilles. The use of humor and irony would also be a pattern in Kierkegaard's mature works.

Finally, the specific motif of the marginalized loner—perhaps best embodied by Kierkegaard himself—would be a lingering presence in the Dane's thought. Through myth and legend, he would continue to explore the intricate depths of the self.

Bibliography

Anonymous, *Den berygtede Mestertyv og Rasphuusfange Morten Frederiksens sandfærdige Levnetshistorie; hvorledes han nemlig, efter at have taget Tjeneste ved det Militaire, flere Gange blev afstraffet som Tyv og Deserteur baade her i Danmark og i Udlandet; hvorledes han herpaa blev hensaat i Slaveriet og senere i Rasphuset, hvorfra han brød ud, for at begaae nye Forbrydelser, indtil han endelig efter mangfoldige sælsomme Eventyr blev hensat i Citadellet*, Copenhagen: no year.

Benzon, Peter Lorentz, "Kort Omrids af Morten Frederiksens Levnetsløb," in *Criminalhistorier uddragne af Danske Justits-Acter*, Copenhagen: Andreas Seidelin 1827, pp. 46–60.

Blicher, Steen Steensen, "Røverstuen," in *Samlede Noveller og Skitser*, vols. 1–3, Copenhagen: Gyldendalske Boghandel Nordisk Forlag 1905, vol. 1, pp. 92–130.

Borup, Morten, *Johan Ludvig Heiberg*, vols. 1–3, Copenhagen: Gyldendal 1973.

Bravo, Nassim, "Heiberg's 'A Soul after Death': A Comedic Wake-Up Call for the Age," in *The Crisis of the Danish Golden Age and its Modern Resonance*, ed. by Jon Stewart and Nathaniel Kramer, Copenhagen: Museum Tusculanum Press 2020 (*Danish Golden Age Studies*, vol. 12), pp. 27–49.

Bravo, Nassim, "Kierkegaard y el proyecto sobre el ladrón maestro (1834–1835): El rebelde marginado frente al orden establecido," *Eidos*, no. 32, 2020, pp. 281–308.

Bravo, Nassim, "The Master-Thief: A One-Man Army against the Established Order," in *Kierkegaard's Literary Figures and Motifs*, Tome II, *Gulliver to Zerlina*, ed. by

Katalin Nun and Jon Stewart, Farnham and Burlington: Ashgate 2015 (*Kierkegaard Research: Sources, Reception and Resources*, vol. 16), pp. 111–20.

Fenger, Henning, *Kierkegaard, The Myths and Their Origins: Studies in the Kierkegaardian Papers and Letters*, trans. by George C. Schoolfield, New Haven and London: Yale University Press 1980.

Fenger, Henning, "Mestertyven. Kierkegaards første dramatiske forsøg," *Edda*, no. 71, 1971, pp. 331–9.

Fenger, Henning, *The Heibergs*, trans. by Frederick J. Marker, New York: Twayne Publishers 1971.

Garff, Joakim, "Andersen, Kierkegaard—and the Deconstructed *Bildungsroman*," in *Kierkegaard Studies Yearbook*, 2006, pp. 83–99.

Hansen, T.P. (ed.), *Archiv for danske og norske Criminalhistorier, eller mærkværdige Domfældtes Levnet, Forbrydelser og Straf*, Copenhagen: published by the editor 1834.

Heiberg, Johan Ludvig, *Om Vaudevillen, som dramatisk Digtart, og om dens Betydning paa den danske Skueplads*, Copenhagen: Ferdinand Printzlau 1826.

Heiberg, Johan Ludvig, *Om Philosophiens Betydning for den nuværende Tid*, Copenhagen: C.A. Reitzel 1833.

Heiberg, Johan Ludvig, *Prosaiske Skrifter*, vols. 1–11, Copenhagen: J.H. Schubothes Boghandling 1841–43.

[Heiberg, Johan Ludvig], *Heiberg's On the Significance of Philosophy for the Present Age and Other Texts*, ed. and trans. by Jon Stewart, Copenhagen: C.A. Reitzel 2005.

Jandrup, Sara Katrine, "The Master Thief, Alias S. Kierkegaard, and his Robbery of the Truth," *Søren Kierkegaard Newsletter*, no. 43, 2002, pp. 7–11.

Jones, Michael, "The Jutland Cipher: Unlocking the Meaning and Power of a Contested Landscape," in *Nordic Landscapes: Region and Belonging on the Northern Edge of Europe*, ed. by Michael Jones and Kenneth R. Olwig, Minneapolis and London: University of Minnesota Press 2008, pp. 12–52.

Kastholm Hansen, Claes, *Den kontrollerede virkelighed. Virkelighedsproblemet i den litterære kritik og den nye danske roman i perioden 1830–1840*, Copenhagen: Akademisk Forlag 1975.

Kierkegaard, Søren, *Early Polemical Writings*, trans. by Julia Watkin, Princeton: Princeton University Press 1990.

Kierkegaard, Søren, *Kierkegaard's Journals and Notebooks*, vols. 1–11, ed. by Niels Jørgen Cappelørn, Alastair Hannay, David Kangas, Bruce H. Kirmmse, George Pattison, Vannesa Rumble and K. Brian Söderquist, Princeton and Oxford: Princeton University Press 2007-.

Kierkegaard, Søren, *Søren Kierkegaards Skrifter*, vols. 1–28, ed. by Niels Jørgen Cappelørn, Joakim Garff, Jette Knudsen, Johnny Kondrup and Alastair McKninnon, Copenhagen: Gad Publishers 1997–2012.

Kirmmse, Bruce H. (ed.), *Encounters with Kierkegaard: A Life as Seen by His Contemporaries*, Princeton: Princeton University Press 1996.

Knight, Stephen and Thomas H. Ohlgren (eds.), *Robin Hood and Other Outlaw Tales*, Kalamazoo: Medieval Institute Publications 1997.

Nagy, András, "Schiller: Kierkegaard's Use of a Paradoxical Poet," in *Kierkegaard and His German Contemporaries*, Tome III, *Literature and Aesthetics*, ed. by Jon Stewart, Aldershot and Burlington: Ashgate 2008 (*Kierkegaard Research: Sources, Reception and Resources*, vol. 6), pp. 171–184.

Nun, Katalin, Gerhard Schreiber and Jon Stewart (eds.), *The Auction Catalogue of Kierkegaard's Library*, Farnham and Burlington: Ashgate 2015 (*Kierkegaard Research: Sources, Reception and Resources*, vol. 20).

Nun, Katalin and and Jon Stewart (eds.), *Kierkegaard's Literary Figures and Motifs*, Tome I, *Agamemnon to Guadalquivir*, Farnham and Burlington: Ashgate 2014 (*Kierkegaard Research: Sources, Reception and Resources*, vol. 16).

Nun, Katalin and and Jon Stewart (eds.), *Kierkegaard's Literary Figures and Motifs*, Tome II, *Gulliver to Zerlina*, Farnham and Burlington: Ashgate 2015 (*Kierkegaard Research: Sources, Reception and Resources*, vol. 16).

Pedersen, Karl Peder, "Forbryderhistorier. Om trykte kilder til kriminelles historie ca. 1800–1850," *Personalhistorisk Tidsskrift*, no. 2, 2010, pp. 218–32.

Ritson, Joseph (ed.), *Robin Hood: A Collection of All the Ancient Poems, Songs and Ballads, now extant, Relative to that Celebrated English Outlaw*, vols. 1–2, London: William Pickering 1832, vol. 1.

Rohde, Hans Peter, "Søren Kierkegaard som Bogsamler," in *Auktionsprotokol over Søren Kierkegaards Bogsamling*, ed. by Hans Peter Rohde, Copenhagen: Det kongelige Bibliotek 1967.

Schrøder, Vibeke, *Tankens våben. Johan Ludvig Heiberg*, Copenhagen: Gyldendal 2001.

Scott, Walter, *Walter Scott's sämmtliche Werke*, vols. 1–173, Stuttgart: Franckh 1826–1833.

Stewart, Jon, *A History of Hegelianism in Golden Age Denmark*, Tome I, *The Heiberg Period: 1824–1836*, Copenhagen: C.A. Reitzel 2007 (*Danish Golden Age Studies*, vol. 3).

Stewart, Jon, "The Finite and the Infinite: Johan Ludvig Heiberg's Enigmatic Relation to Hegelianism," *Filosofiske Studier*, 2008, pp. 267–280.

Stewart, Jon, "Johan Ludvig Heiberg· Kierkegaard's Criticism of Hegel's Danish Apologist," in *Kierkegaard and his Danish Contemporaries*, Tome I, *Philosophy, Politics and Social Theory*, ed. by Jon Stewart, Farnham and Burlington: Ashgate 2009 (*Kierkegaard Research: Sources, Reception and Resources*, vol. 7), pp. 35–76.

Stewart, Jon, "Heiberg's Conception of Speculative Drama and the Crisis of the Age: Martensen's Analysis of *Fata Morgana*," in *The Heibergs and the Theater. Between Vaudeville, Romantic Comedy and National Drama*, ed. by Jon Stewart,

Copenhagen: Museum Tusculanum Press 2012 (*Danish Golden Age Studies*, vol. 7), pp. 139–60.

Thulstrup, Niels and Marie Mikulová Thulstrup (eds.), *Kierkegaard: Literary Miscellany*, Copenhagen: C.A. Reitzel 1981 (*Bibliotheca Kierkegaardiana*, vol. 9).

Visby, Carl Holger, "Psychologiske Bemærkninger over den, med Øxen henrettede, Morder Søren Andersen Kagerup," *Borgervennen*, nos. 20–24, 1832, pp. 141–87.

[Von Schiller, Friedrich], *Schillers sämtliche Werke in zwölf Bänden*, vols. 1–12, Stuttgart and Tübingen: Verlag der J.G. Cotta'schen Buchhandlung 1838.

Worth, Chris, "*Ivanhoe* and the Making of Britain," *Links & Letters*, no. 2, 1995, pp. 63–76.

Index